I0800512

IMAGES
of America

LA CROSSE
WISCONSIN

IMAGES
of America

LA CROSSE
WISCONSIN

La Crosse County Historical Society

ARCADIA
PUBLISHING

Copyright © 1999 by La Crosse County Historical Society
ISBN 978-0-7385-5022-0

Published by Arcadia Publishing
Charleston, South Carolina

Printed in the United States of America

Library of Congress Catalog Card Number: 2007921767

For all general information contact Arcadia Publishing at:
Telephone 843-853-2070
Fax 843-853-0044
E-mail sales@arcadiapublishing.com
For customer service and orders:
Toll-Free 1-888-313-2665

Visit us on the Internet at www.arcadiapublishing.com

Contents

INTRODUCTION

As the 20th century comes to an end and we contemplate the next millennium, perhaps it is necessary that we glance back over the waning century. While the early years of La Crosse history have been well documented, both in book and in photographs, the 20th-century history of the area has been largely understudied. Some local scholars, collectors, and educators have, however, taken up the challenge of sifting through data and information contained in archival records, newspapers, photographs, and oral history recordings and have begun to piece together our recent story. It was with this challenge in mind that the La Crosse County Historical Society undertook this project in 1998. We are proud to present, as our contribution to the ongoing local documentary process, this photographic essay of some of the events and people of the present century.

This book does not represent an attempt to be complete in our photographic history of the area. This was not even an attempt to cover every historic event, turning point, important person, or influence of the 20th century in the Coulee Country. We began and ended by utilizing only the photographic archives in the possession of the La Crosse County Historical Society, and this parameter gave us the border and scope of this photographic essay.

In addition to the chronological focus of the last 100 years in the La Crosse area, we also set our sights on images that depicted or shed light on everyday life. Using this theme provided a more democratic and inclusive representation of our diverse local population. To be sure, we have included images of prominent local personalities and well-documented events, but in choosing these, we sought to focus on the human story conveyed in the photos, rather than on the prominence or newsworthiness of their subjects.

The turn of the 20th century brought optimism and hope to the residents of the La Crosse area, as they looked forward to seemingly unending prosperity and technological advances. Transportation changed dramatically with the common use of the automobile, the introduction of the airplane, and the many railroad lines available to travelers. Trolley cars brought shoppers and workers downtown, and buses replaced them as the "modern" form of mass transportation. Streets were paved, electrical lines were installed below ground, and an extensive park system was designed. Three institutions of higher education came into being, and numerous factories employed thousands of workers. Local soldiers fought in the Mexican Border War, World War I, World War II, Korea, Vietnam, and the Persian Gulf, while those on the home front supported them in myriad ways. Women took their places in factories, on farms, in homes, government, medicine, business, athletics, entertainment, and education. Presidents came to town, and citizens delighted in celebrations and enjoyed parades. A new bridge was built to span the Mississippi River; hospitals and clinics expanded to serve the medical needs of a growing area, and new schools were erected to accommodate the children. Citizens were born, matured, played, married, raised families, worked, worshiped, studied, sang, and left their mark. Disasters took place, including flood, fire, illness, and epidemic. Immigrants took up residence looking for new beginnings, among them were Germans, Bohemians, Norwegians, and Hmong. Attitudes changed, along with hem lengths, hair styles, and ambitions. But through the technological advances, urbanization, and population shifts, the La Crosse area has remained a home for Midwestern families and their positive outlook.

Like most historical service institutions, the La Crosse County Historical Society continues to seek not only photographs, but personal papers, diaries, and correspondence collections that shed light on the last 100 years. Materials that document the local experiences of immigrant groups, African Americans, American Indians, the working classes, and women are especially welcome. As you enjoy this pictorial history, we hope that you will keep this need in mind and consider supporting our organization—as well as other local repositories—with donations of historical materials that add to the growing story of our recent local past.

One

The Learning Years

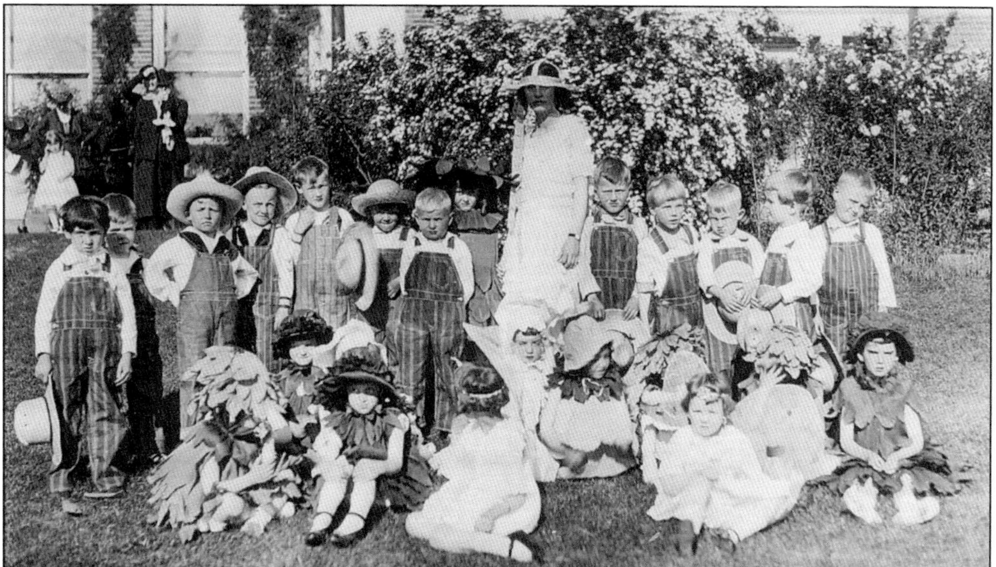

All the little boys dressed as farmers and the girls as flowers in this June 1920 photograph of a training school class at La Crosse's State Normal School. The teacher's dress reflects the latest fashion style.

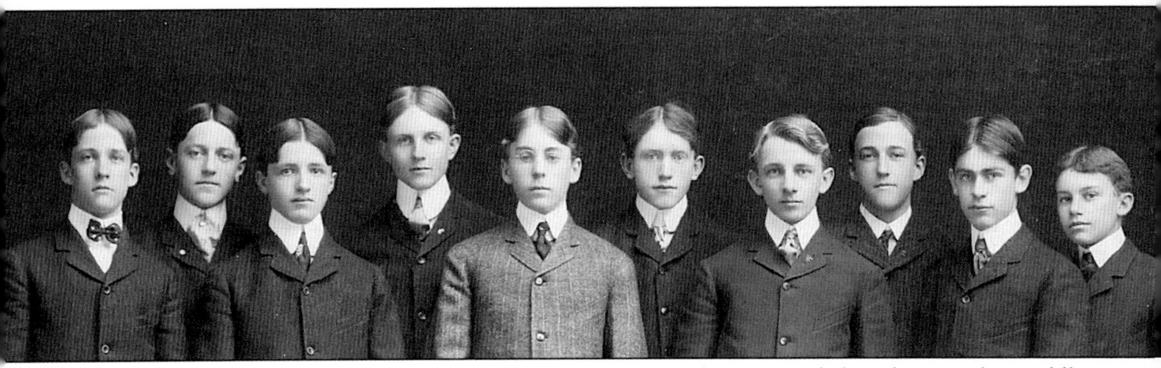

The majority of these La Crosse High School fraternity boys parted their hair in the middle, an example of the prevailing tonsorial trend in 1902. Nicknames were apparently popular; the identification on the reverse of the photo lists the boys' names as follows: "Sheep" Lamb, Earl "Sonny" Pryor, "Keck" Holley, "Bill" White, "Mike" Hayes, "Russ" James, "Ole" Holcomb, "Smush" Borreson, "Matt" Hosely, and "Hod" Holley.

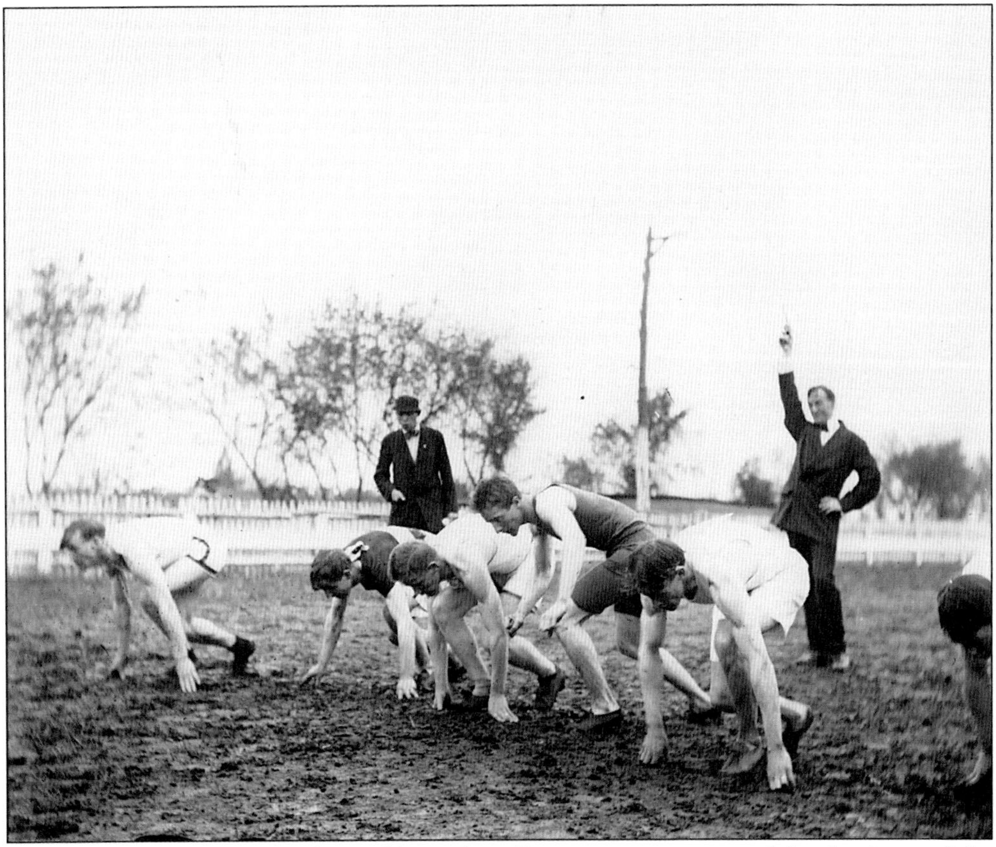

Poised on the Normal School's muddy track, college competitors waited for the firing of the starting pistol c. 1913. Louis P. Benezet, superintendent of La Crosse's Public Schools from 1911 until his death in 1915, fired the shot.

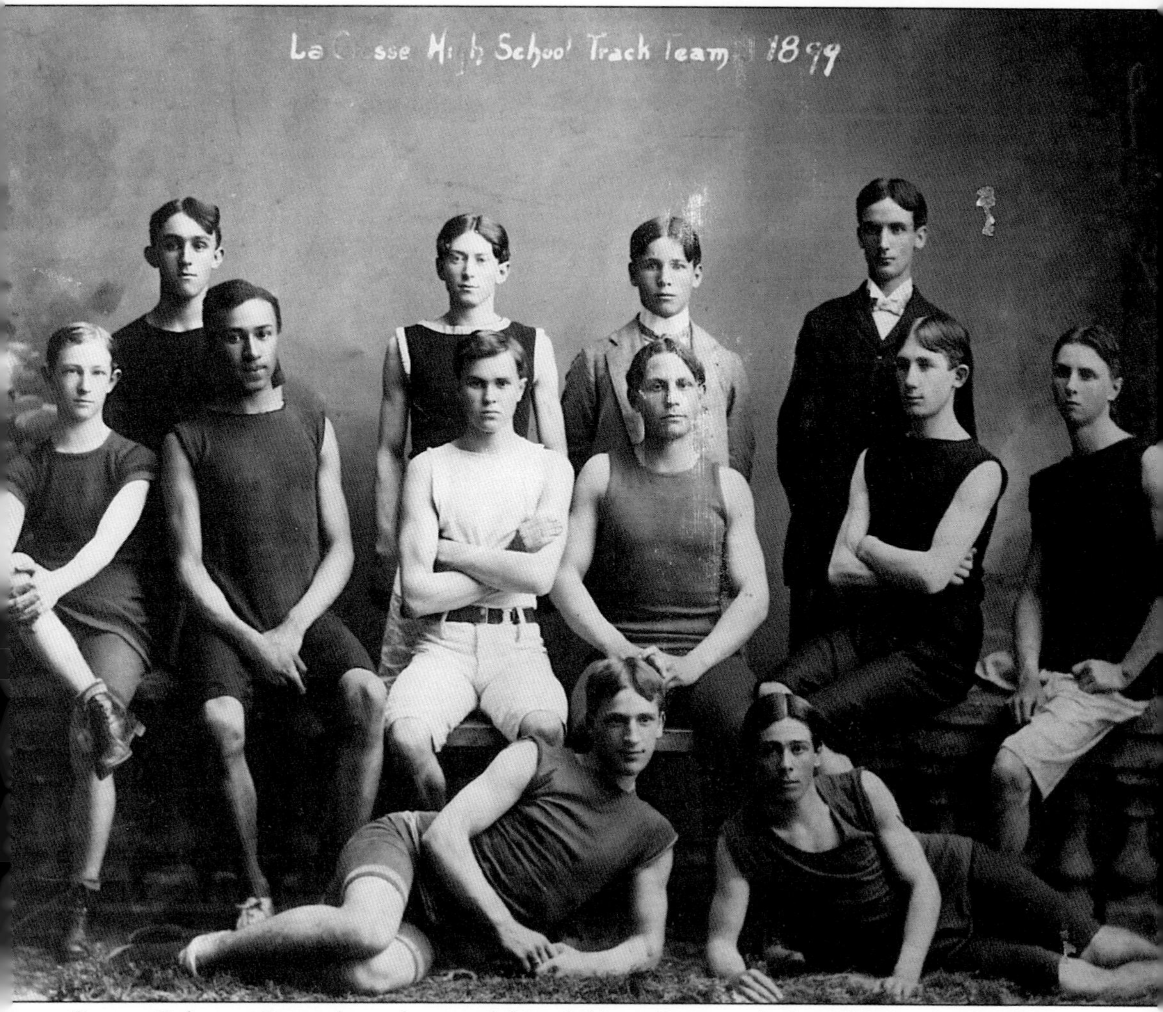

George Coleman Poage (seated, second from left) is shown with the 1899 La Crosse High School track team. Poage placed third in both the 200-meter and 400-meter hurdles at the 1904 Olympic Games, winning the first medals to be garnered by an African-American competitor.

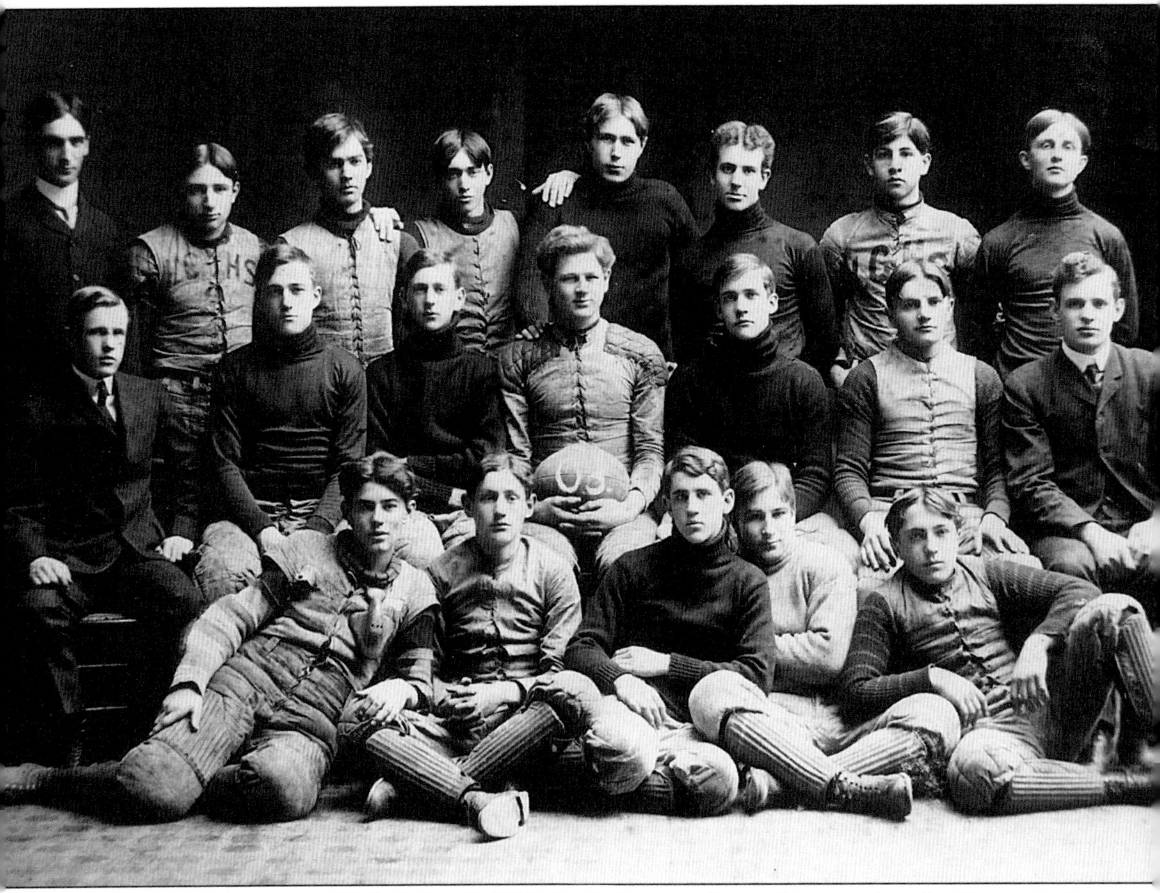

Pictured is La Crosse High School's 1903 football team. Several interesting details catch the observer's eye: hair was parted in the middle, the protective gear wasn't very protective, and their shoes had no cleats.

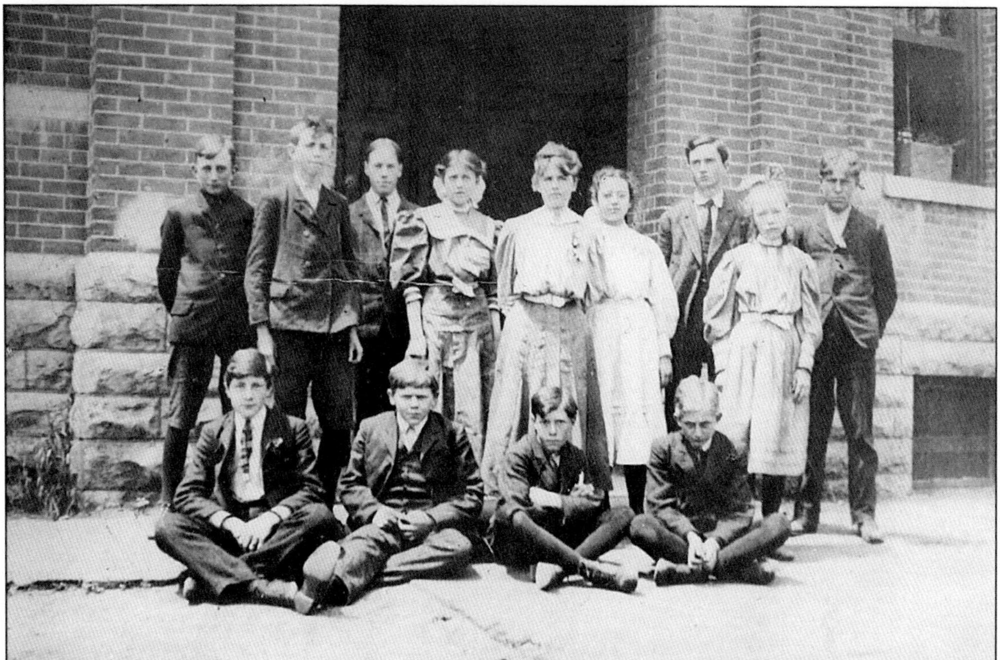

This North La Crosse eighth-grade graduation photograph was taken in June 1906. Pictured from left to right are, (seated) William Stevenson, Oscar Swennes, John Allen, and Joe Davidson; (standing) Louis Robinson, Paul Redpath, Al Evenson, Ethel Curran, Stasia Felzer, Norma Partridge, George Wilson, Stella Sheely, and Rudolph Schlabach.

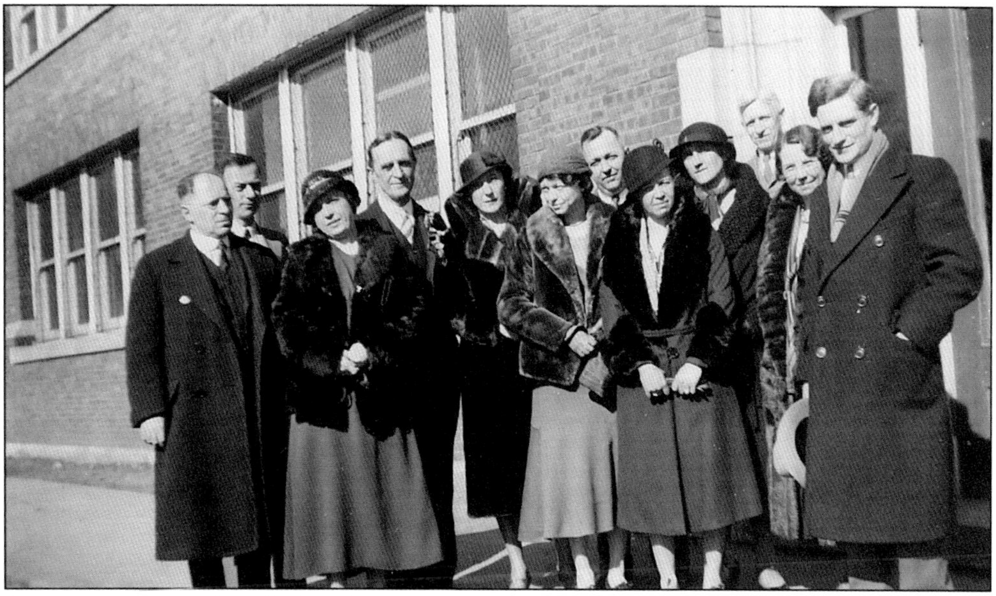

Only two men are identified in this La Crosse High School reunion photograph, one of whom is also in the preceding 1906 eighth-grade graduation photo. Presumably, in the high school class of 1910, these classmates posed outside the south gym of the original Central High School. George Howe is seen in the center of the back row, and William Stevenson is on the far right, in the front row.

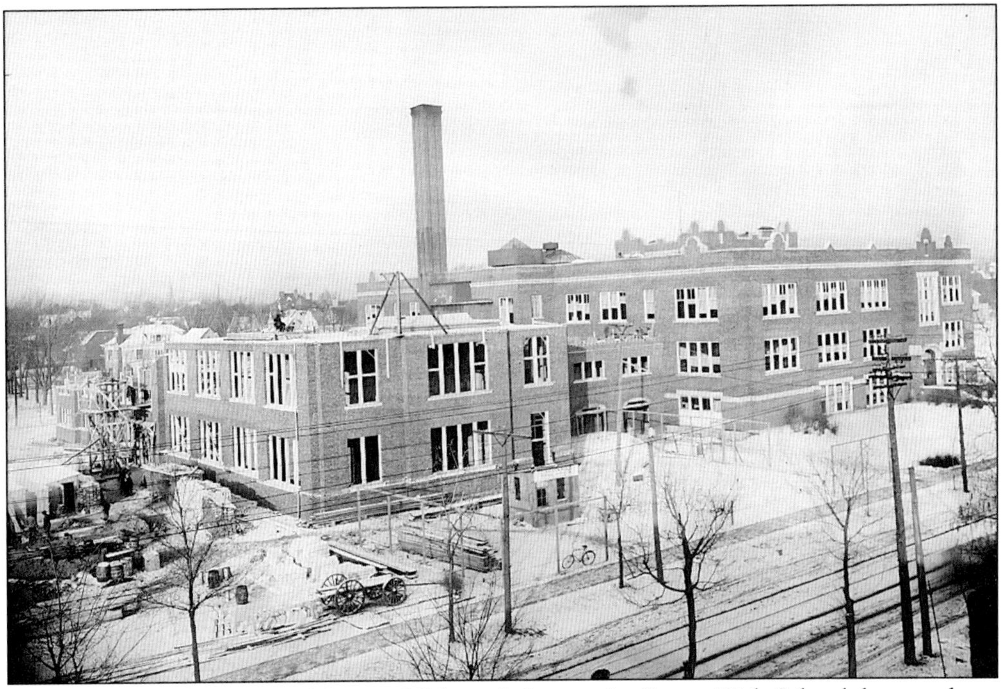

Built in 1906 at the corner of Cass and Fifteenth Streets, La Crosse High School drew students from the entire city. A high school remained at the same location for nearly 60 years.

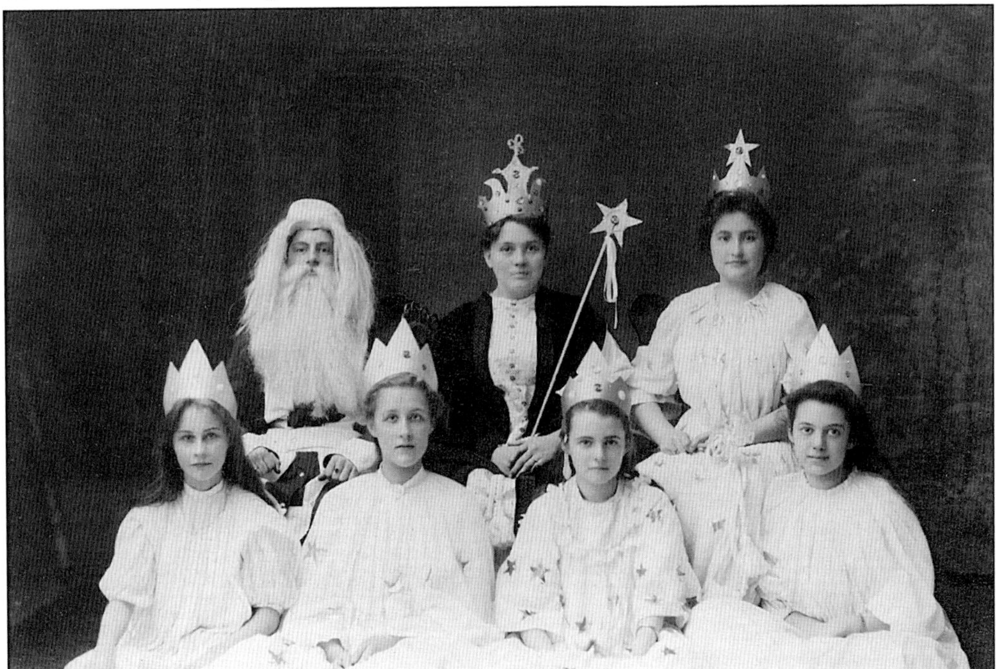

These seven Northsiders were performers in the 1907 cantata, *The Christmas Fairy*. William Stevenson was cast as Santa, Etta Nesler was the Fairy Queen, and Ella Gage played Evening Star. In the front row are Carolla Bangsberg as Serena, Ethel Mulder as Luna, Mildred Eberhart as Sunbeam, and Norma Partridge as Lily.

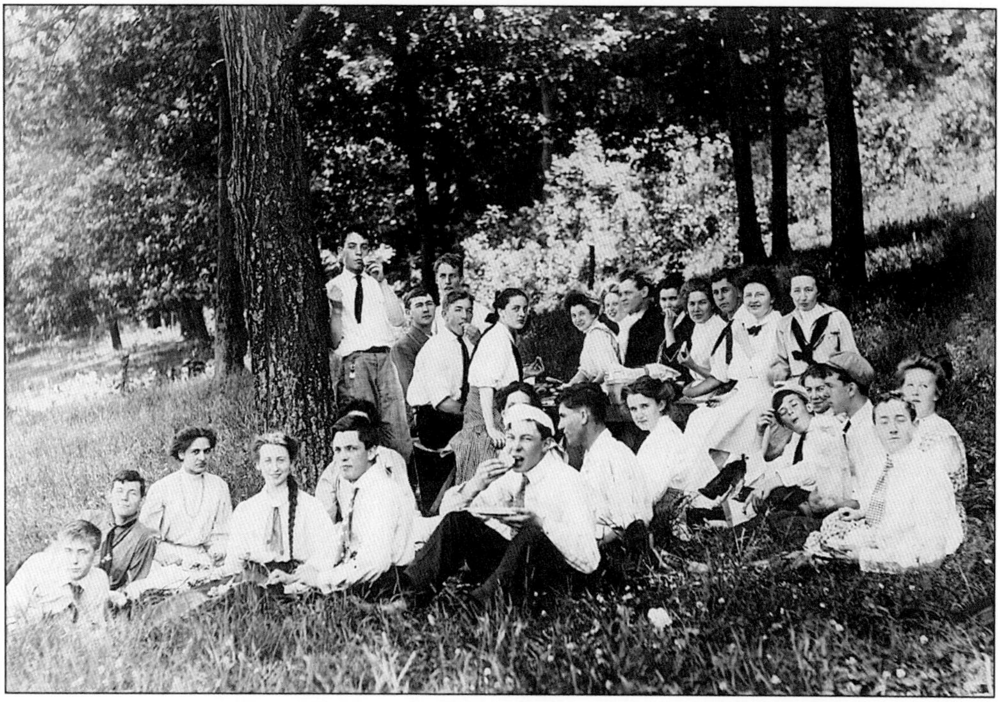

La Crosse High School's Lincoln-Douglas Debate Team enjoyed a picnic in 1908. Pictured from left to right are, (front row) Ben Stevens, Gus Schultze, Stella Tane, Daisy Gage, Sig Stavrum, Florence Heating, Eugne Luening, Cora Hempter, Walter "Squally" Miller, Florence Meyers, Arthur Gelatte, Dorothy Smith, Mason Sivermore, Ted Cronon, and Edith Dickens; (back row) Victor Jacobson, P. MacArthur, Irving Teteur, Fred Dickens, Grace Gesell, Margery Hammons, Daisy Jacobson, Mr. Schubert, Mrs. Stam, Edna Dickens, Norman Kelley, H.F. MacArthur, and S. MacArthur.

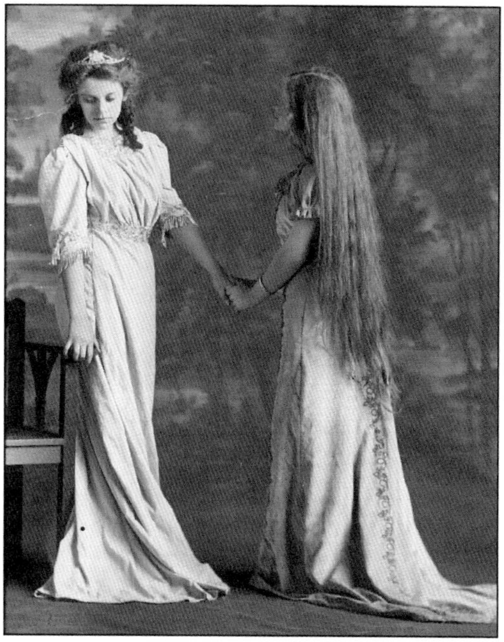

Pearl Cook and Lula Belle Bucklin strike a theatrical pose for the Shakespearean play, *As You Like It,* produced at the State Normal School c. 1910.

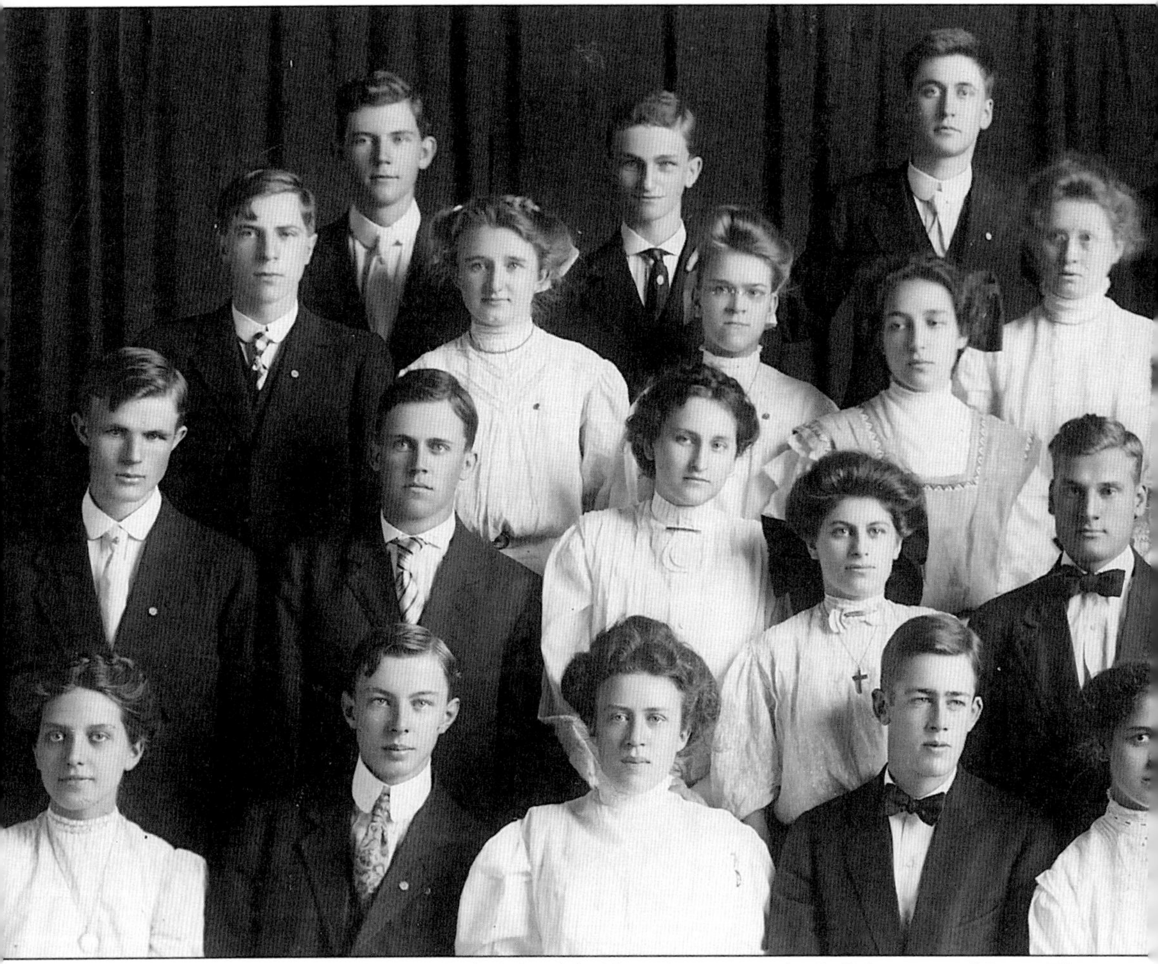

Early in the century, La Crosse High School held graduations in both February and June. The 1908 graduates from both sections are featured here, from left to right: (first row) Cora Kempter, Eugene Luening, Mabel Bryant, Howard Eidemiller, Stella Trane, Cora Schulze, Gertrude Smith, Joe Fowler, and Emma Zeisler; (second row) Orrin Nelson, Charles Tanberg, Katharine

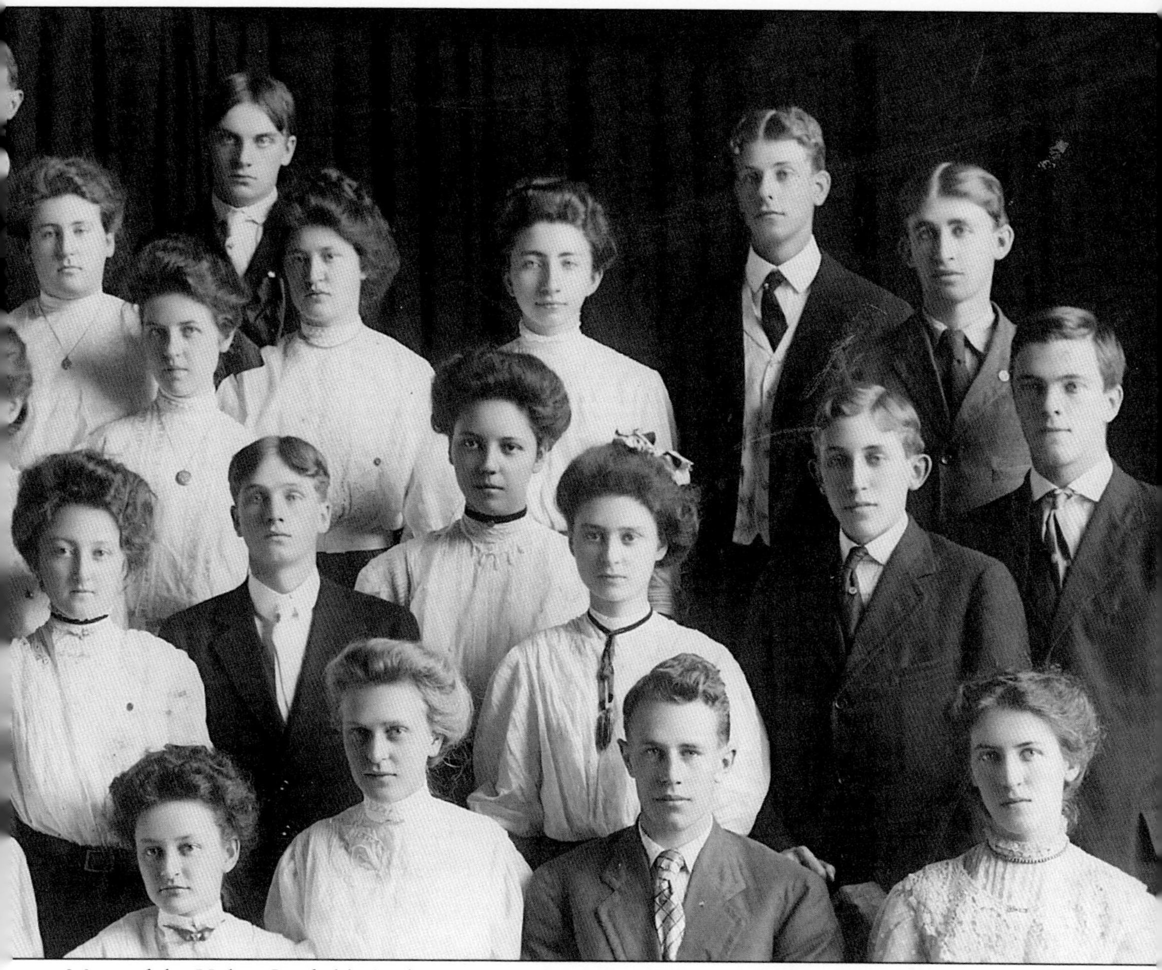

Martindale, Helen Scofield, Archie Larsen, Magdalene Tillman, William Bonneville, Florence Keating, Lillian Waters, Charles Bradish, and Sigmund Stavrum; (third row) Mary Anderson, Emma May James, and Ella Horn; (fourth row) Hugo Schaldach, Clarence Weber, Ben Stevens, Principal L.P. Benezet, and Hubert Morley.

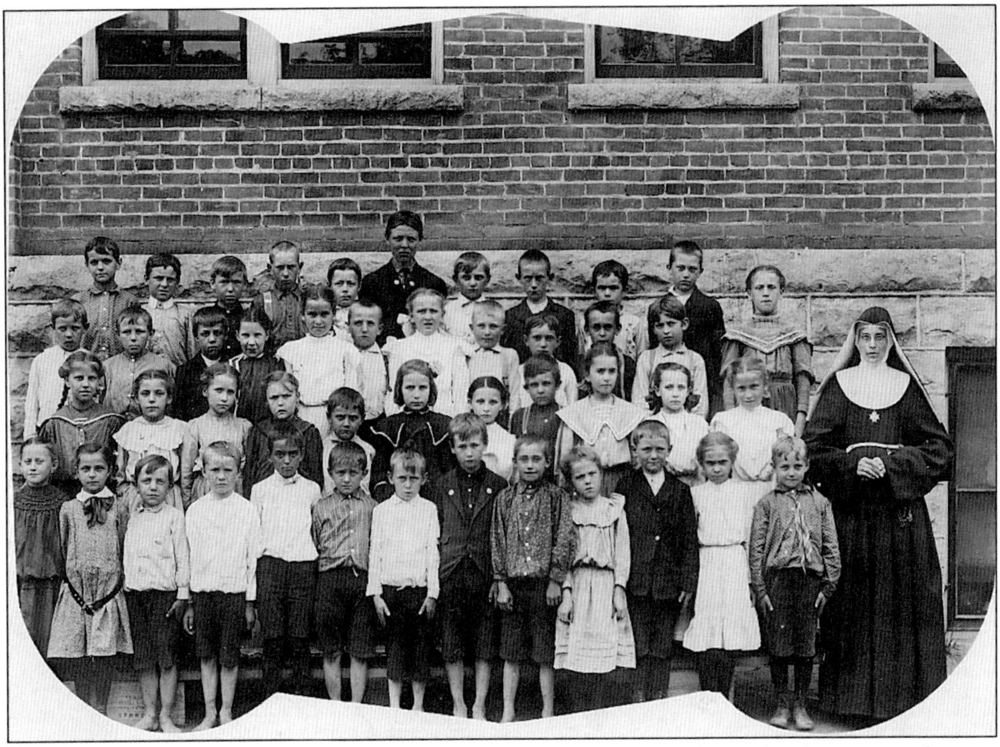

The Franciscan Sisters of Perpetual Adoration staffed St. Wenceslaus school, among others in La Crosse. This school was located at 801 South Tenth Street, and this photograph was taken c. 1910. Notice the bare feet and short pants on the boys in the front row.

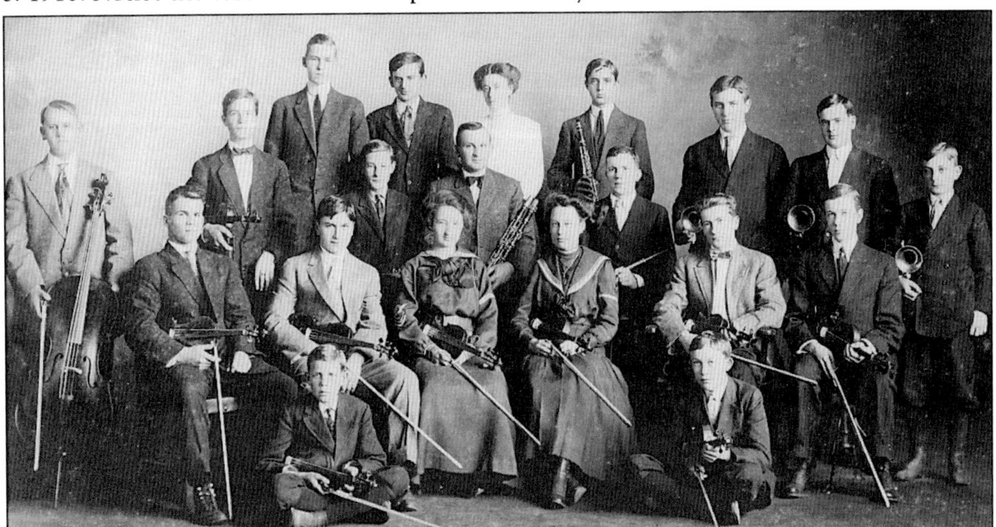

The La Crosse High School Orchestra posed for this portrait in June 1911. Members are pictured as follows: (first row) Paul Egbert, Malcolm Maine, Miss Martha Rollins, Raymond Merman, Borge Gunderson, Harry Marshall, and Harry Johnson; (second row) Reuben Thompson, Joseph Spika, Russell Anderson, Professor Horton Kline, and Eugene McNean; (third row) Albert Weimar, Albert Dittman, Louise MacArthur, Vera Andersen, Walter Williams, and Glen Halik; (seated) George Kreutz and William Tomsicek.

In this *c.* 1912 photograph developed from a glass plate negative, this dreamy young woman (unidentified) was a participant in a State Normal School pageant.

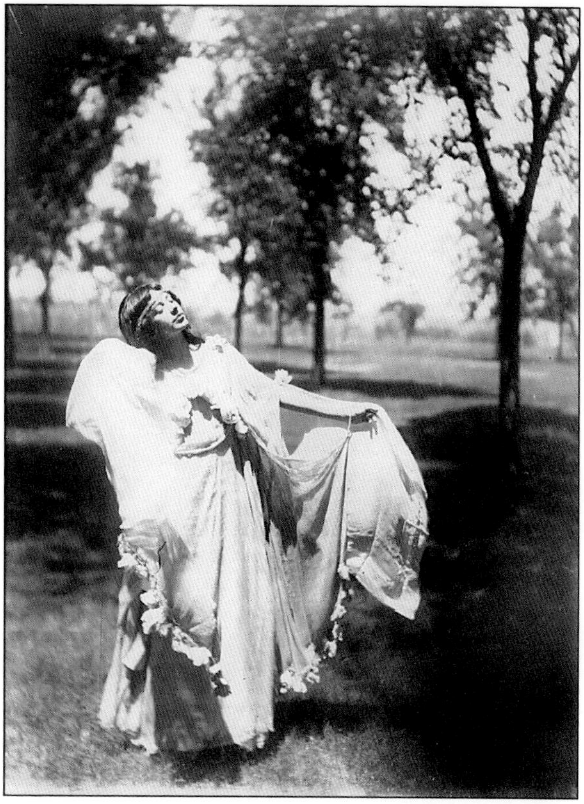

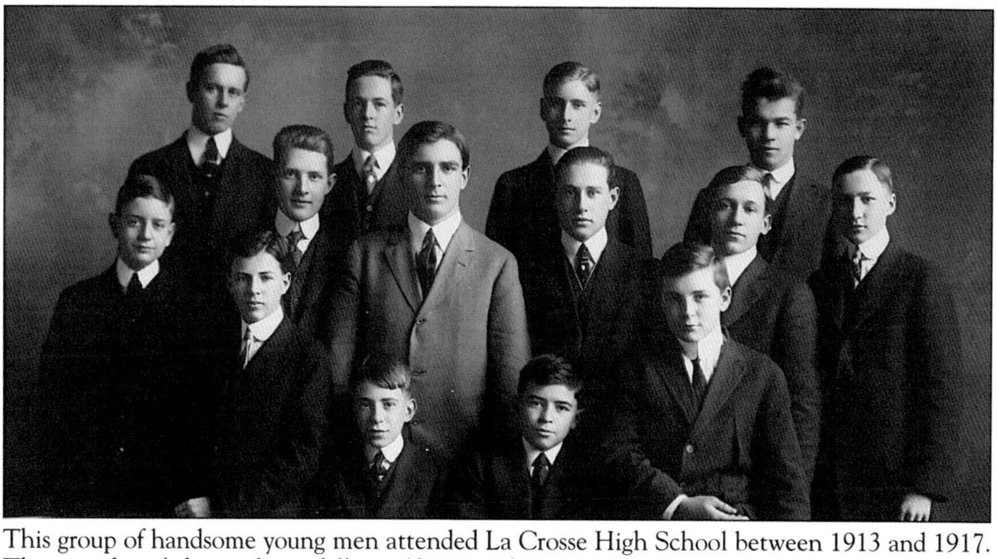

This group of handsome young men attended La Crosse High School between 1913 and 1917. They are, from left to right, as follows: (front row) Leroy Yerby, Jack Brindley, Earl Hirshheimer, and George Bunge; (middle row) Paul Gatterdam, Frank Funke, Borge Gunderson, Ronald Valier, Joe Bruha, and Otto Werner; (back row) Andrew Boyd, Arthur Evans, Burton James, and Harry W. Hirschheimer.

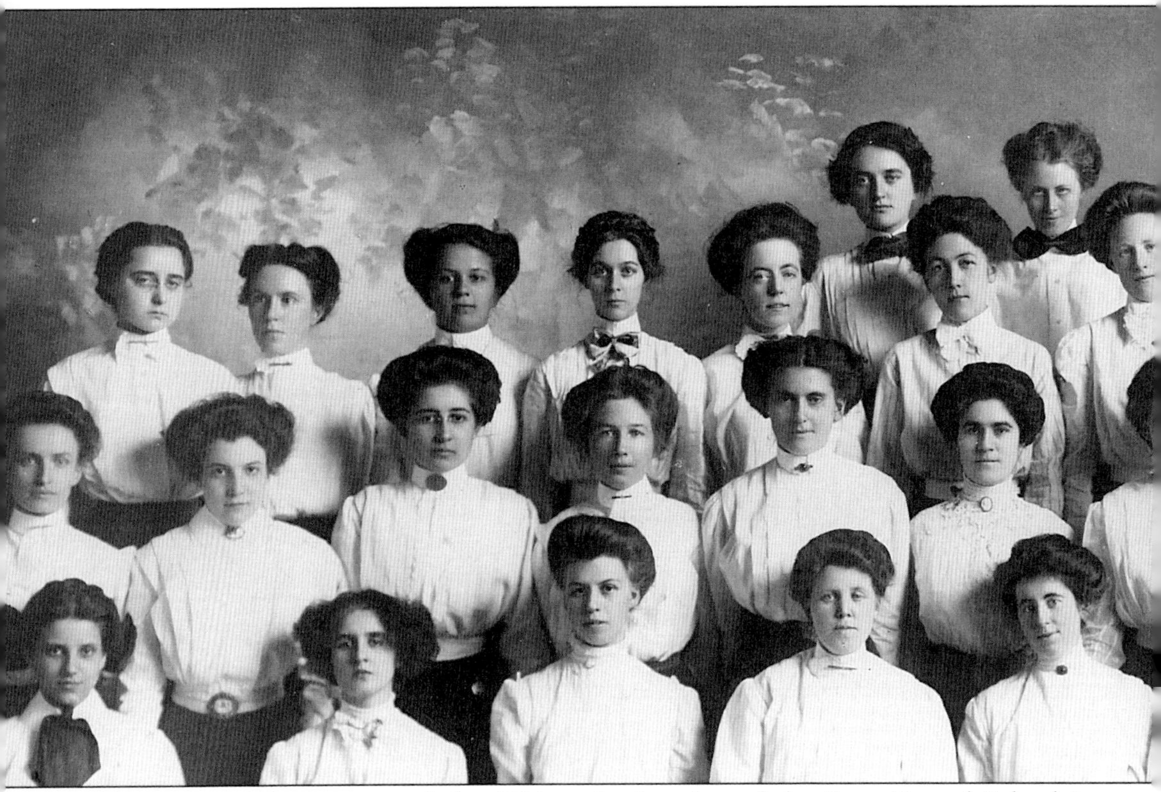

Forty young ladies constituted the 1911 graduating class of the State Normal School in

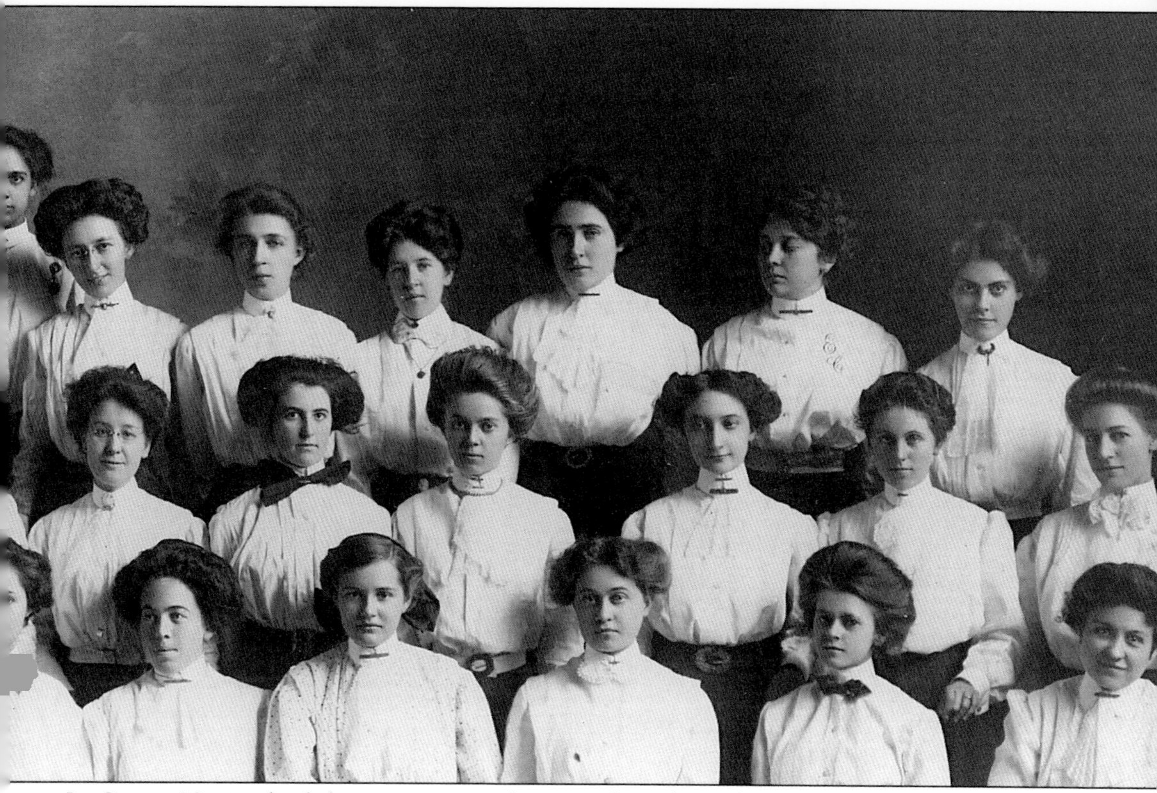

La Crosse. Notice the fashion statement of upswept hair-dos and white shirt-waists.

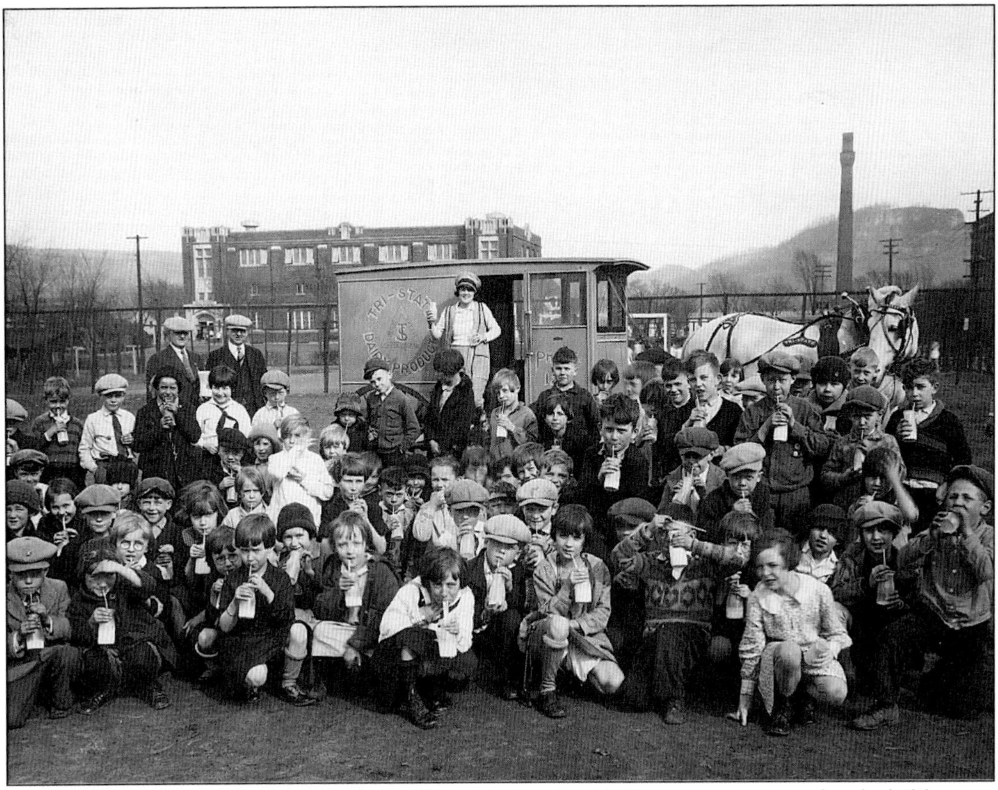

Actress Eloda Beach spearheaded a milk campaign in 1922 to encourage school children to drink more milk. Shown here on the State Normal School campus (with Wittich Hall in the background), the actress is surrounded by young students.

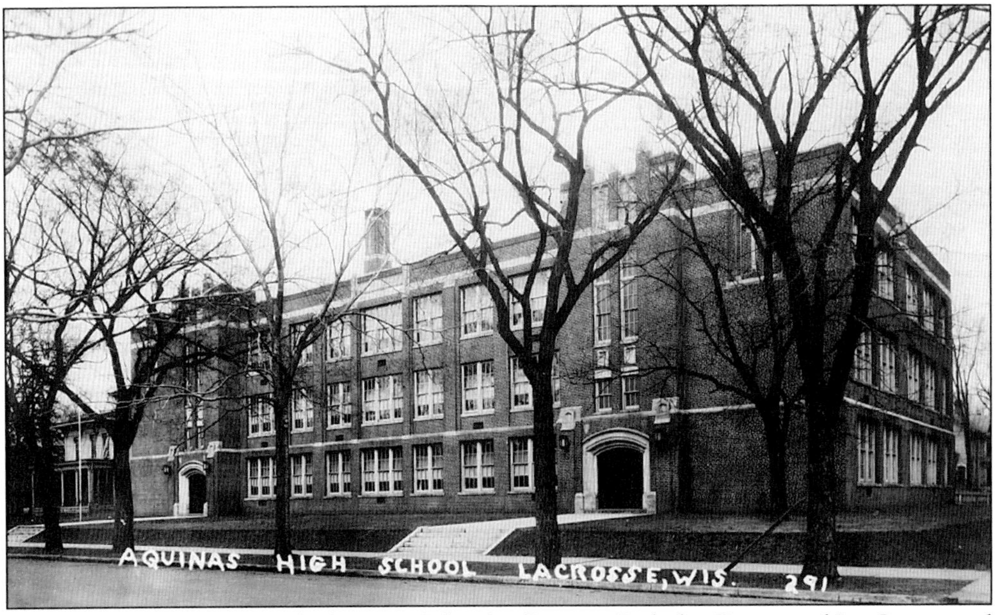

Aquinas High School was built *c.* 1927 by the Roman Catholic Diocese of La Crosse and continues to serve not only city high school students, but many from outlying areas.

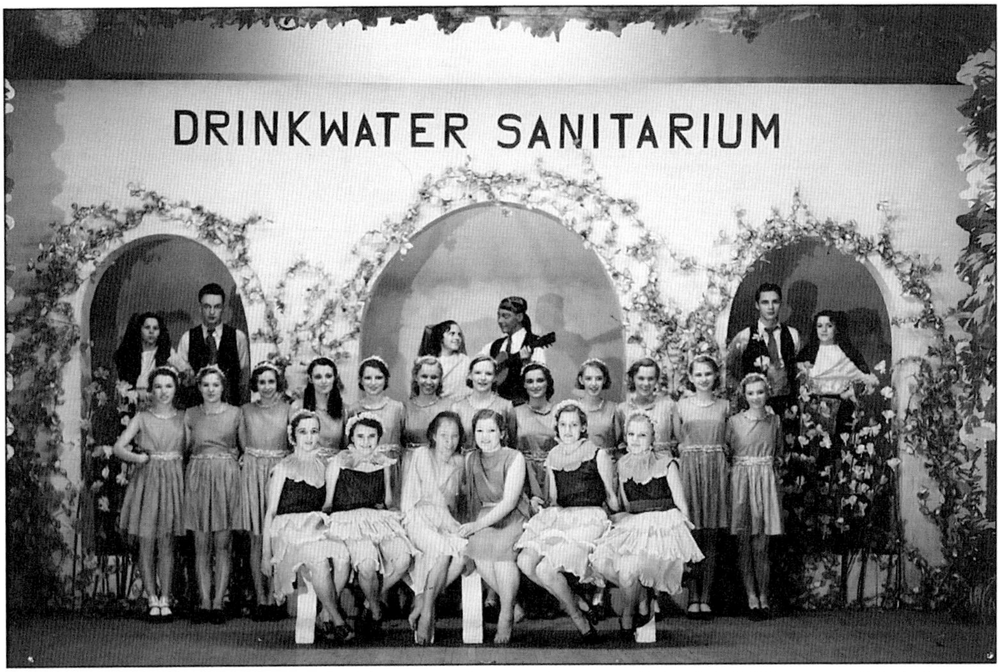

Elaborate costumes and a "cast of thousands" were showcased in this 1933 Logan High School operetta, *Oh, Doctor*. Cast members are, from left to right, (first row) Arlene Forss, Marian Ebner, Audrey Collins, Audrey Kuschel, Adeline Mlsna, and Eileen Mekvold; (second row) Fern Lumley, Jean Lindsay, Marcella Hammersburg, Gwenyth McGaughren, Mildred Limpert, Lillian Hilbert, Dorothy Briggs, Geraldine Schermerhorn, Doris Nieland, Janet de Ranitz, Bertha Groeschner, and Dorothy Simon; (third row) Margaret Dohlby, Donald Schroeder, Beryl Mittelbach, Eugene Bohrnstedt, Arthur Johnson, and Adeline Dunham.

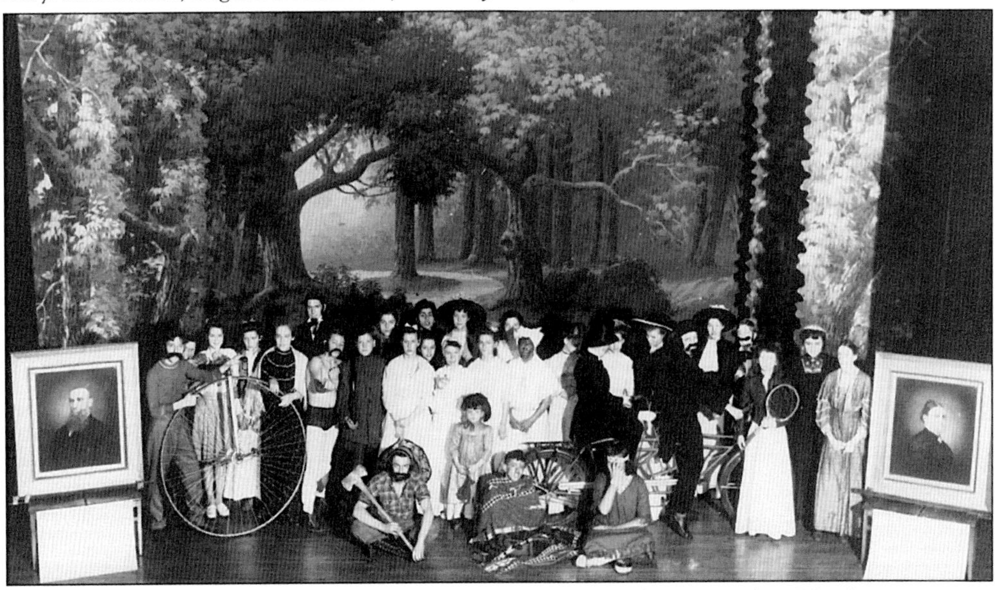

Lincoln School students depict La Crosse's early history in this 1942 play. The large portraits are of Nathan Myrick (generally counted as the first permanent white settler in La Crosse) and his wife, Rebecca.

Dick Brown, shortstop for Logan High School in the early 1940s, hams it up during baseball practice.

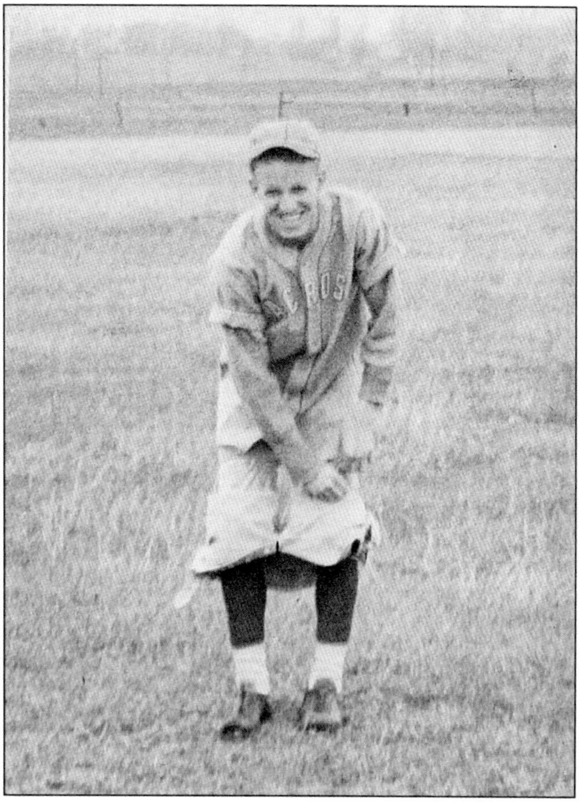

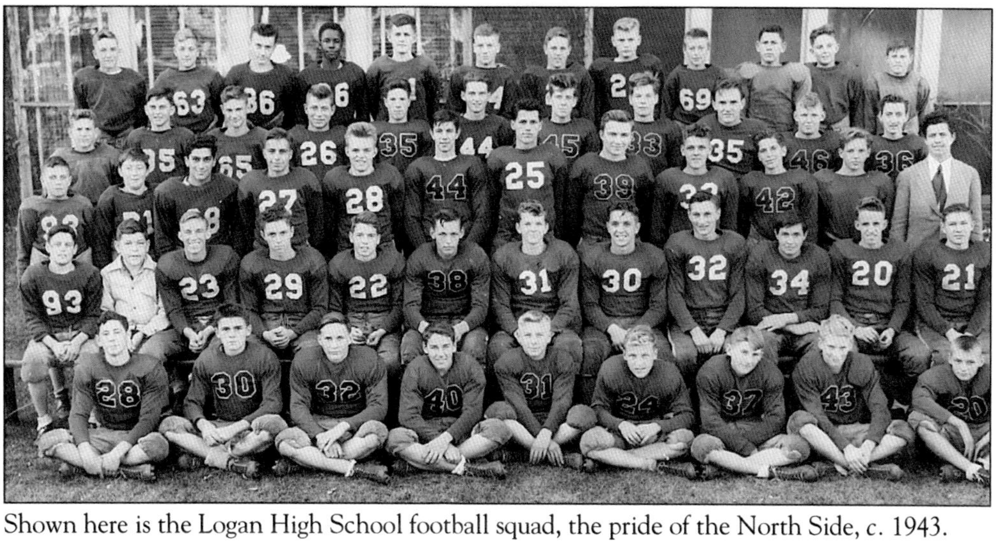

Shown here is the Logan High School football squad, the pride of the North Side, *c.* 1943.

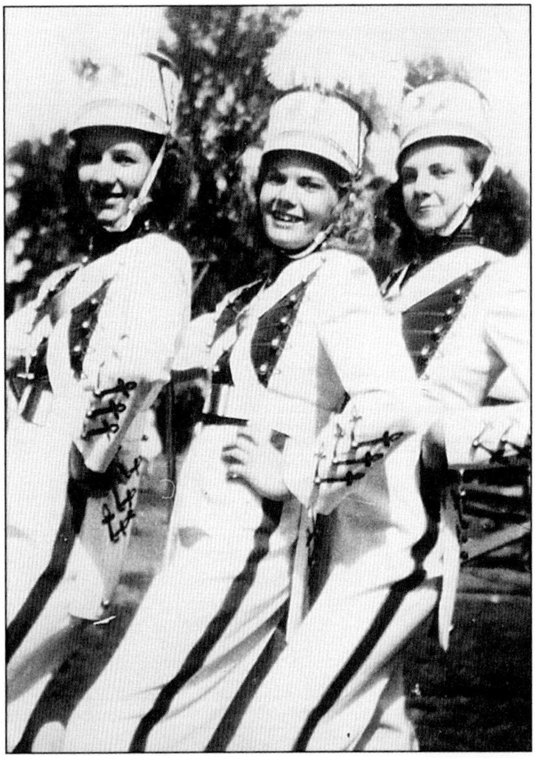

Three Logan High School majorettes strike the traditional pose during a 1940s football game.

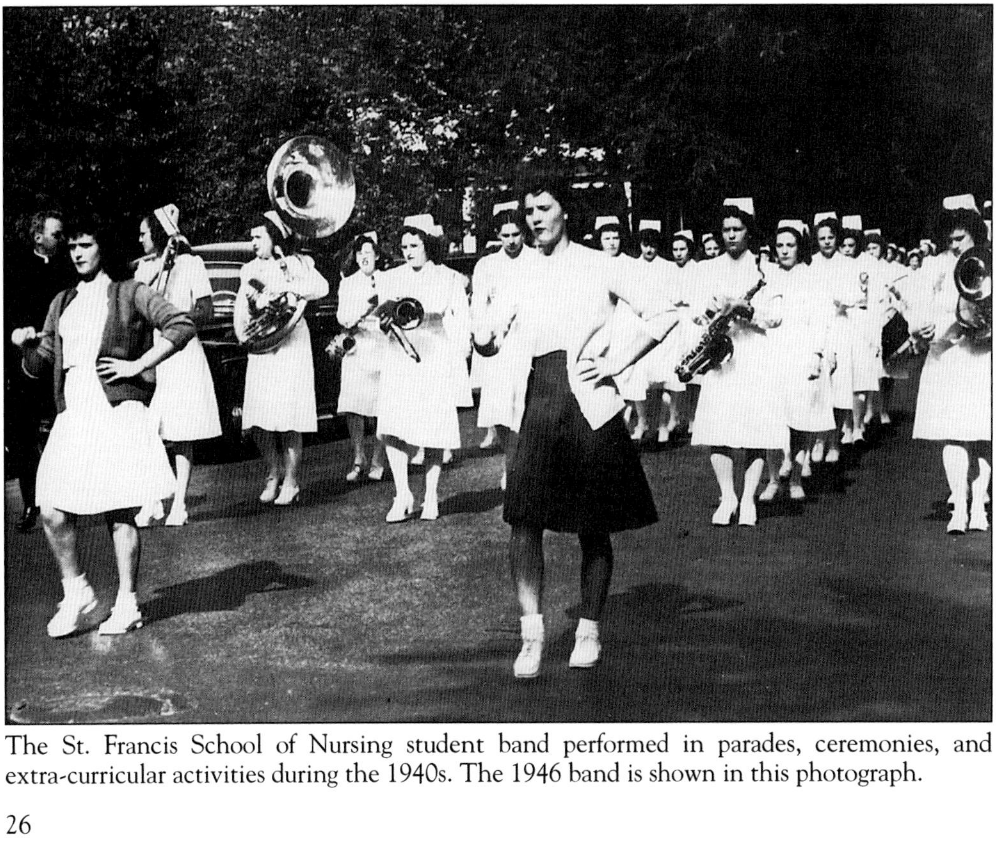

The St. Francis School of Nursing student band performed in parades, ceremonies, and extra-curricular activities during the 1940s. The 1946 band is shown in this photograph.

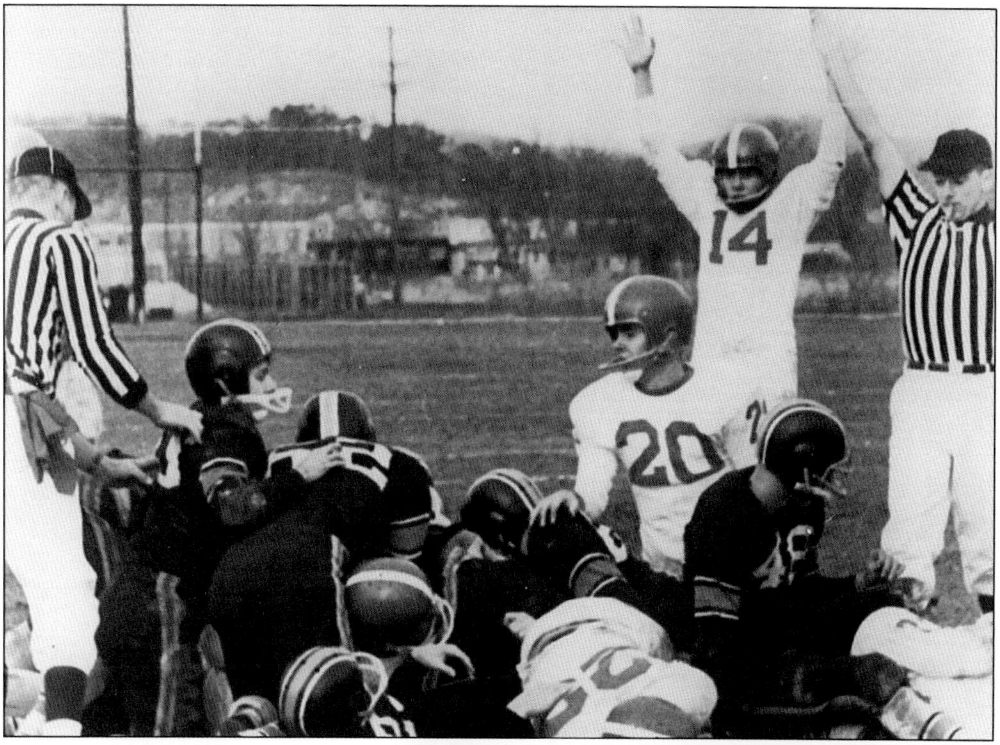

The 1960 Logan High School Rangers' football season was mixed with victory as well as defeat. In this photograph, Dave Jensen's assessment of the play corresponded with the referee's.

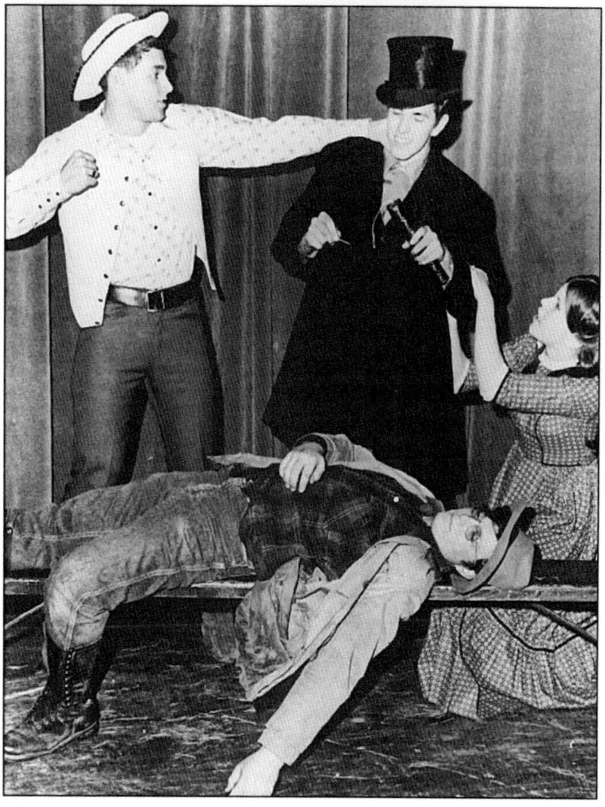

Budding Thespians Phil Blackman, Eric Knutson, Nancy Jorgenson, and Bill Barney starred in the 1967 Logan High School production of *The Miner's Daughter*, a one-act play directed by students.

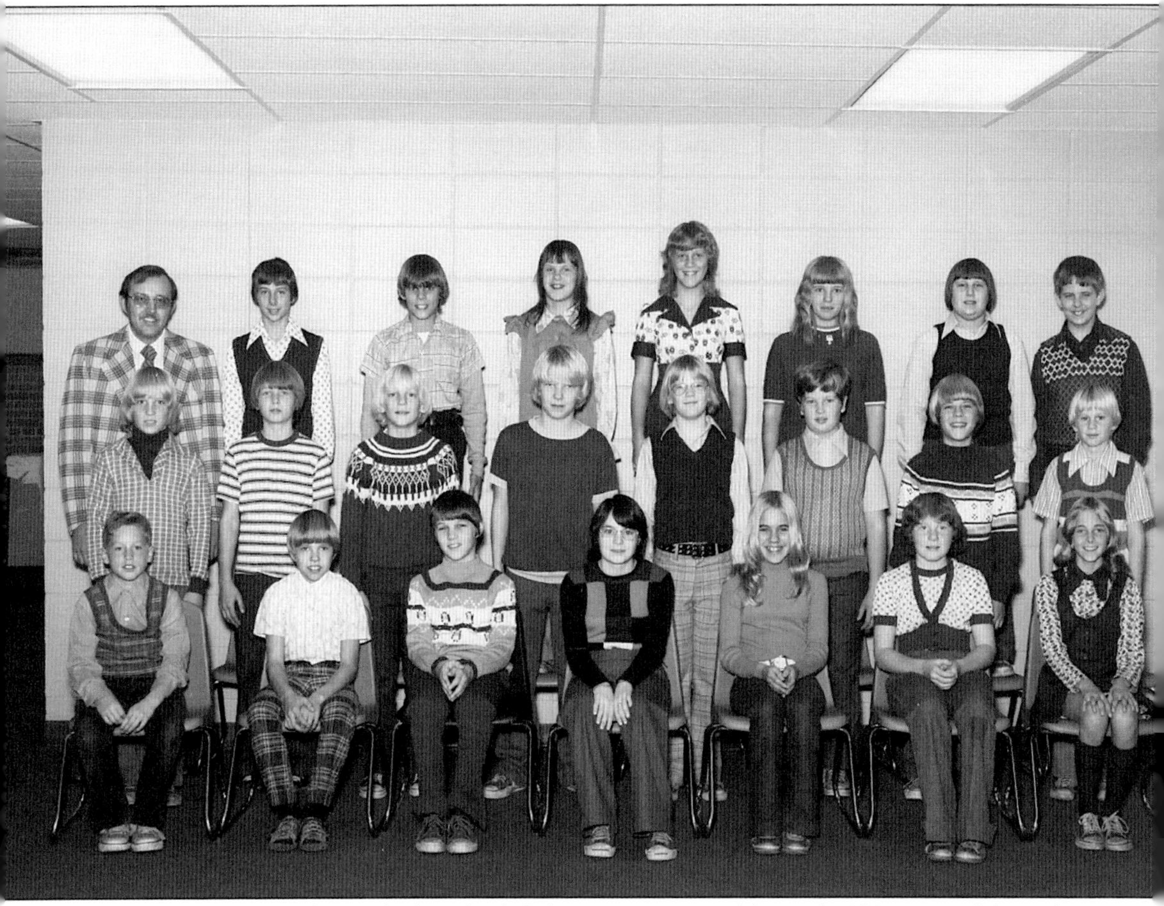

Wide lapels and stick-straight hair, both fashion statements of the mid-1970s, are widely evident in this photo of a sixth-grade class at Harry Spence school. Taken during the 1974–75 school year in the newly built Instructional Materials Center (IMC), the photo shows the following students, from left to right: (front row) Craig Griffin, Marty Brown, Todd Smrcina, Diane Hodge, Mary Jelen, Bonnie Wright, and Nancy Kolkind; (middle row) Dan Quam, Mike Thompson, Mark Fiers, John Bruring, Greg McCabe, Bob Stahl, Don Harmon, and Dave Lawrence; (back row) Mr. John Schultz, Bruce Noonan, Todd Hundt, Bonnie Blexrud, Laurie Wiedman, Jackie Johnson, Mark Kuschel, and Rick Brown.

Two

Stone, Wood, Bricks, and Mortar

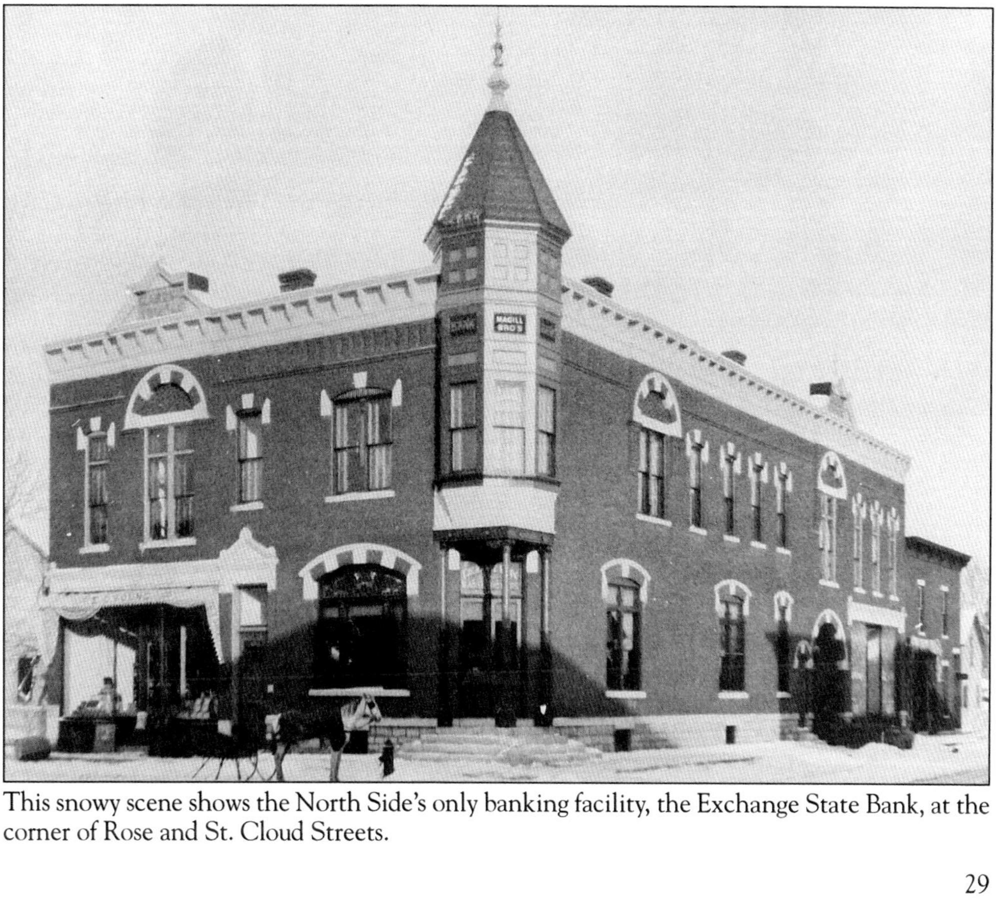

This snowy scene shows the North Side's only banking facility, the Exchange State Bank, at the corner of Rose and St. Cloud Streets.

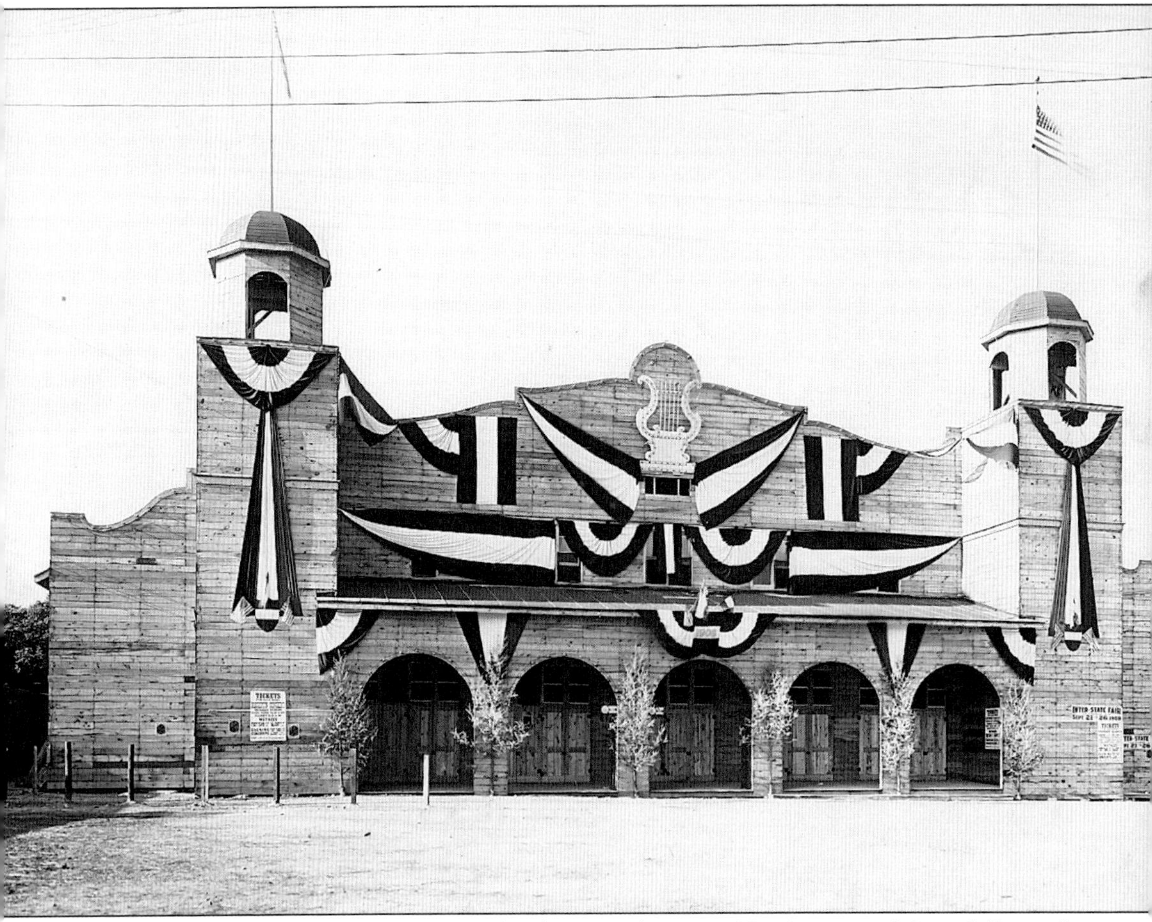

In 1908, La Crosse was chosen to play host to the great Northwestern Musical Festival—Saengerfest—and was told to expect 5,000 visitors and 3,000 singers. In his enthusiasm to offer La Crosse as host, the president of the chorus had overlooked the fact that the city had no auditorium! The La Crosse Board of Trade was handed the problem and decided to hastily build a hall. In a few short months, a huge building was knocked together on Market Square (Fourth and Jay Streets), decorated with bunting, and welcomed thousands of Norwegian singers and spectators.

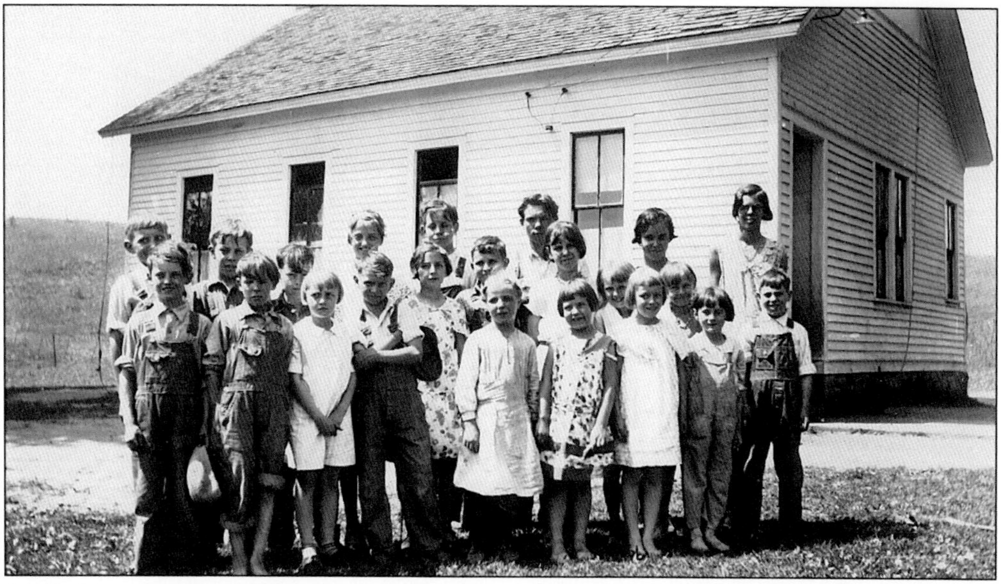

Pupils from the town of Hamilton pose in front of Neshonoc School in 1931. The school was located 1 mile northeast of West Salem.

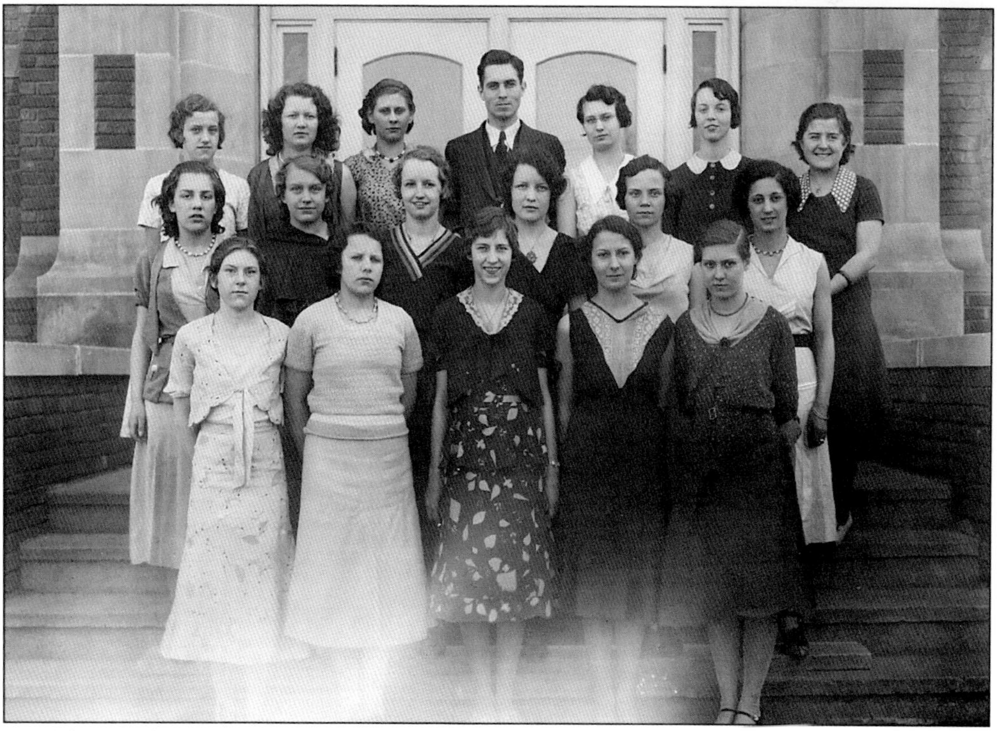

Harold Youngberg directed the musical program at Logan High School for many years. In this 1931 Girls' Glee Club photo, Mr. Youngberg is pictured with his students. They are, from left to right, (front row) Marion Schwarz, Adeline Johnson, Gretchen Kinder, Harriett Swanson, and Evelyn Richards; (middle row) Marion Johnson, Della Bergholz, Marian Widrick, Carol Taylor, Fern Kinney, and Jacqueline Swaydon; (back row) Ellen Finanger, Evelyn Baker, Wilma Vanderbilt, Dorothy Beck, Alice Hayden, and Dorothy Loeffler.

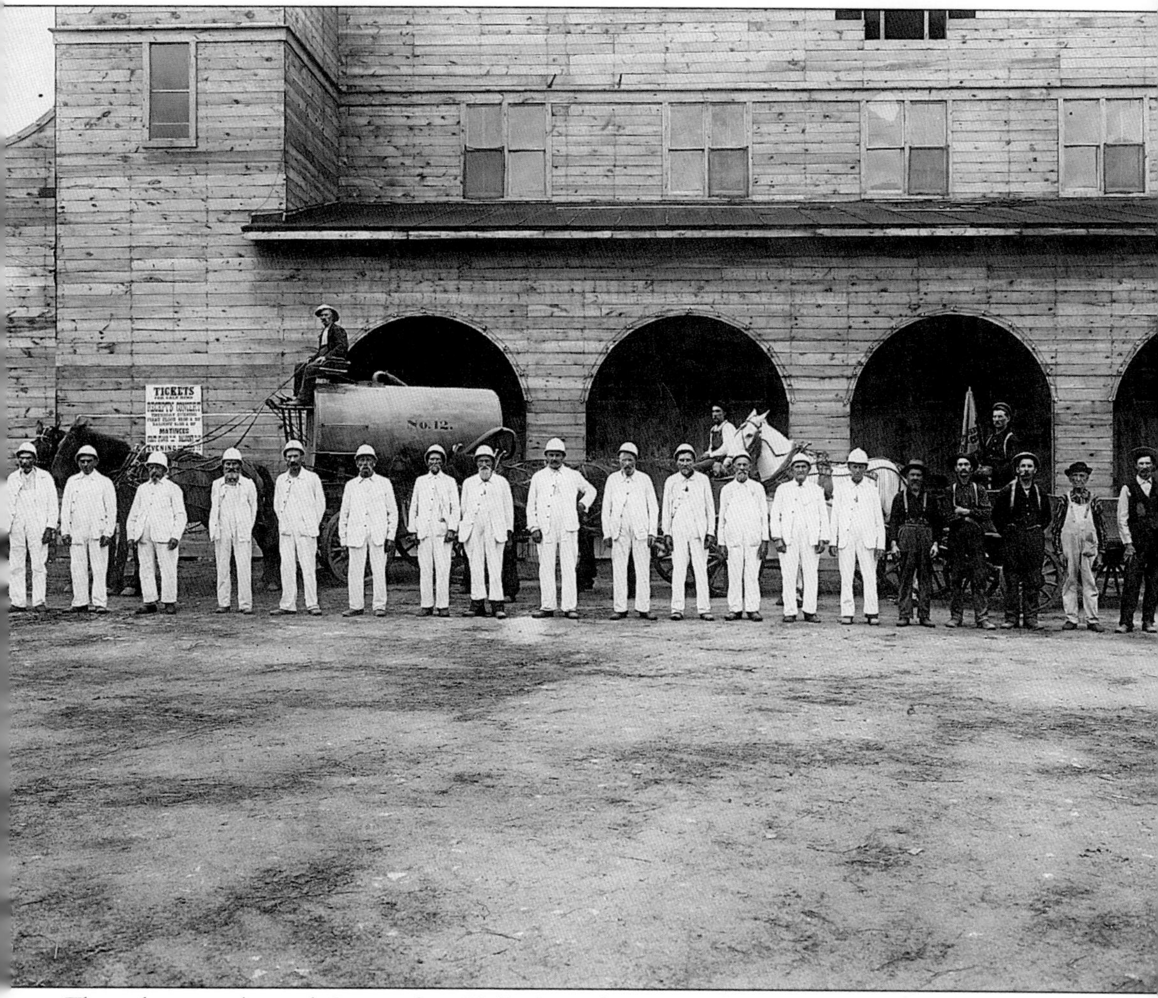

This close-up shot of Saengerfest Hall showed city employees in front of the newly completed building.

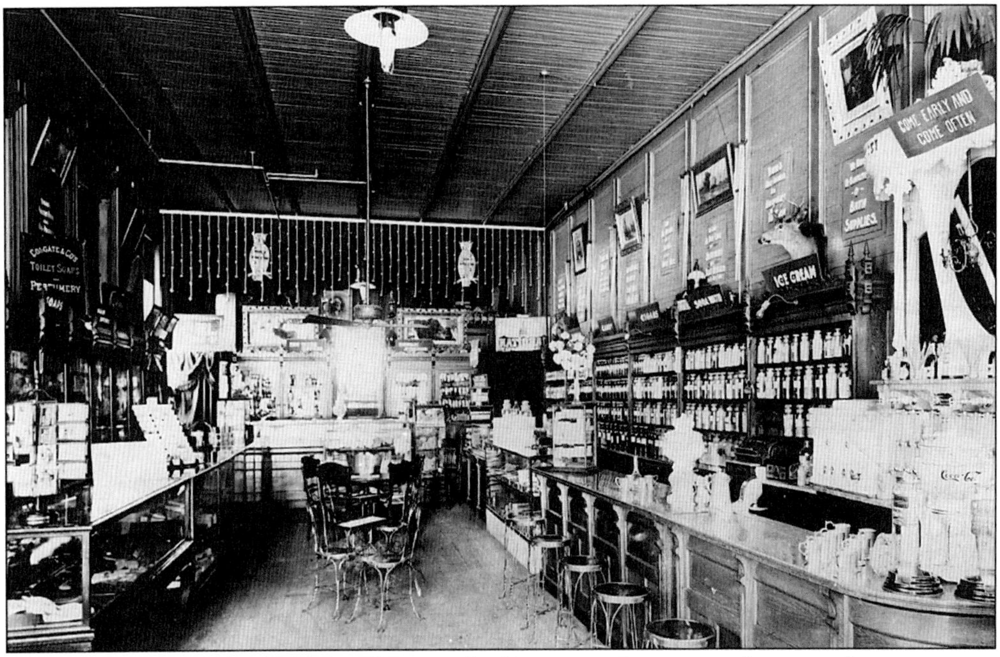

This building, located at 301 Main Street in La Crosse, was home to a pharmacy for many years. In 1900, Mrs. M. Cargen and Edward M. Young worked as pharmacists in the building. At the time of this photo, c. 1910, Mr. Young ran the establishment as a successful business that catered to both the ice cream and pharmaceutical needs of the city. Carl Boerner joined Mr. Young in the business in 1915, and Boerner's Drug Store was at the same location until c. 1959.

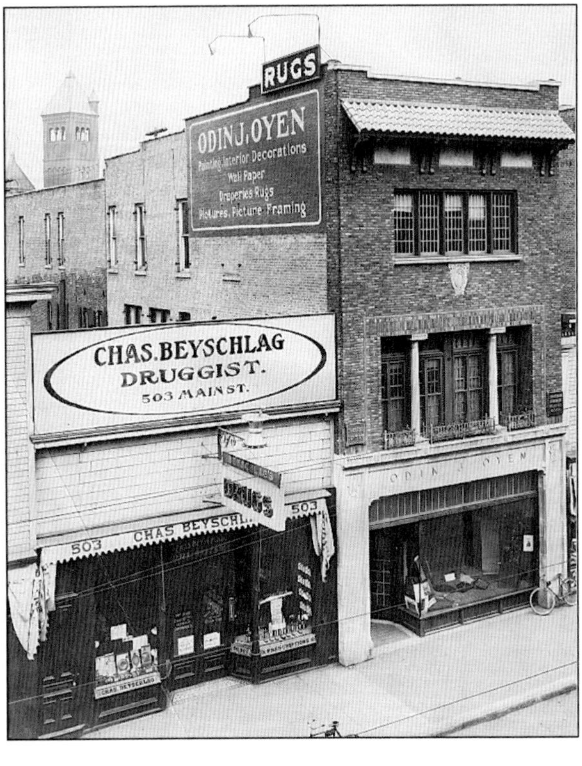

This c. 1913 photo shows Charles Beyschlag's drugstore and Odin J.Oyen's art and interior design shop at 503 Main Street. Oyen and his fellow craftsmen were popular decorators whose artwork adorned many churches, courthouses, theaters, public buildings, and residences throughout the Midwest. La Crosse homes graced with Oyen embellishments included the Henry Gund, the McMillan, Gelatt, Schilling, Gideon Hixon, Ott, and Bartl homes.

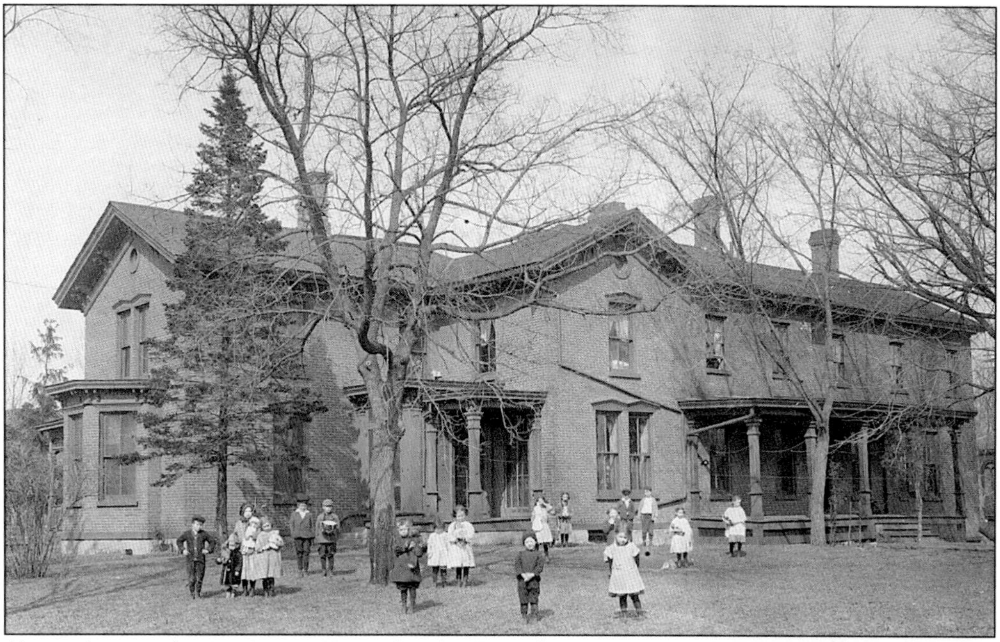

Shown here is the La Crosse Home for the Friendless at 609 South Eleventh Street in 1912. Some of the children are holding their treasured toys. The melancholy name of the building was later changed to the Home for Children.

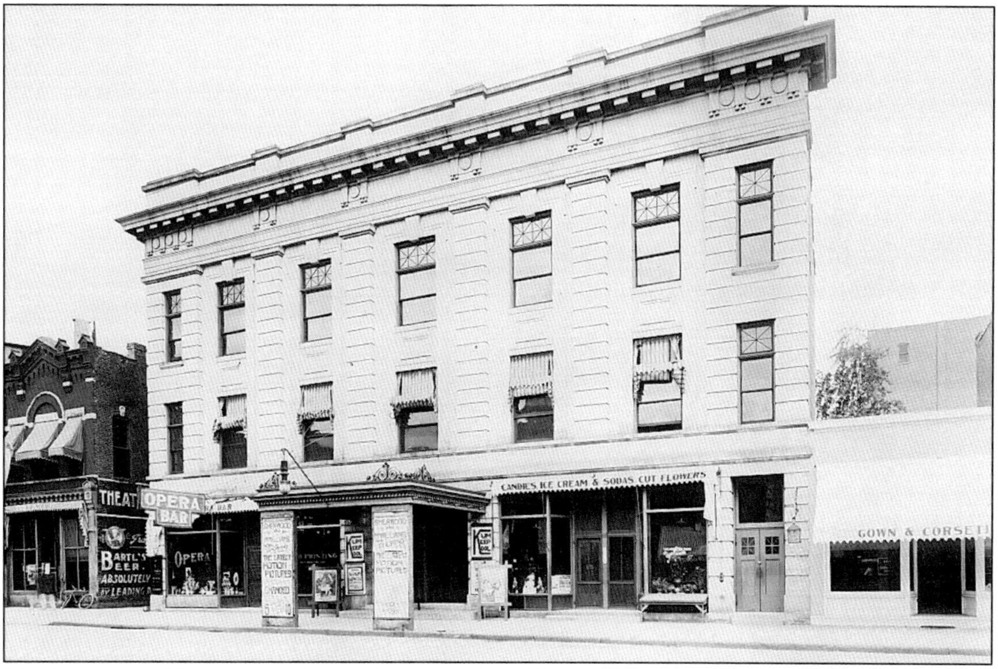

The La Crosse Theater stood at 115-121 South Fifth Street. In this c. 1913 photo, the theater's neighbors were two taverns (one owned by Albert Nekola and the other by Samuel Grant), John Knothe's printing shop, Laura Larsen's candy shop, Theodore Kienahs' florist shop, and Miss Marian Oswald's corset shop. The theater marquee bears the following advertisements: "The Latest Motion Pictures. Changed daily. Prices 5¢ and 10¢" and "Kum Keep Kool."

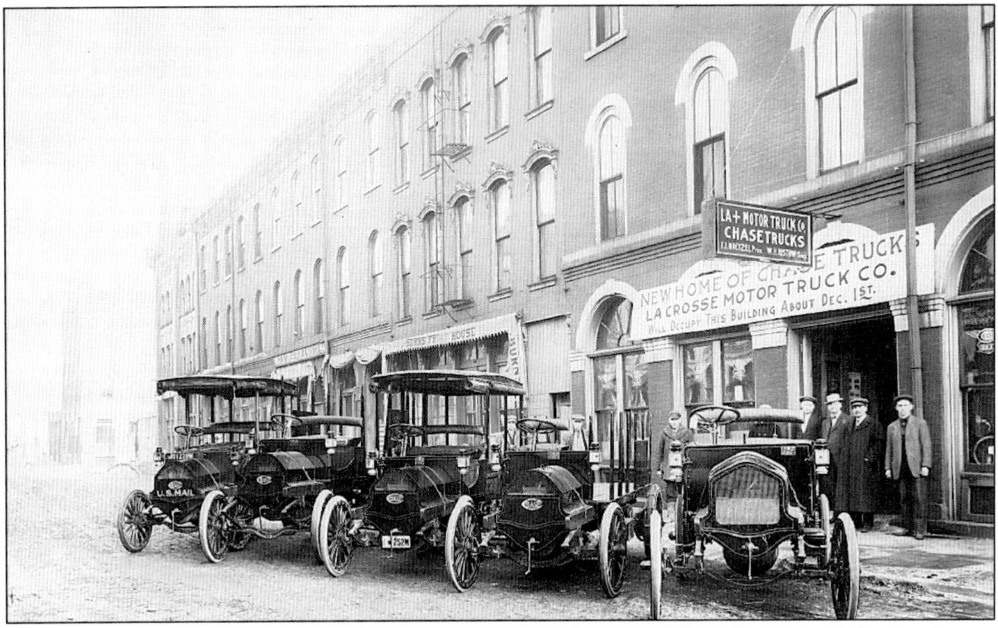

Fred J. Noetzel was a pioneer in the auto business in the city. When he opened the La Crosse Motor Truck Company at 106 North Front Street, his company sold Chase trucks. The post office had already purchased one of the 1914 hand-cranking models seen in front of the new establishment.

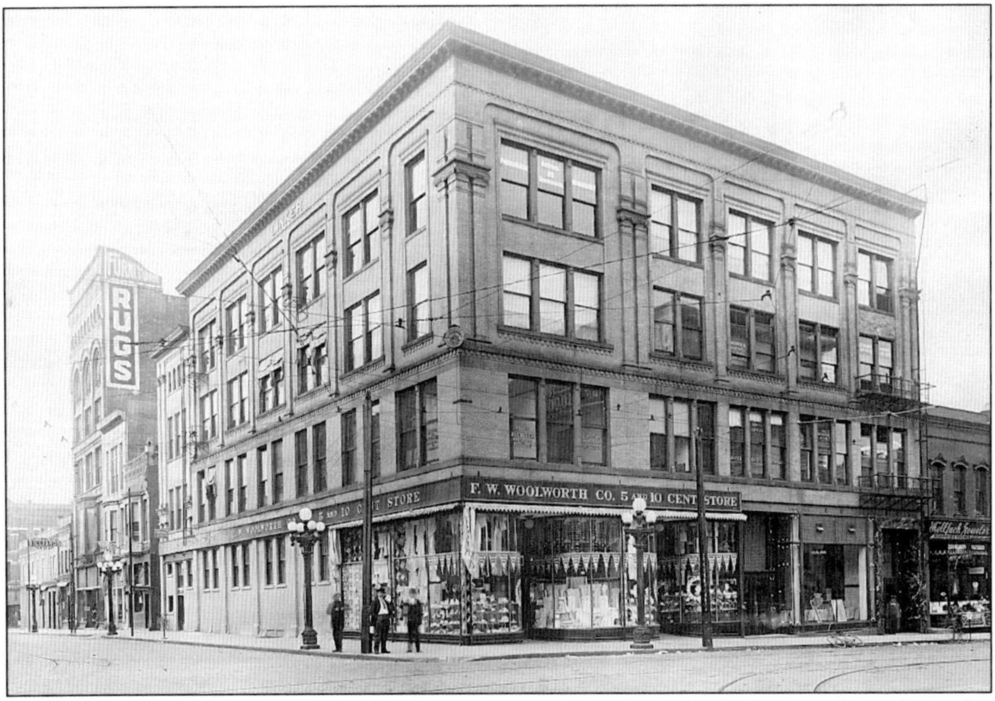

F.W. Woolworth Company, the famous American "Five and Dime," had stores throughout the country, with the La Crosse branch in the Linker Building. This c. 1917 photograph shows Woolworth's at 328 Main Street and Hellfach's Jewelers at 322, just a few doors down.

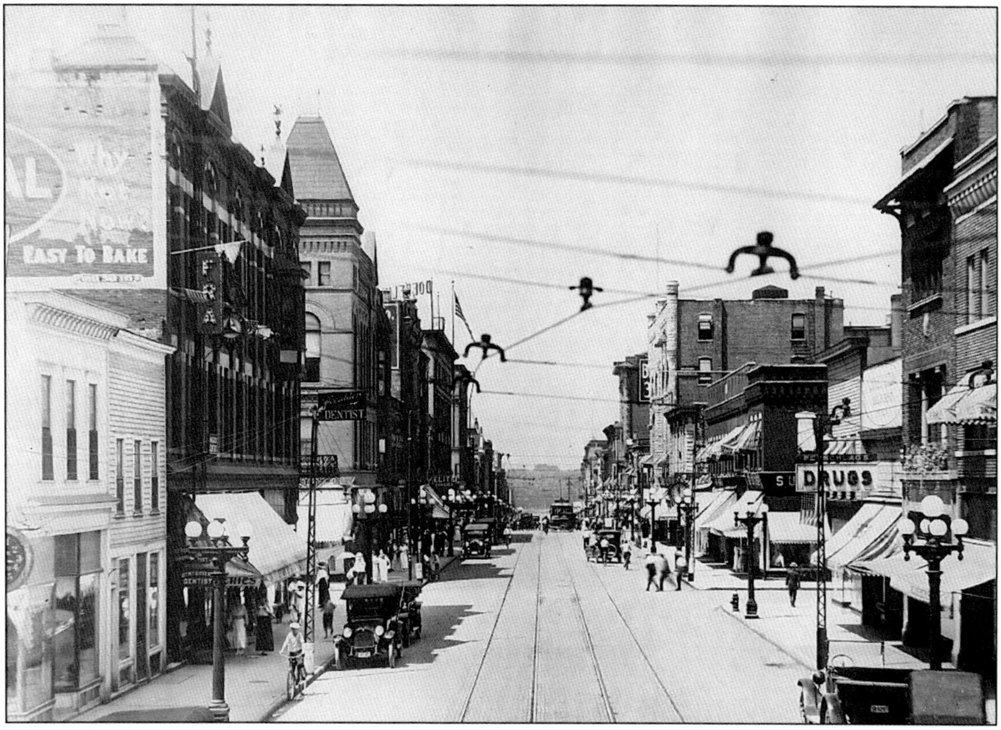

Shown here are Fifth and Main Streets in downtown La Crosse, *c.* 1918. Many kinds of transportation are evident in this scene, including bicycles, automobiles, horse-drawn carriages, and trolley cars, as well as people on foot.

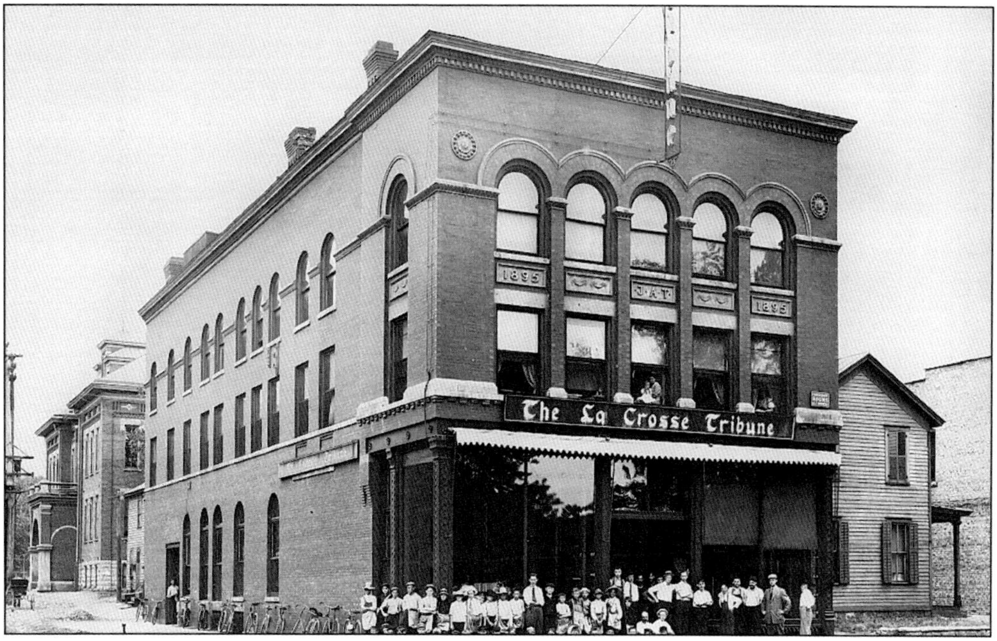

The *La Crosse Tribune* moved to this 201 South Fifth Street location in about 1909. This *c.* 1920 photo shows the newspaper's employees, including the army of 40 newsboys and some of their bicycles.

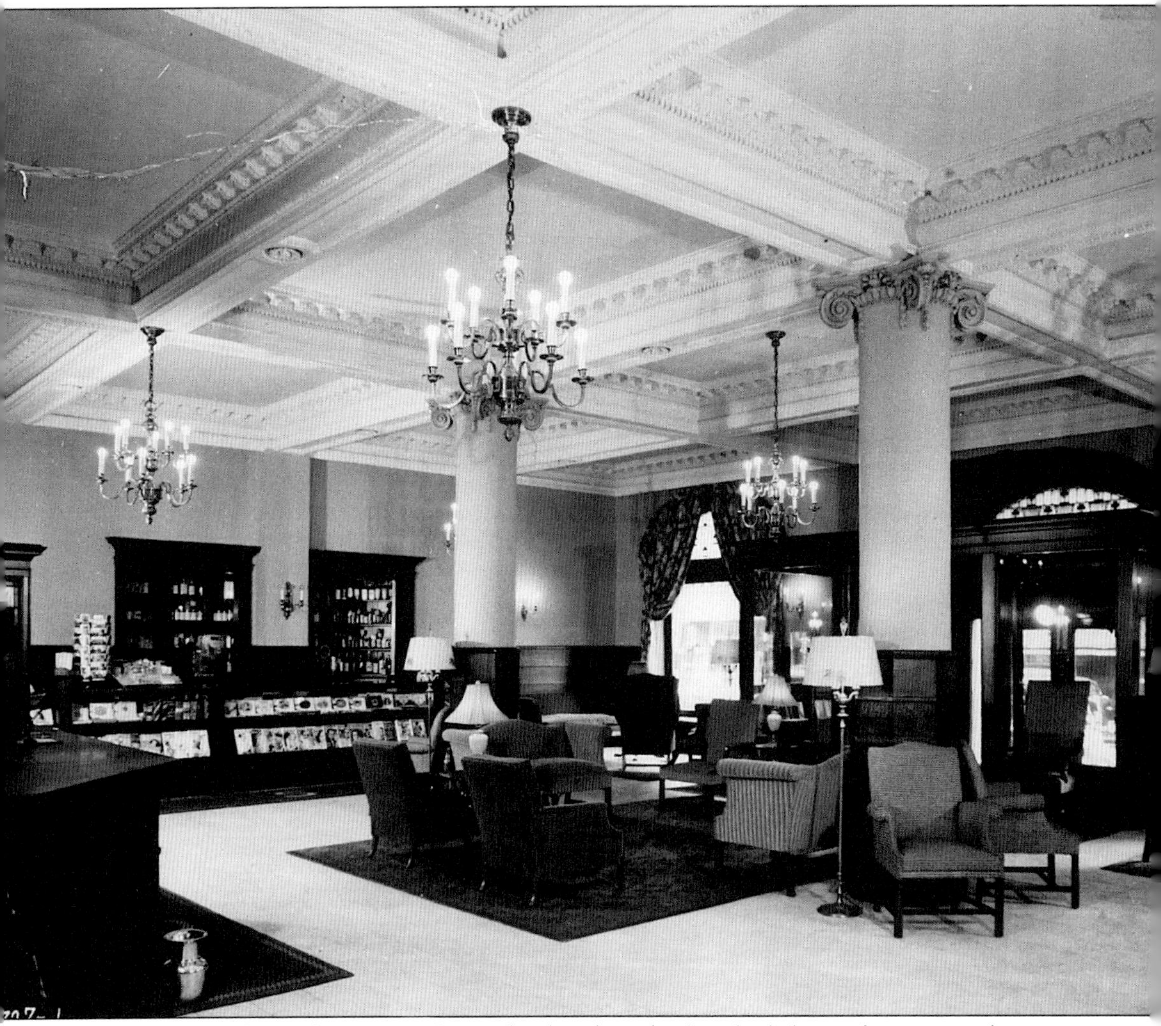

The Stoddard Hotel was a La Crosse landmark and a hotel of choice for visiting dignitaries for many years. In this c. 1940 photo, the lobby is pictured with its grand pillars and graceful chandeliers.

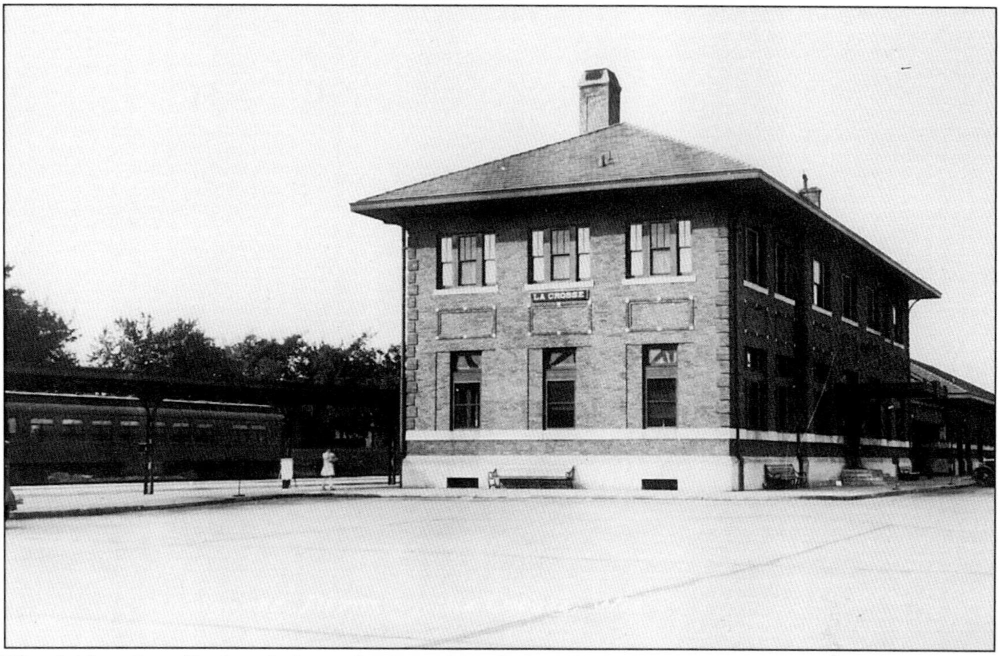

The Milwaukee Railroad depot built in North La Crosse continues to serve passenger-rail travelers today.

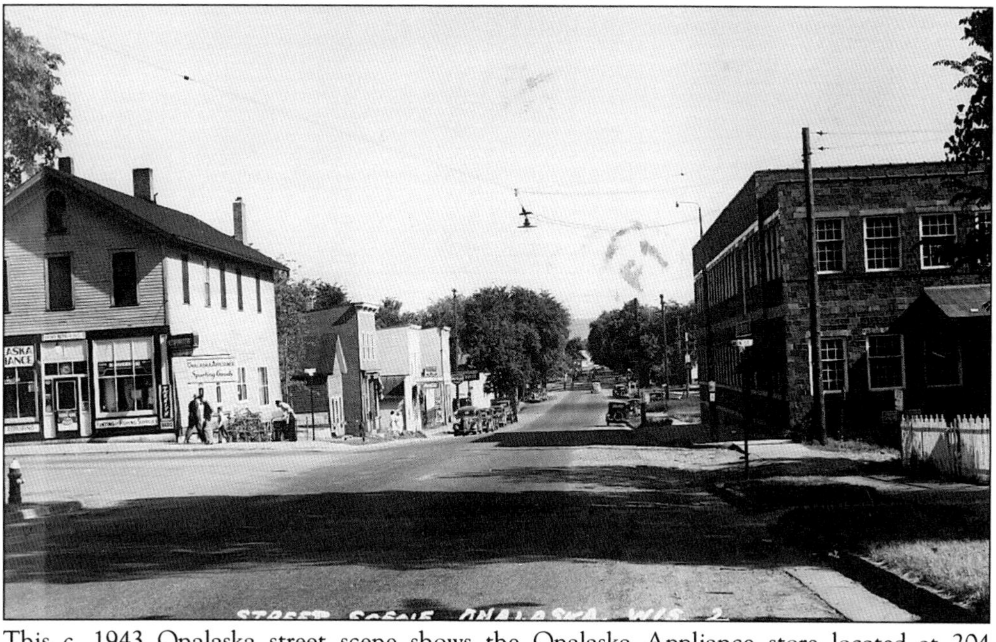

This c. 1943 Onalaska street scene shows the Onalaska Appliance store located at 204 Main Street.

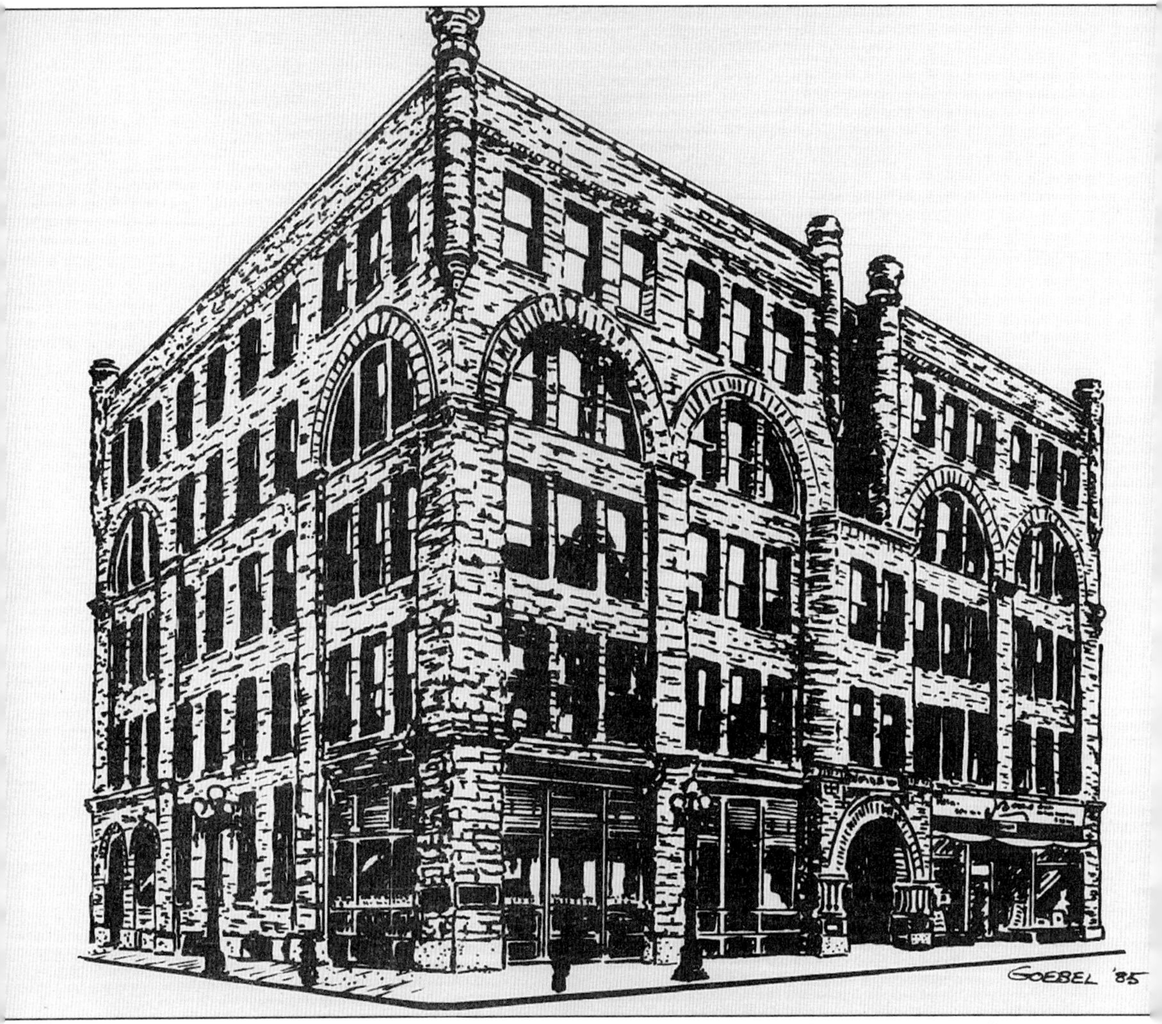

The McMillan Building, located at the northeast corner of Fourth and Main Streets in downtown La Crosse, has recently undergone renovation. The building's restoration team worked hard to reclaim the former beauty of the stately corner block, which houses State Bank of La Crosse.

Three

Defining Moments

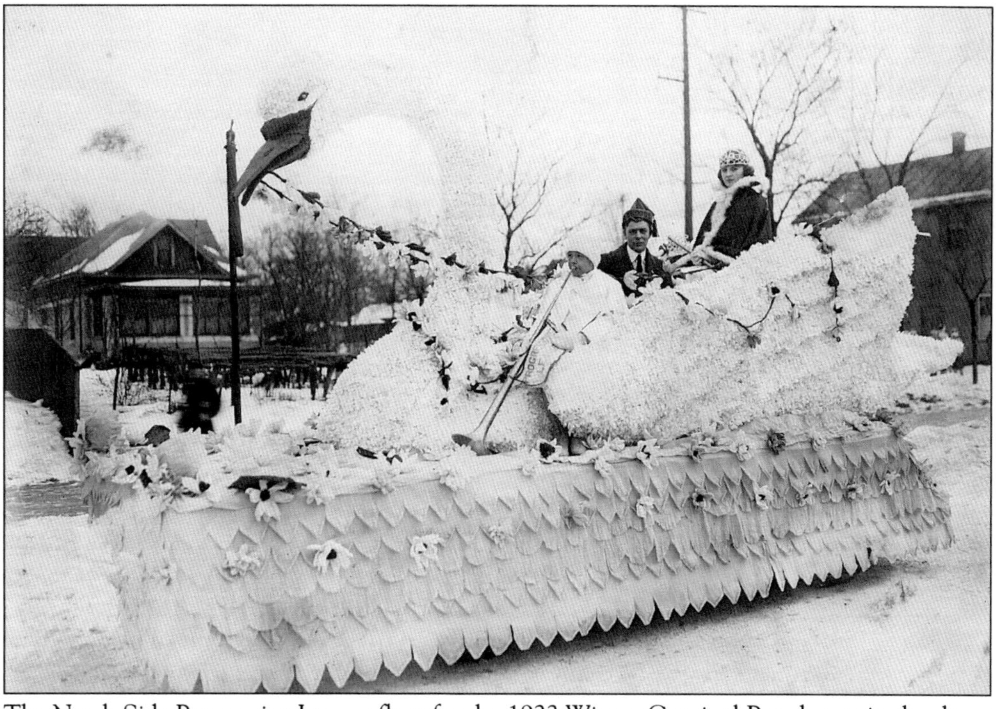

The North Side Progressive League float for the 1922 Winter Carnival Parade was in the shape of a swan and carried Ruth Curtis Allemand as Queen.

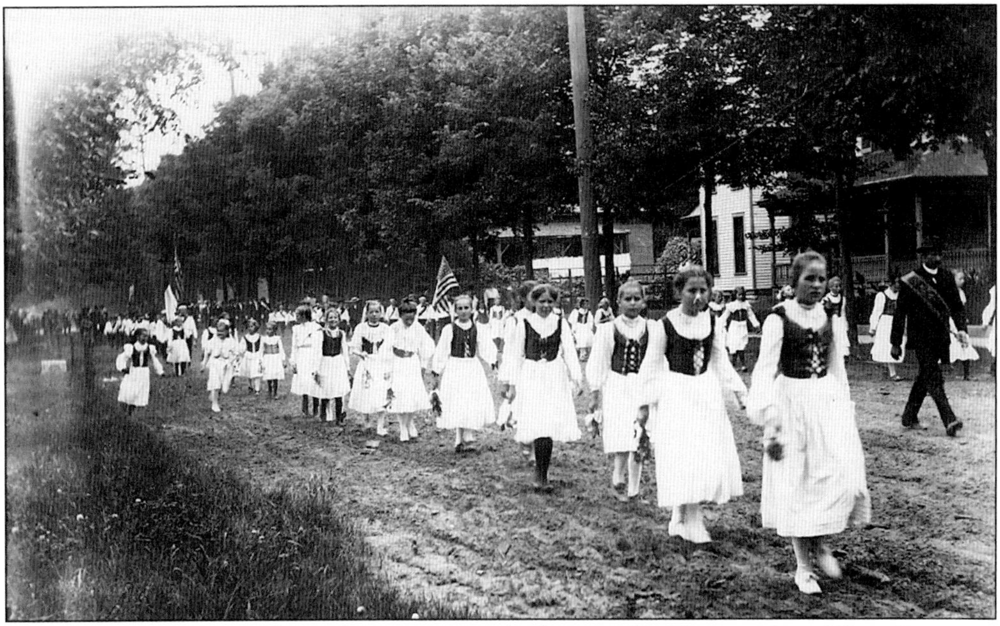

These girls, dressed in traditional costume, march along muddy Thirteenth and Ferry Streets in the Polish Parade held on July 10, 1905.

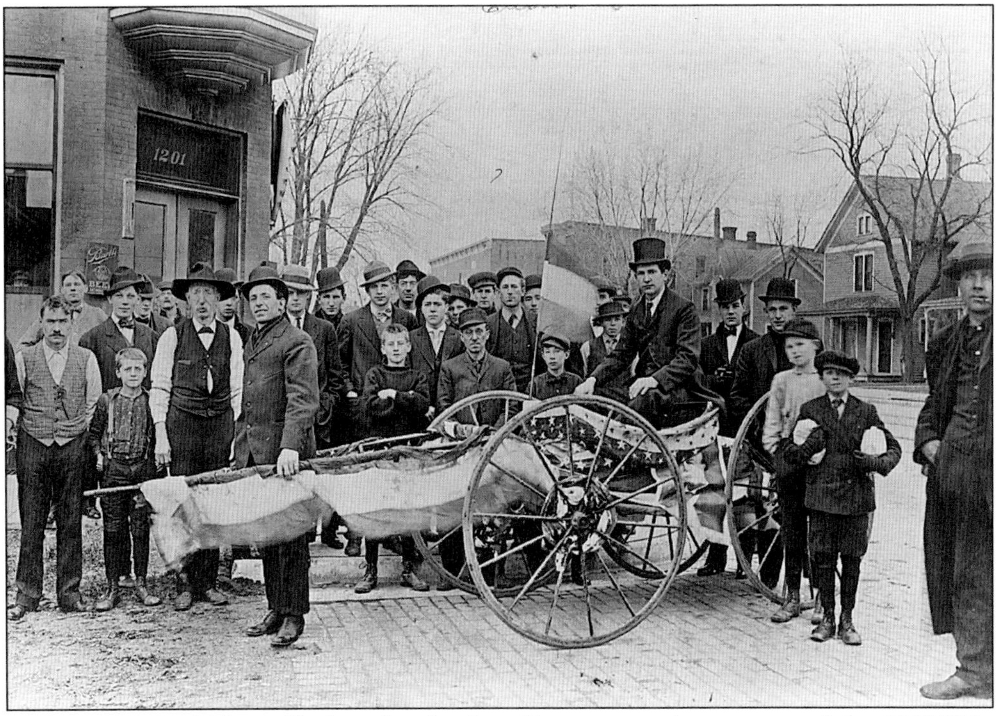

Carl Swanson and Henry Knebes placed a friendly wager on the outcome of the 1908 Taft-Bryan presidential race. Taft and Knebes won, so, as the loser, Swanson supplied the horsepower. Taken at Caledonia and St. Paul Streets, some of the onlookers include Bert Bice (at left, plaid vest), his son Edmond Bice, John Desmond (dark vest), Carl Swanson, and Ray Bice (another son of Bert).

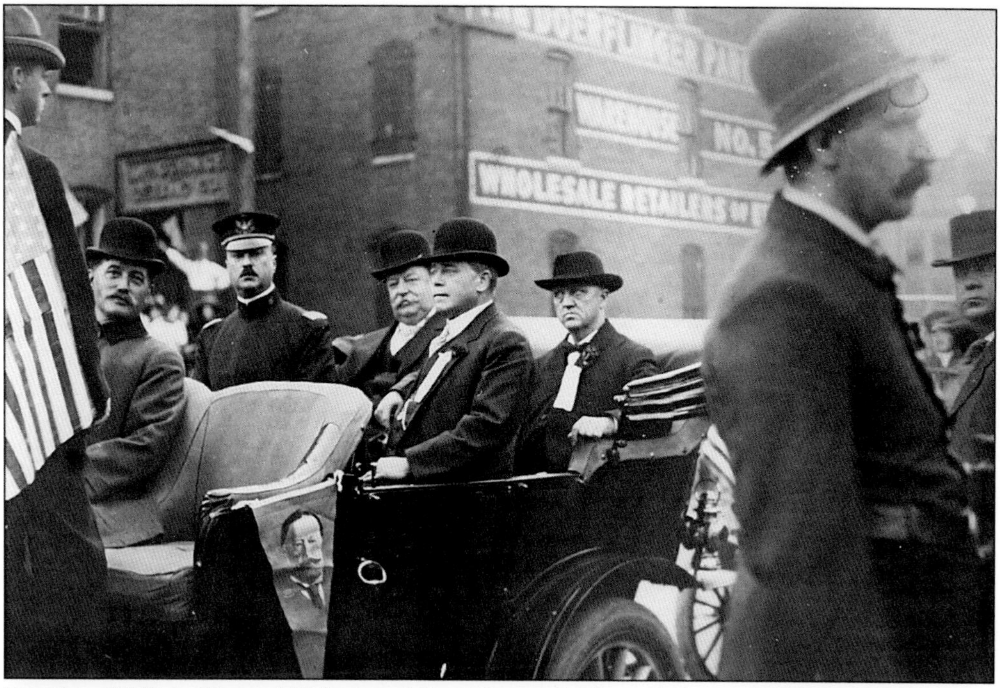

President William Howard Taft visited La Crosse in 1909 to dedicate the YMCA building on Seventh and Main Streets. Frank Hixon is seated in the front seat of the flag-bedecked car. The other riders are Presidential Aide Captain Archie Butt, George Burton (a classmate of the president at Yale), President Taft, and La Crosse Mayor Ori Sorenson.

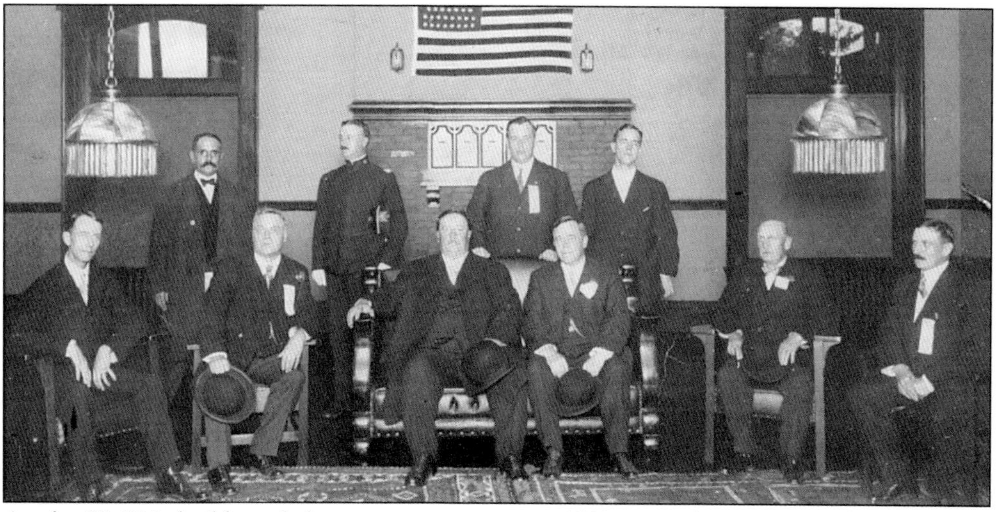

At the YMCA building dedication ceremonies in 1909, area dignitaries gathered to greet President Taft. Those photographed among the leather settees and Oriental carpets in the new building are, from left to right, as follows: (seated) F.G. Tiffany, manager of the Batavian Bank; Congressman John Esch; President Taft; George W. Burton, president of National Bank of La Crosse; W.W. Cargill, president of his own company; and Frank Scofield of the New York Life Insurance Company; (standing) Congressman Tawney from Winona; Presidential Aide Captain Archie Butt; Abner Gran, secretary of the YMCA; and John M. Holley, cashier at State Bank of La Crosse.

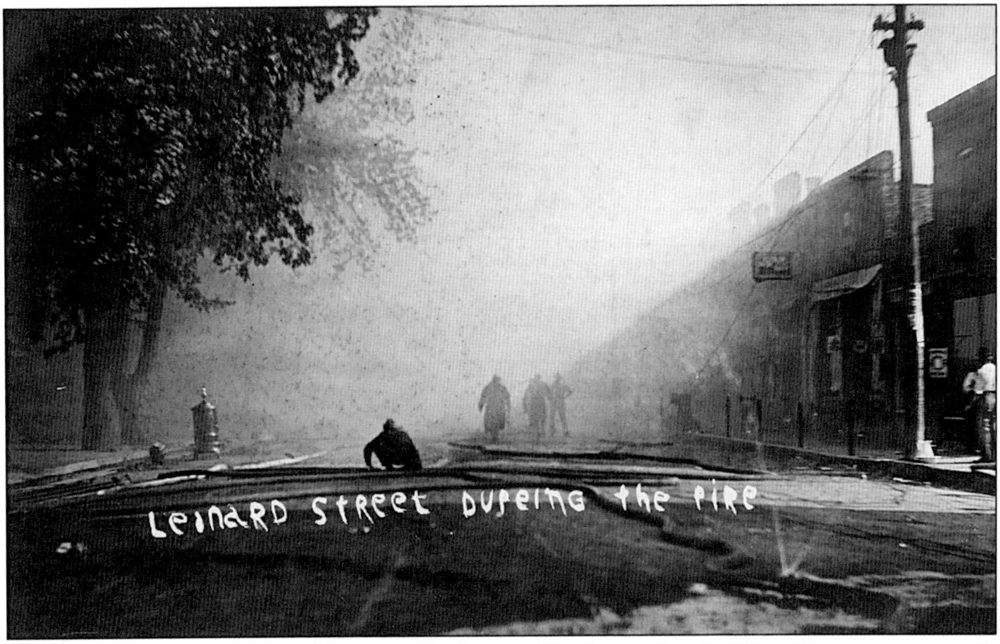

The town of West Salem was almost totally destroyed by fire on July 1, 1911. These two postcards depict Leonard Street during the conflagration. In the top image, firemen battle the smoke and fire, and below are the ruined remains of the Cook and Pratt Livery Barn.

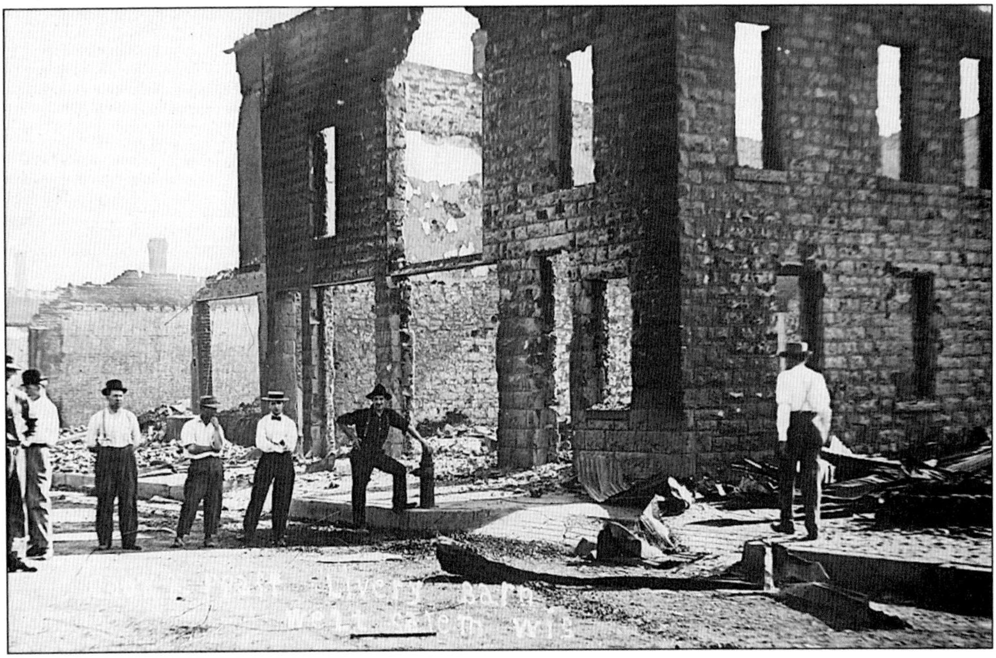

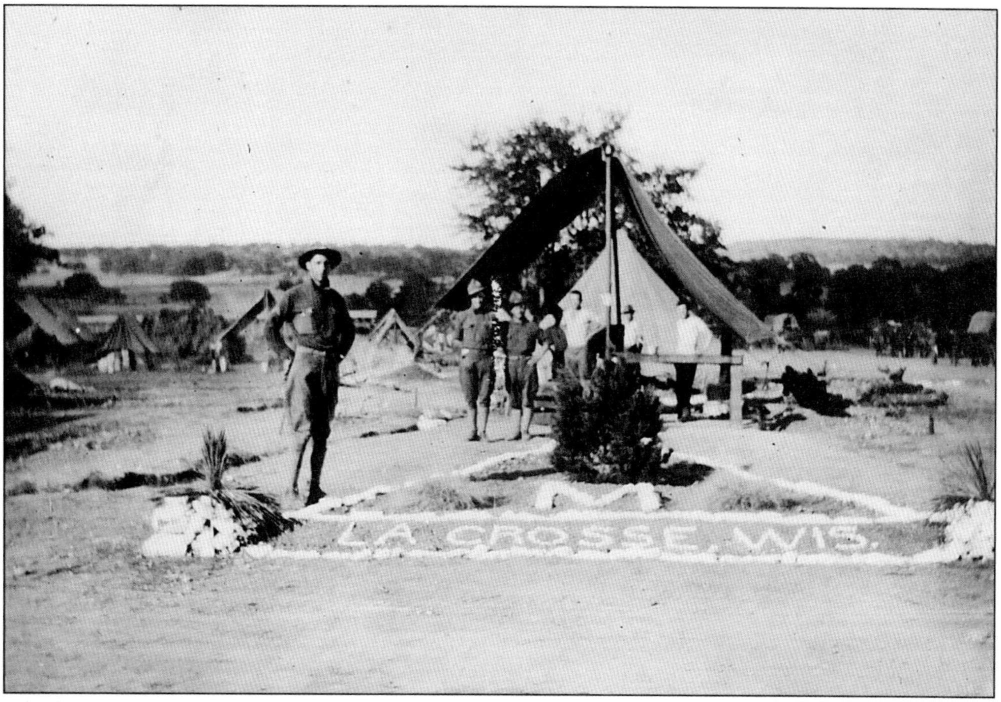

Alvah M. Hill of Onalaska was first sergeant in Company M, Third Wisconsin Infantry, when it was mustered into active service in 1916 to take part in the Mexican Border Wars. He is shown here in Texas with fellow soldiers awaiting duty.

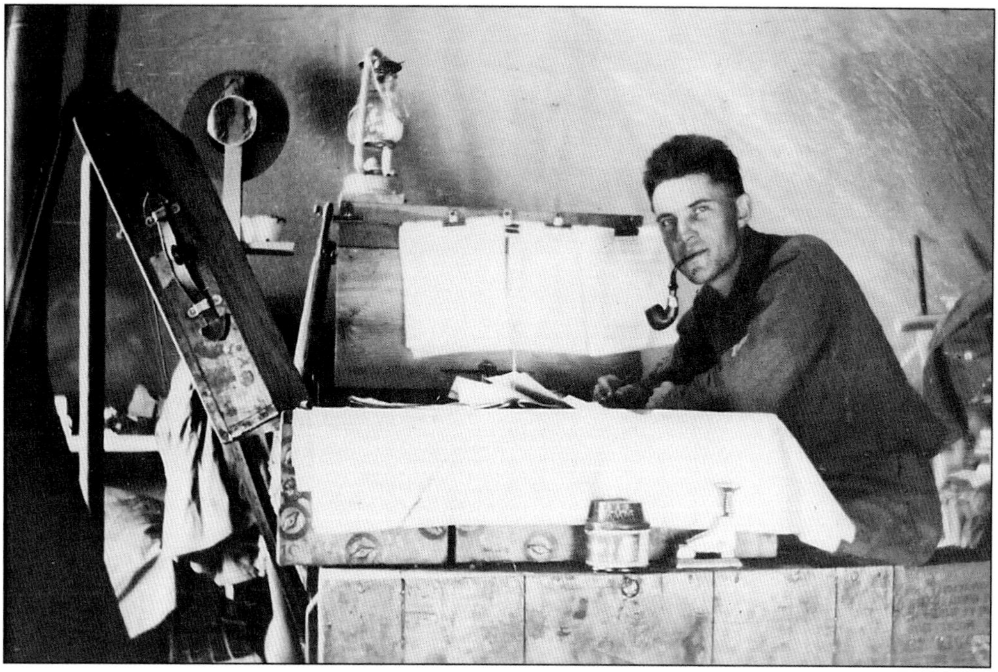

Sergeant Hill, pictured in his tent in 1916, wrote the following message on the back of this postcard: "Yours truly at home. My desk is made of boxes containing 10,800 rounds of cartridges."

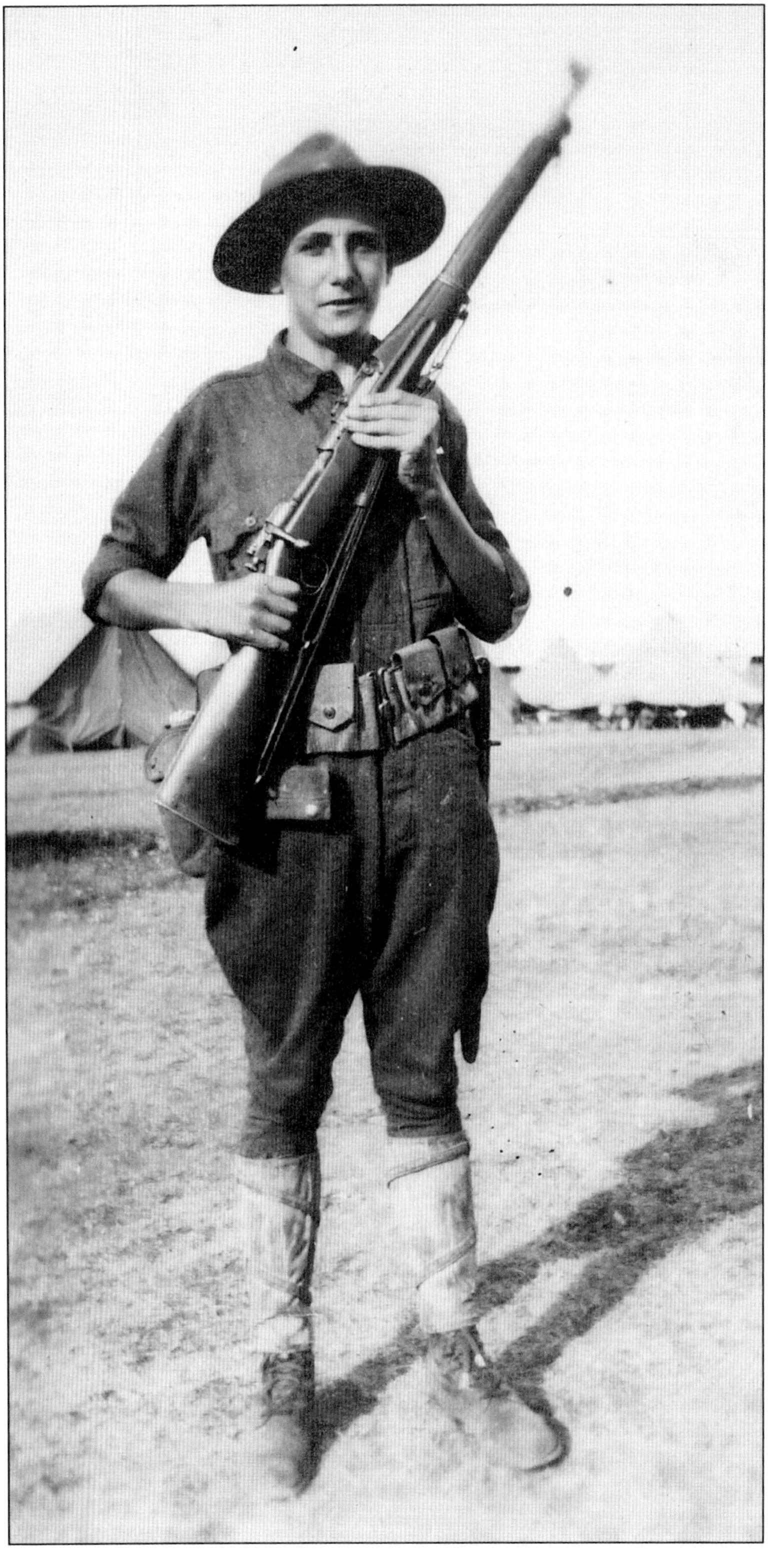

Wenzel Prucha is shown in the uniform worn by soldiers during the Mexican Border War. This photograph was taken on August 1, 1916.

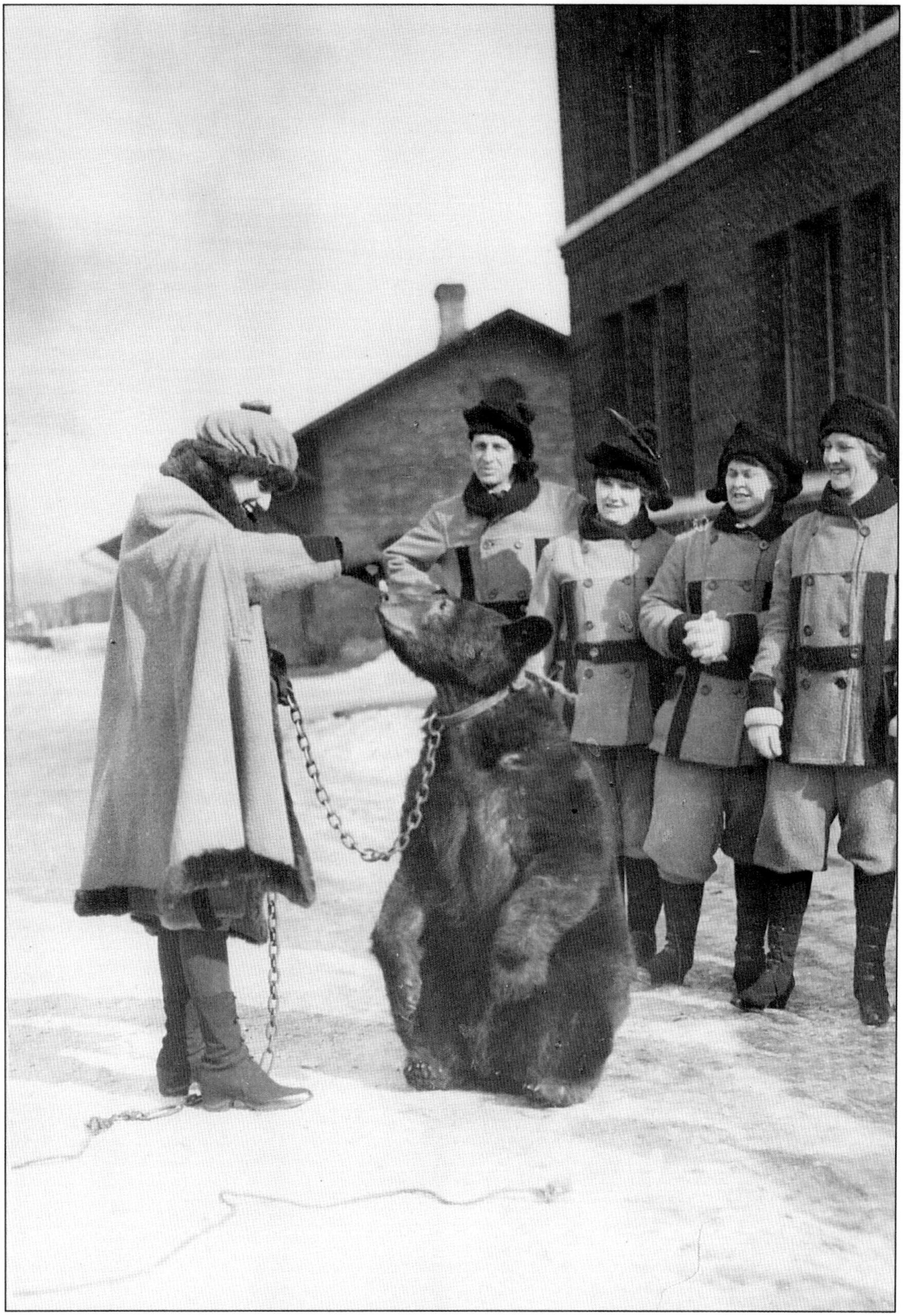

A Winter Carnival was held in La Crosse in 1921 and 1922, complete with winter sports competitions, parades, royalty, floats, and costumes. The W.A. Roosevelt employees wore matching costumes and accompanied a trained bear as the mascot for the 1922 parade.

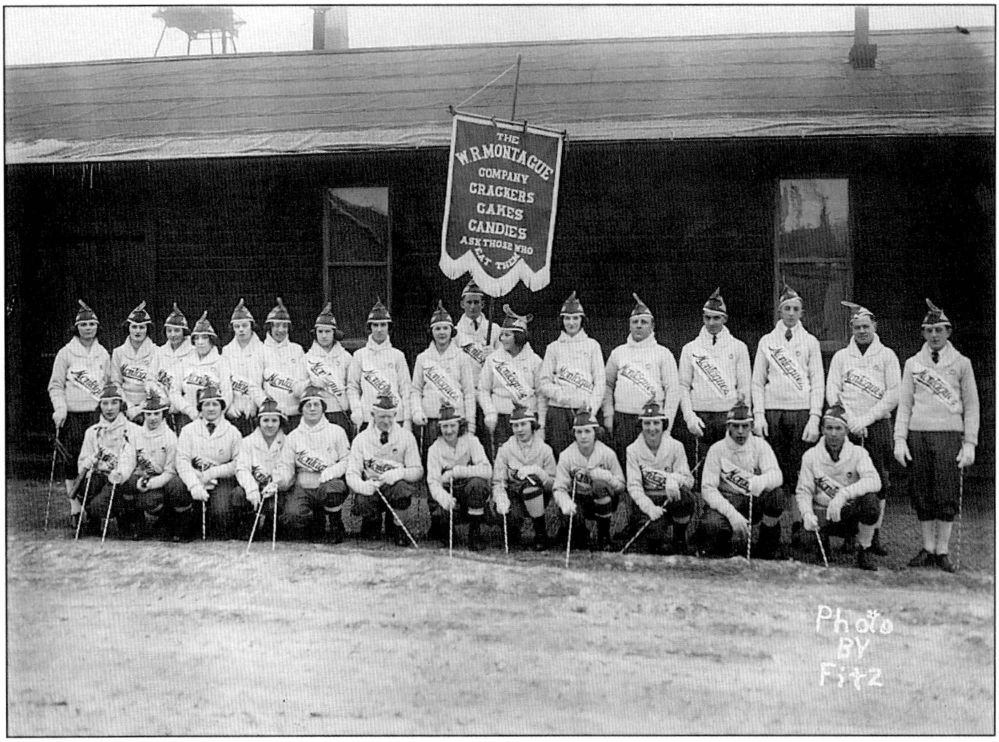

The W.R. Montague Company, which made crackers, cakes, and candies, asked all of their employees, male and female, to wear identical outfits when they marched in the Winter Carnival Parade. Everyone is wearing a white sweater, knickers, white socks, white gloves, and pointed hats.

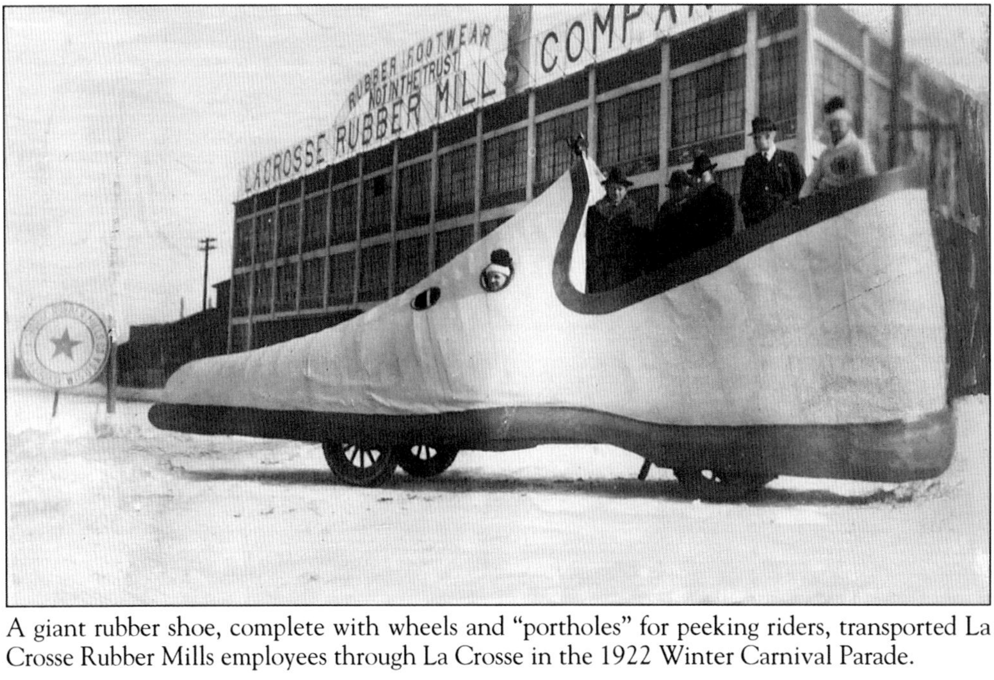

A giant rubber shoe, complete with wheels and "portholes" for peeking riders, transported La Crosse Rubber Mills employees through La Crosse in the 1922 Winter Carnival Parade.

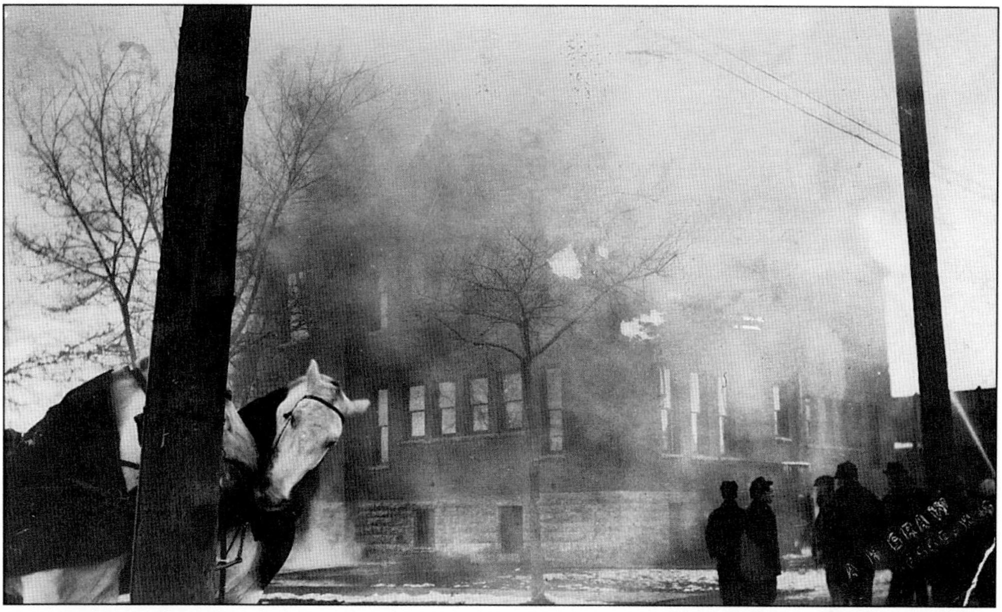

Two firehouse horses nuzzle each other as they stand outside the First Ward School during a fire in 1922. Located at the corner of Sixteenth and Vine Streets, the school was named Washington School earlier in the century. At that time, several city schools were named after famous Americans, including Lincoln, Jefferson, Franklin, and Hamilton.

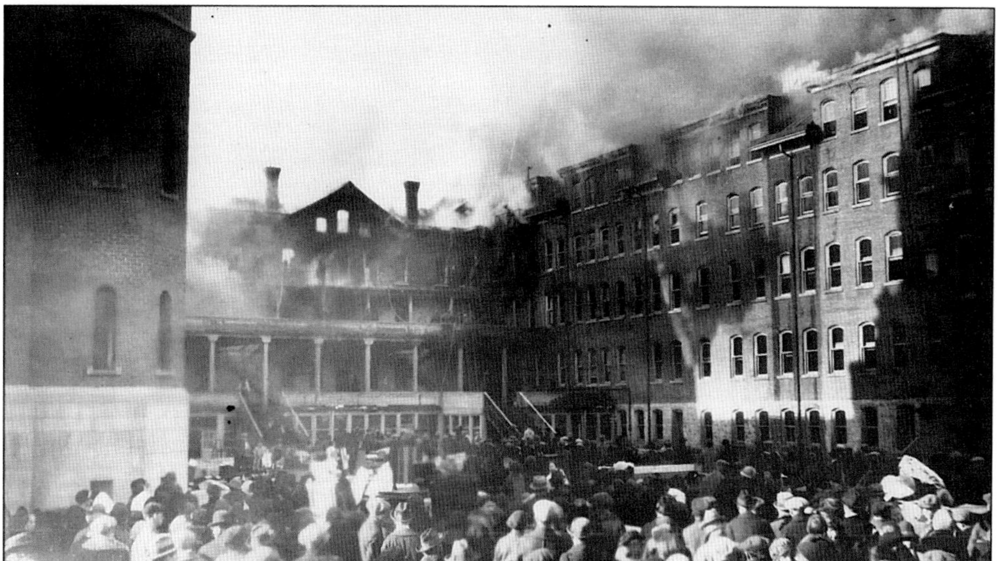

Crowds of onlookers gather in the St. Rose Convent courtyard on December 2, 1923, to gape at the smoldering buildings. After being severely damaged by the fire, the convent was razed. The new facility was rebuilt in record time, and the sisters were in their new home by March 1, 1925.

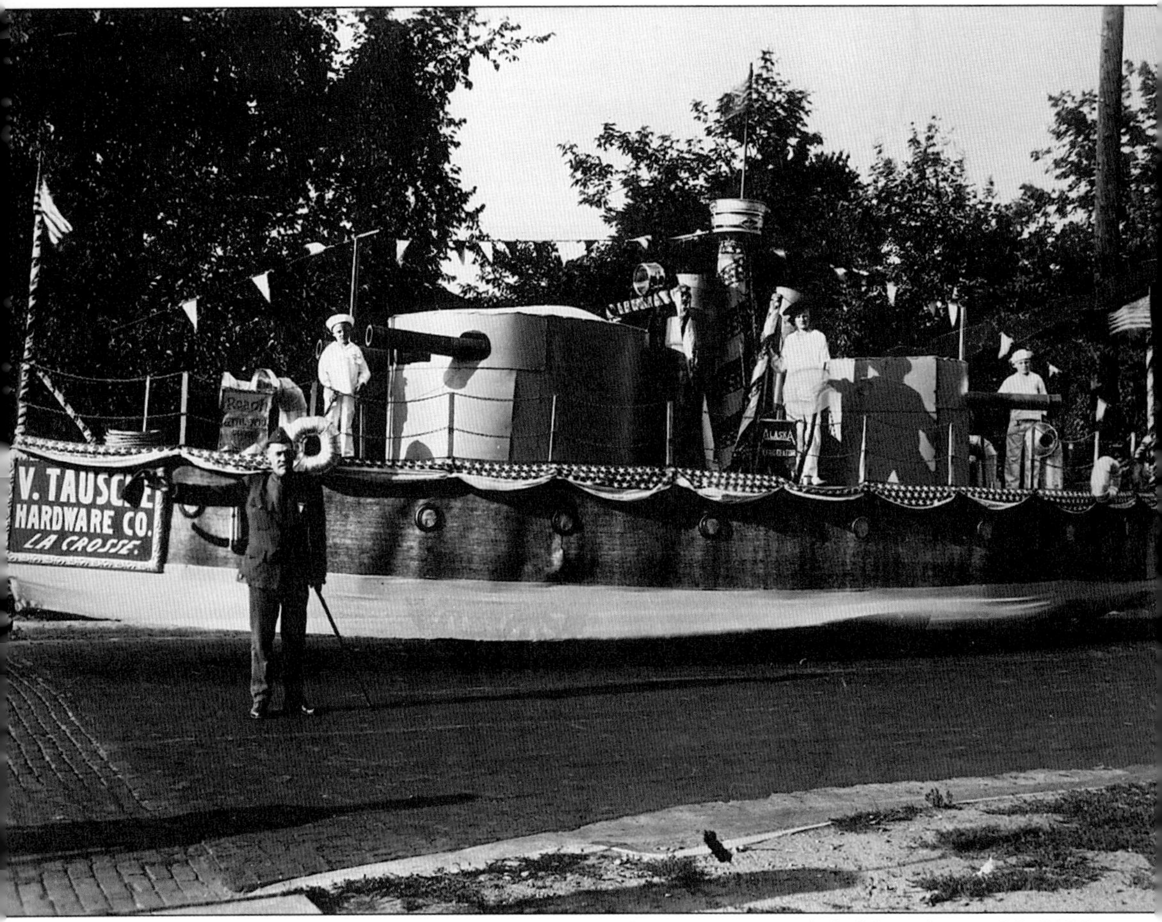

This float won first prize in the American Legion Convention parade held on August 27, 1926. Shaped like a Navy ship, the float carried three boys dressed in sailor outfits and advertised Alaska Refrigerators and Reach Athletic Goods. The float was sponsored by the Tausche Hardware Company.

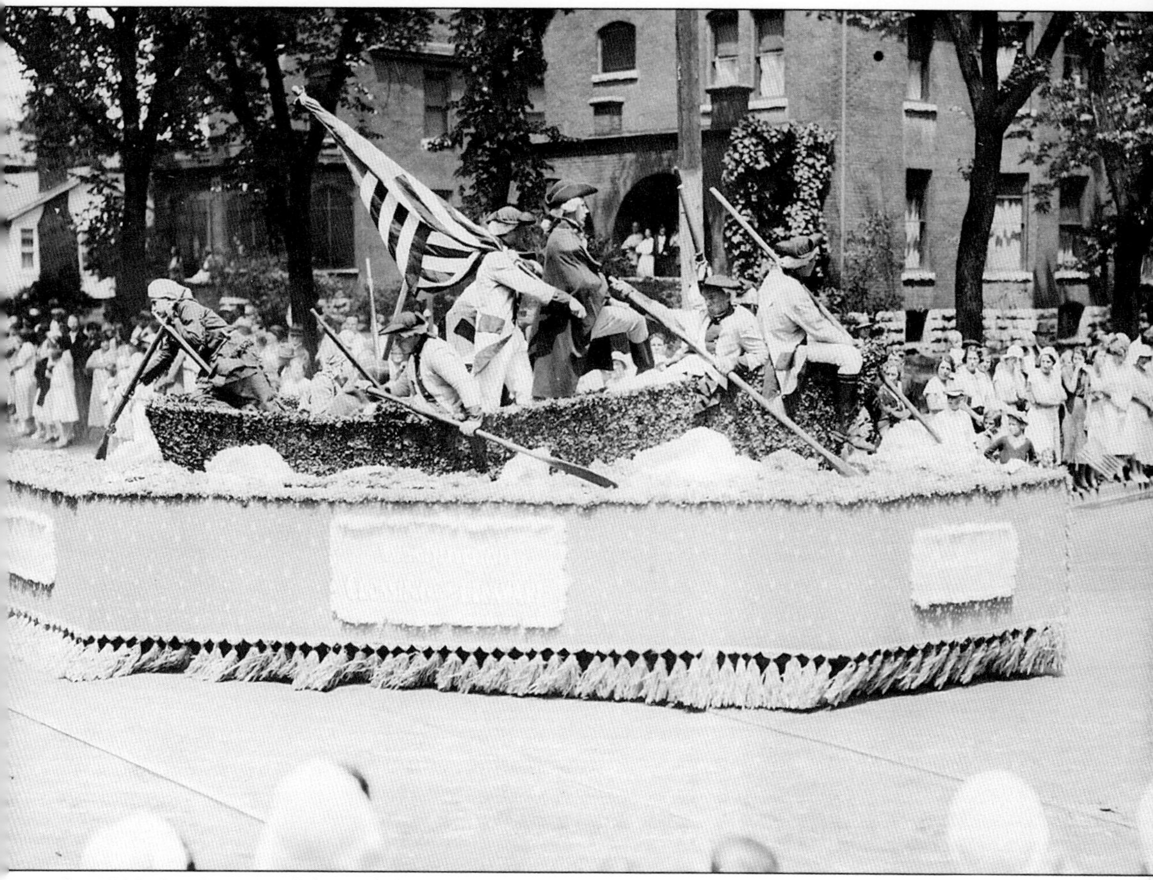

In 1932, La Crosse celebrated the 200th anniversary of George Washington's birth with a big parade. This float, shown here turning the corner of West Avenue and Main Street, represented Washington crossing the Delaware and was sponsored by Doerflinger's Department Store.

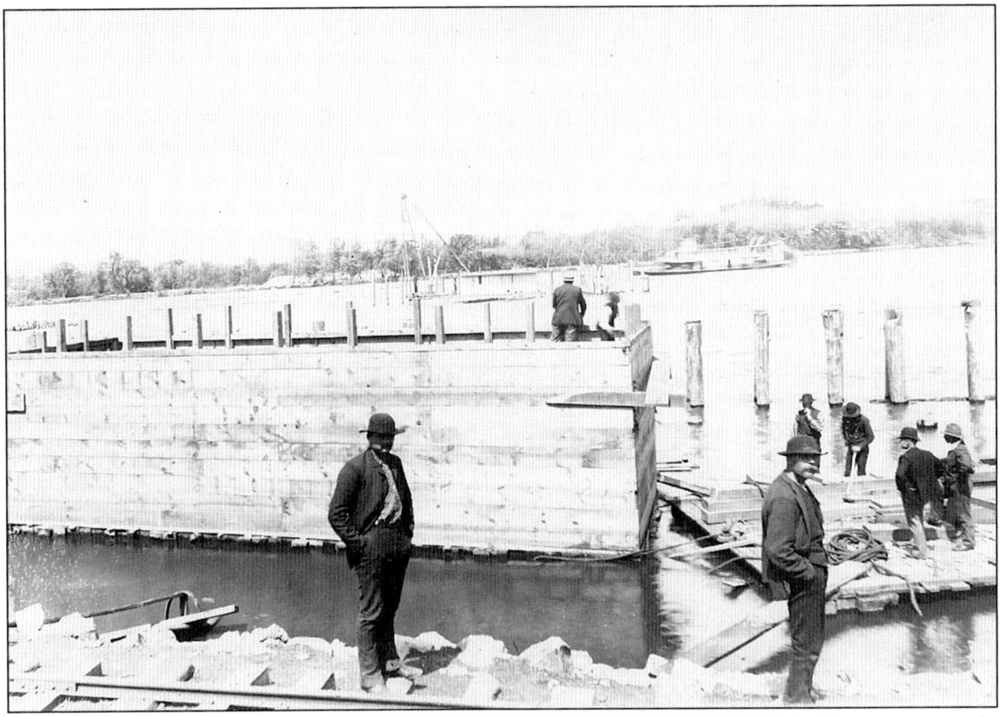

With a new century around the corner, a bridge spanning the Mississippi River was sorely needed in La Crosse. Built in 1891 and dedicated on the Fourth of July, the bridge gave easy access back and forth from Minnesota. Toll charges were listed as follows: sheep and hogs on foot, 5¢; cattle and horses, 10¢; horse and rider, 15¢; wagon team and driver (with his lady), 25¢.

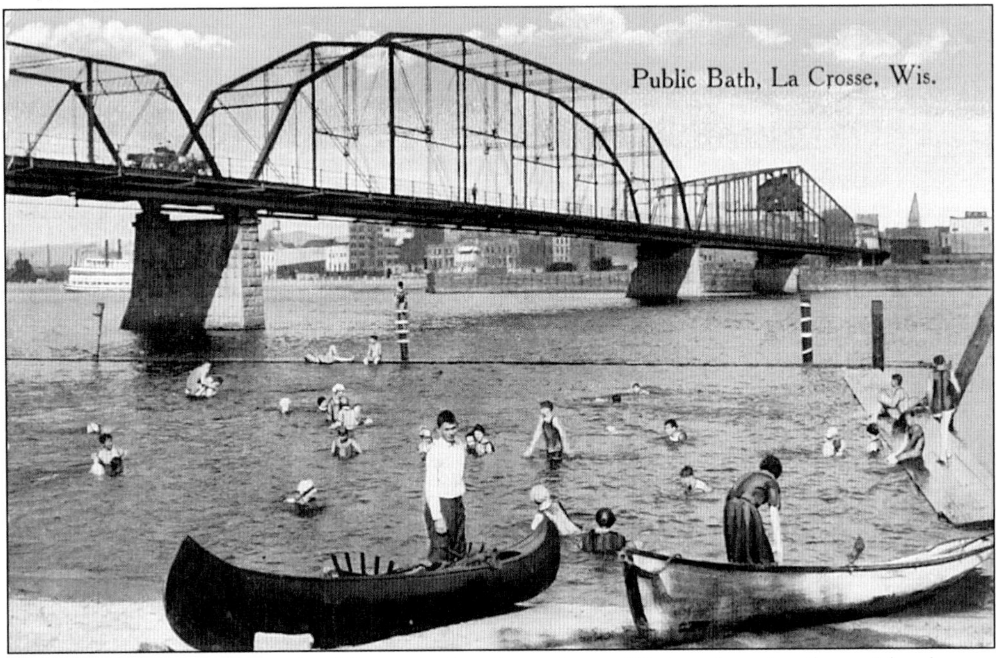

This 1917 postcard depicts the Wagon Bridge above the public beach at Pettibone Island.

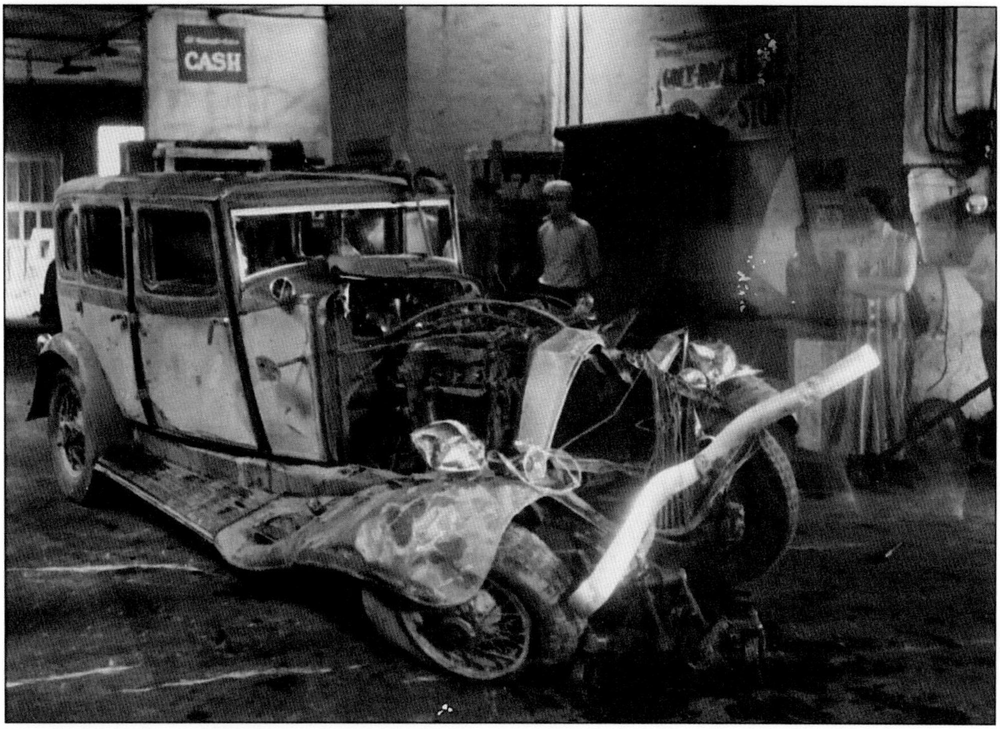

Until 1935, the only bridge crossing the Mississippi River between La Crosse and La Crescent, Minnesota, was the Wagon Bridge. Around midnight on August 9 of that year, this car hit a guard rail on the west approach, collapsing the bridge. The need for a modern span capable of carrying heavier cars and trucks suddenly became critical.

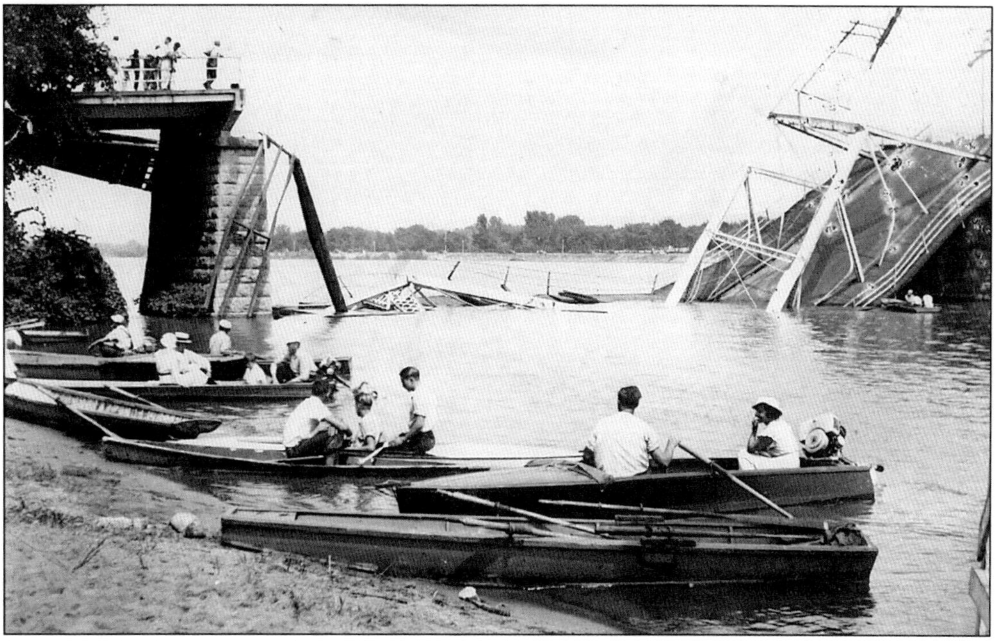

Curious onlookers inspect the collapsed wagon bridge from motor boats, row boats, and bridge footing. Two people were killed when their automobile collided with the bridge in 1935.

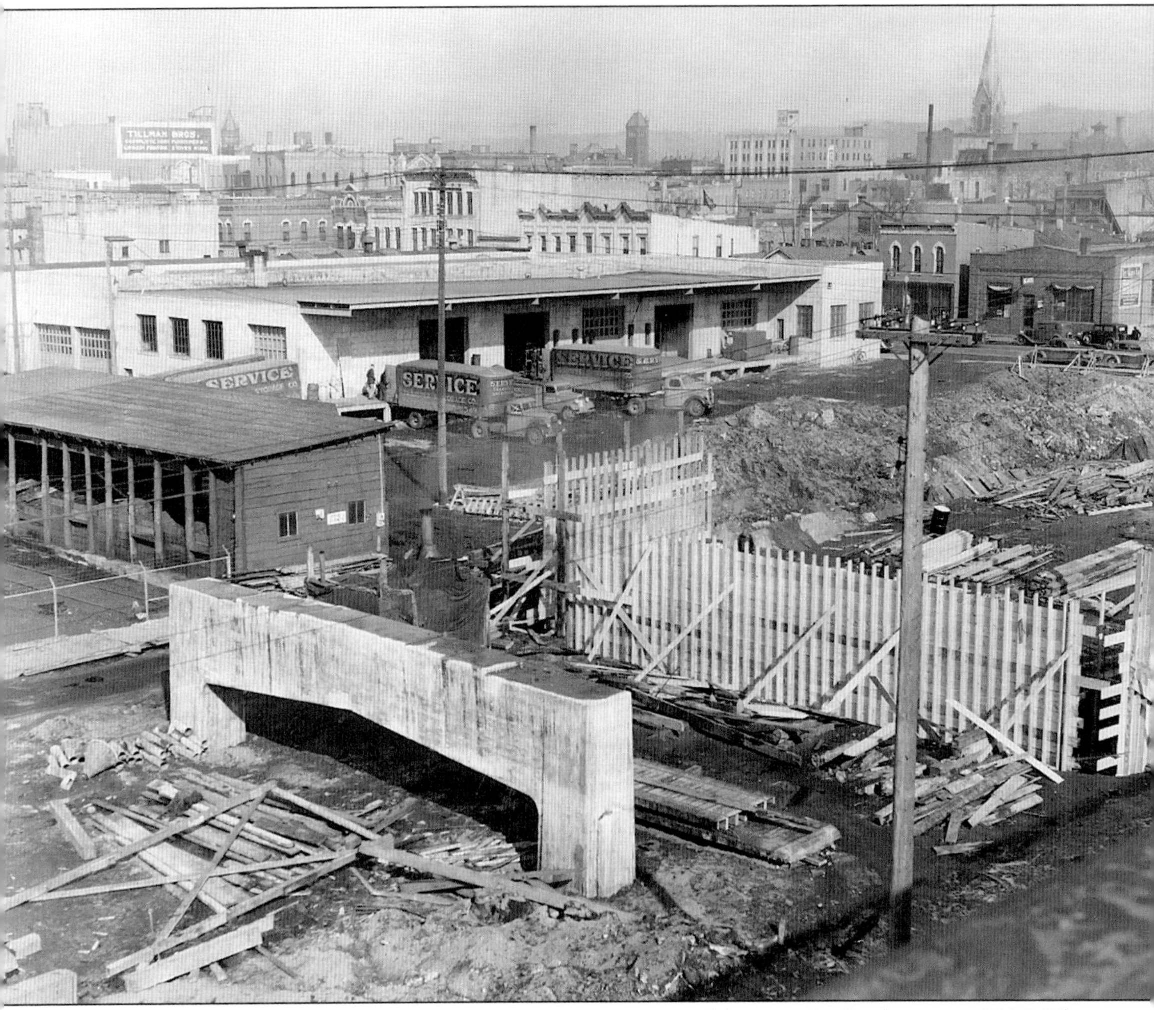

After two years of planning and legalities, construction of the new bridge began in 1937. This photo shows the first in a series of concrete piers completed. The Service Transfer and Storage Company on Third Street is seen in the background.

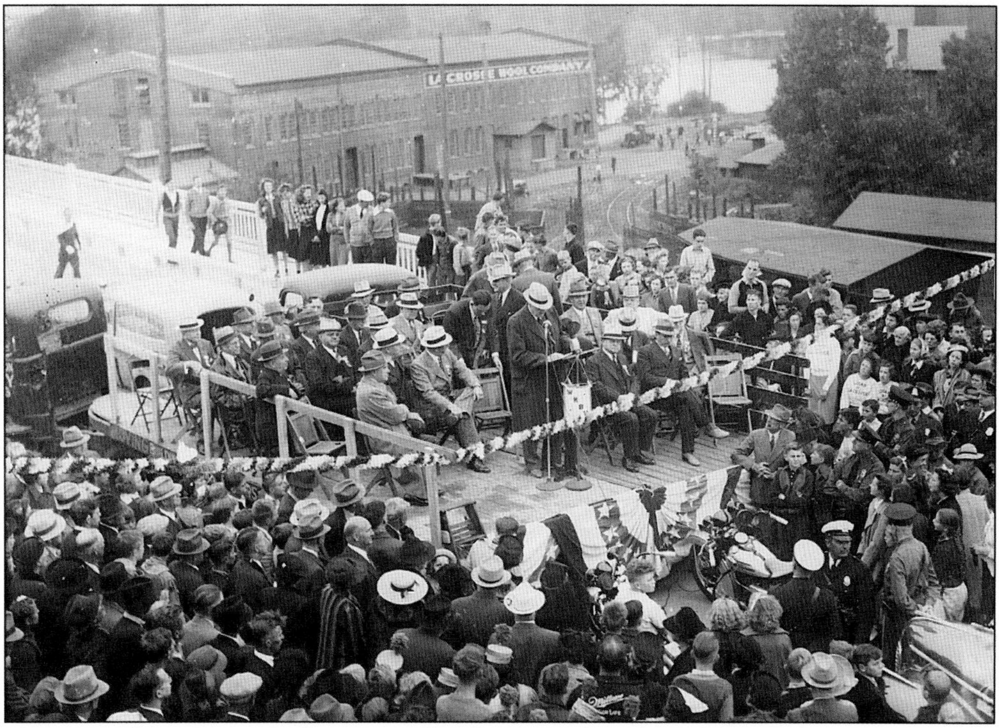

The new Cass Street bridge was officially opened with a huge dedication ceremony on September 23, 1939. Dignitaries crowd the stand as the radio station broadcasts the momentous occasion.

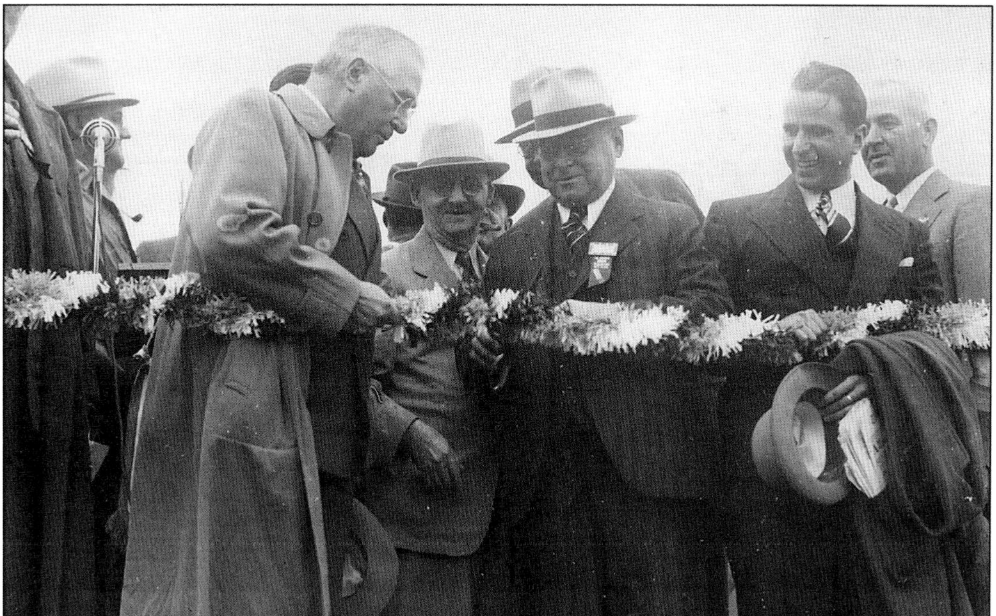

Wisconsin Governor Julius Heil and La Crosse Mayor J.J. Verchota cut the opening ribbon as part of a day filled with parades, band concerts, airplane aerobics, water sports, and pow-wows. Looking on with a big smile is R.W. Davis, the chairman of the board of supervisors.

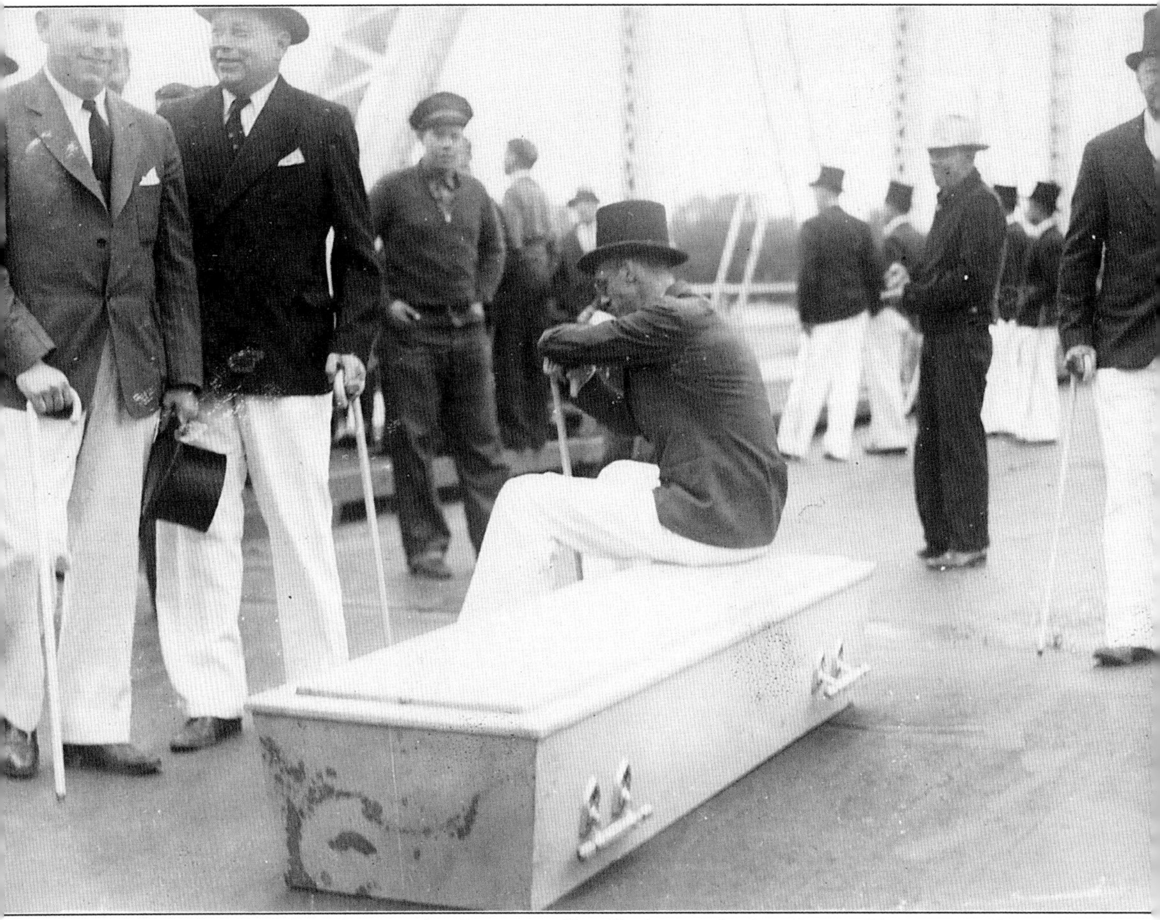

Fifteen minutes after the new bridge was officially born, the La Crosse Plugs carried a casket (representing the death of the old Wagon Bridge) across the bridge just before the swing span opened for the last time.

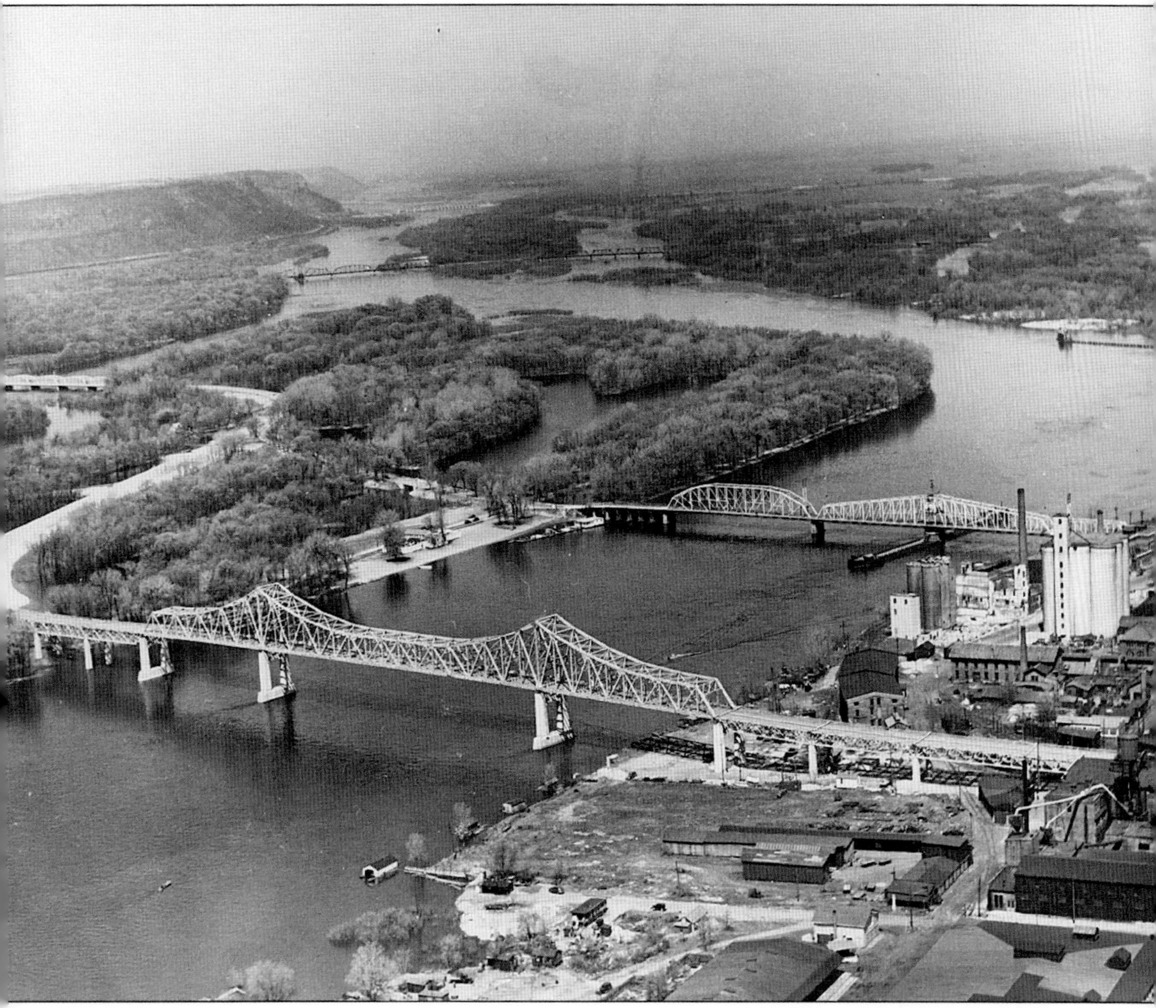

The Wagon Bridge was reinforced in 1935 until the modern Main Channel Bridge could be completed. The project was built with Wisconsin highway money and regular Federal Aid funds, employing more than 300 workers. Over 288,000 man hours and $280,000 were spent on erecting the 2,533-foot-long bridge. Both the new and old spans are shown in this photograph taken before the destruction of the Wagon Bridge.

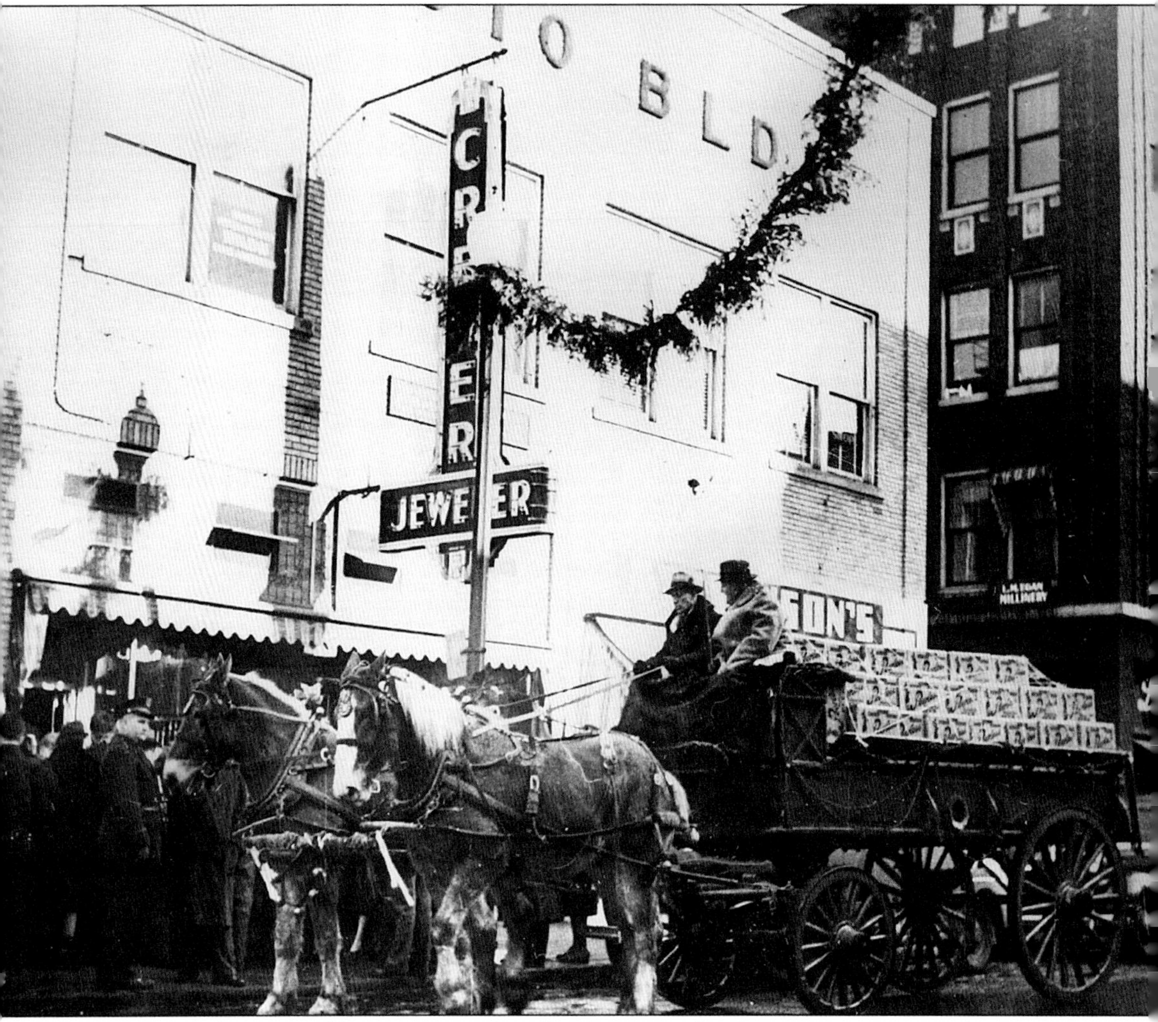

The manufacturing of beer was introduced to La Crosse by German immigrants. At one time, the city was second only to Milwaukee in beer production. The industry was still in full swing with five working breweries when Prohibition became the law of the land in 1920. During Prohibition, the G. Heileman brewery made "near-beer," and thus stayed in production. Although the Gund Brewery did not open after Prohibition, their Peerless beer was made by Carl Michel's La Crosse Brewery after beer-making was again made legal. This 1933 photo, entitled "The Repeal of Prohibition," shows a wagon making its way down Main Street, loaded with Peerless beer.

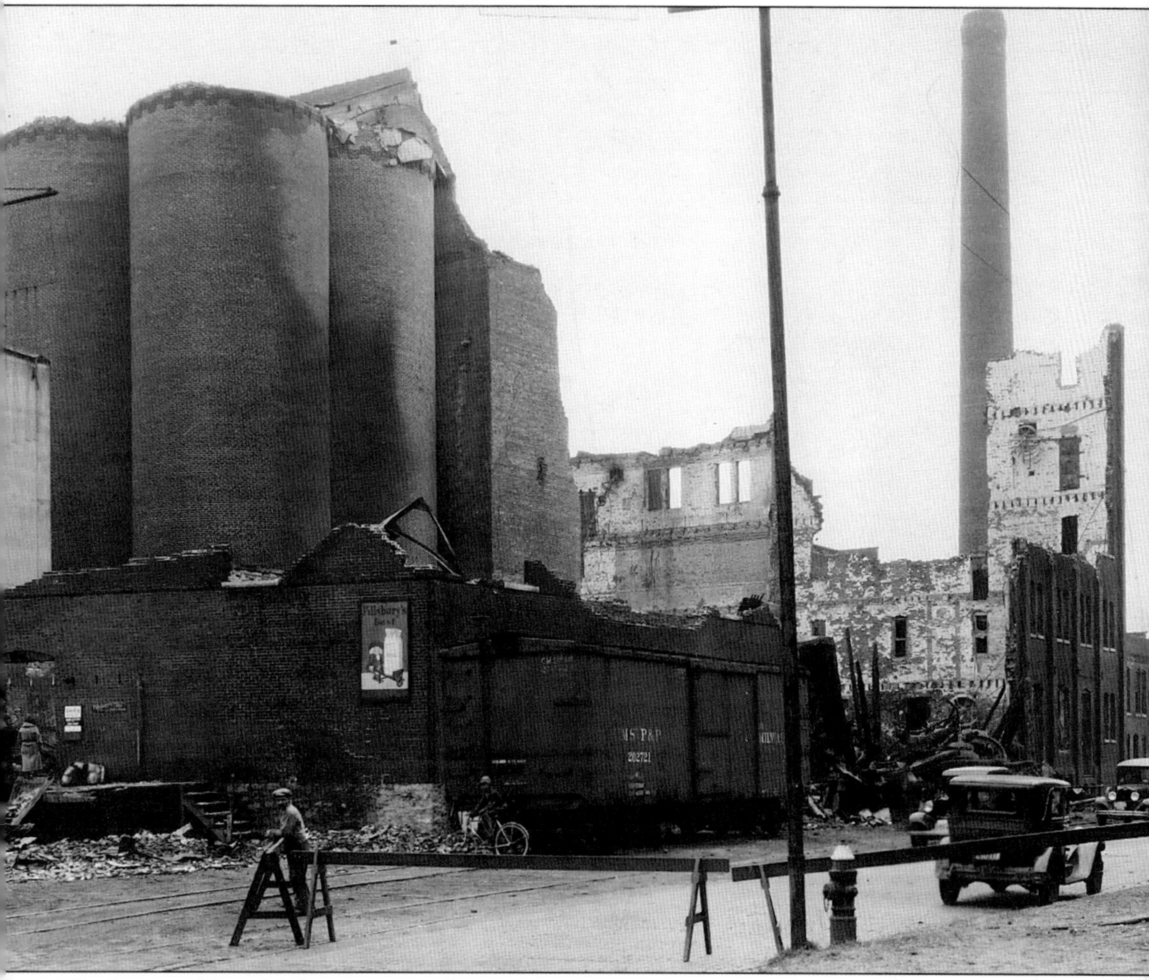

The Listman Flour Mill, a major employer in La Crosse, was destroyed by fire in 1934. After the smoke had cleared and the embers had cooled, the brick shell was all that remained of the large complex. Notice the unscorched Pillsbury flour ad on the wall.

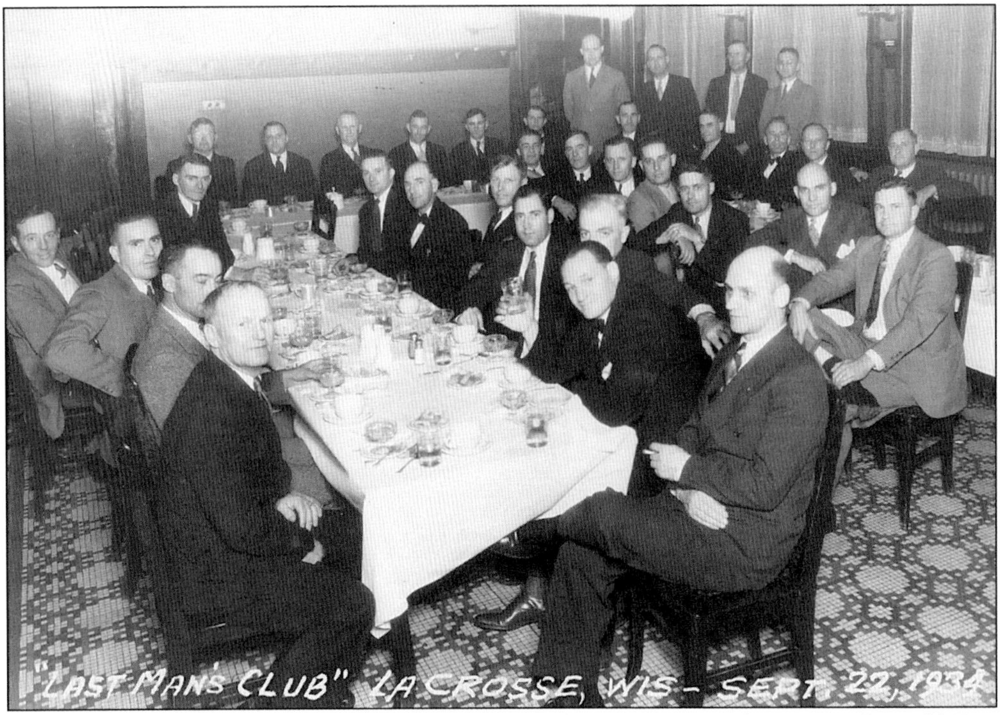

The "Last Man's Club" was made up of veterans of the Mexican Border War and World War I who met annually to toast their fallen comrades and reminisce. This photograph shows the 1934 members.

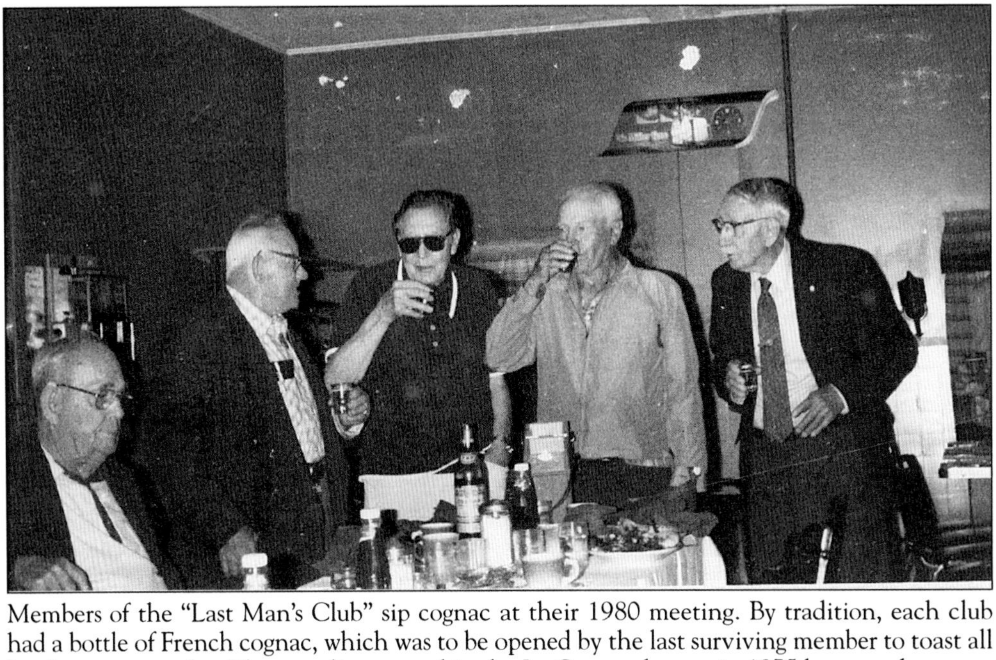

Members of the "Last Man's Club" sip cognac at their 1980 meeting. By tradition, each club had a bottle of French cognac, which was to be opened by the last surviving member to toast all his former comrades. The sampling started in the La Crosse chapter in 1975 because they were afraid the sole survivor wouldn't be able to get the cork out of the bottle! Pictured are Lavern Smay, Joseph Raith, Clarence McCall, Fred Dietz, and Herchal Bold.

When this photo was taken in 1935, Benton Minor was 20 years old and worked in the Civilian Conservation Corps at Camp New Wood.

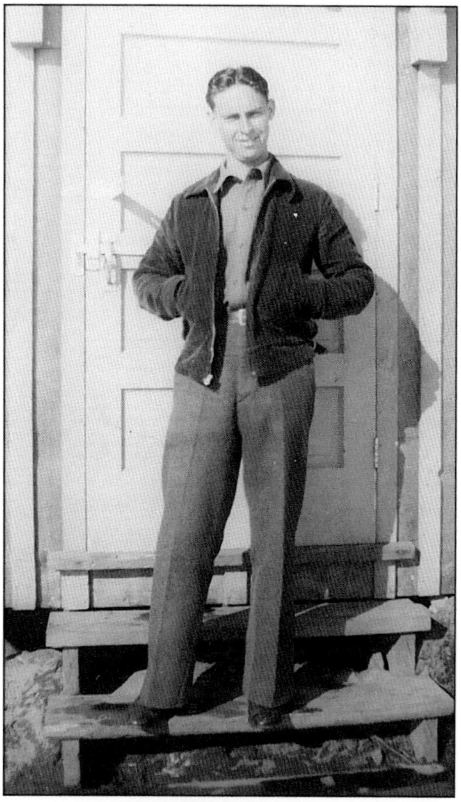

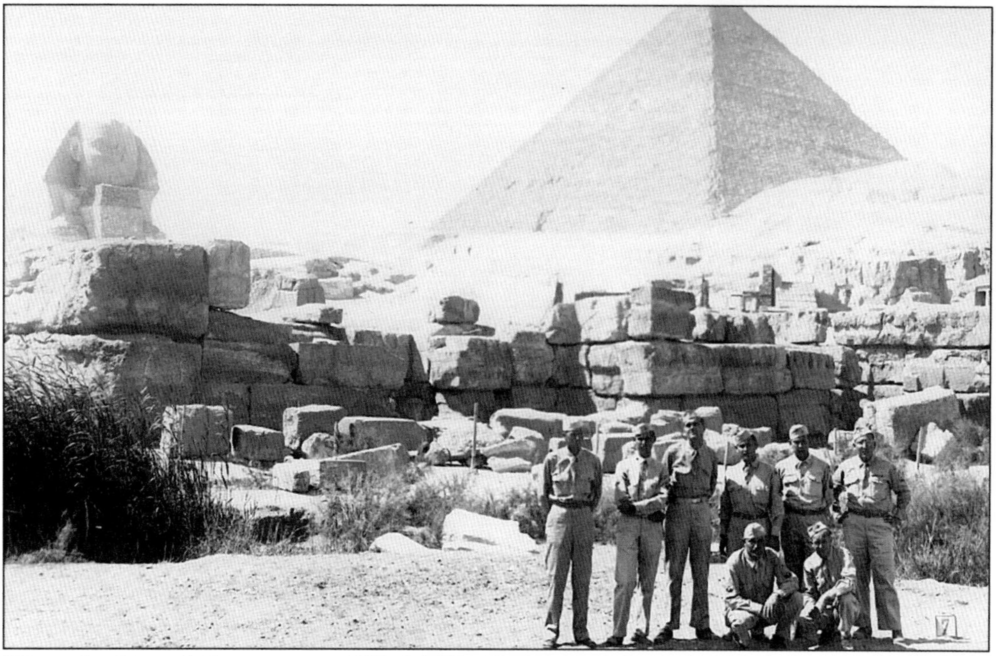

When the United States entered World War II, Benton Minor joined the Army and went to places far from hometown La Crosse. Shown in Cairo, Egypt, in September 1944, Minor listed the people in the photograph as "Caldwell, Myself, Weaver, Cassidy, Frank, Dan, Pop, Jones."

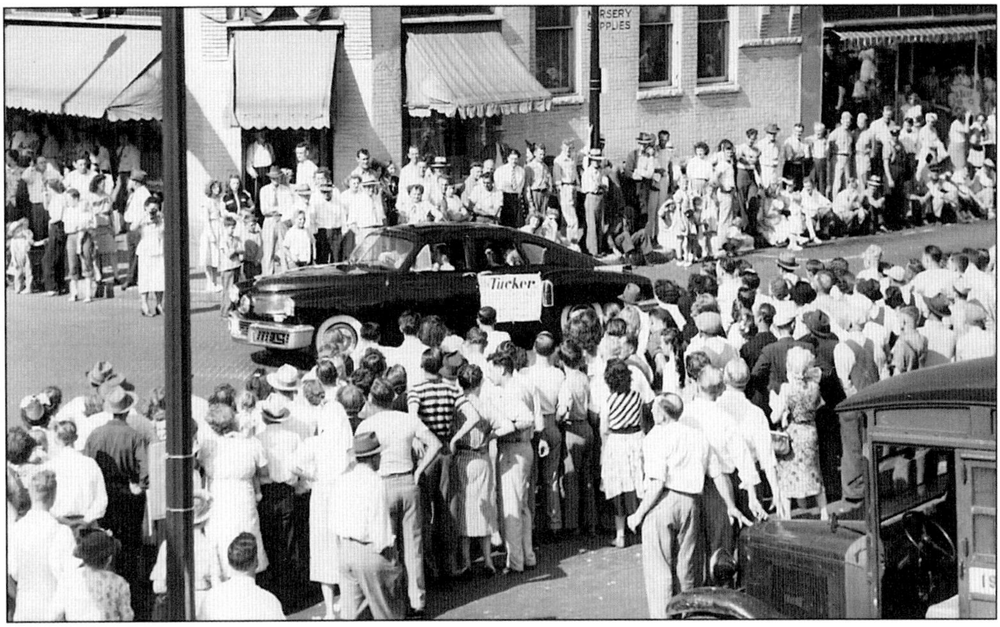

As part of Wisconsin's 1948 Centennial celebration, a parade was held in La Crosse's downtown business district. This photo, taken at the corner of Fourth and Jay Streets, spotlights the new, streamlined—and short-lived—Tucker automobile.

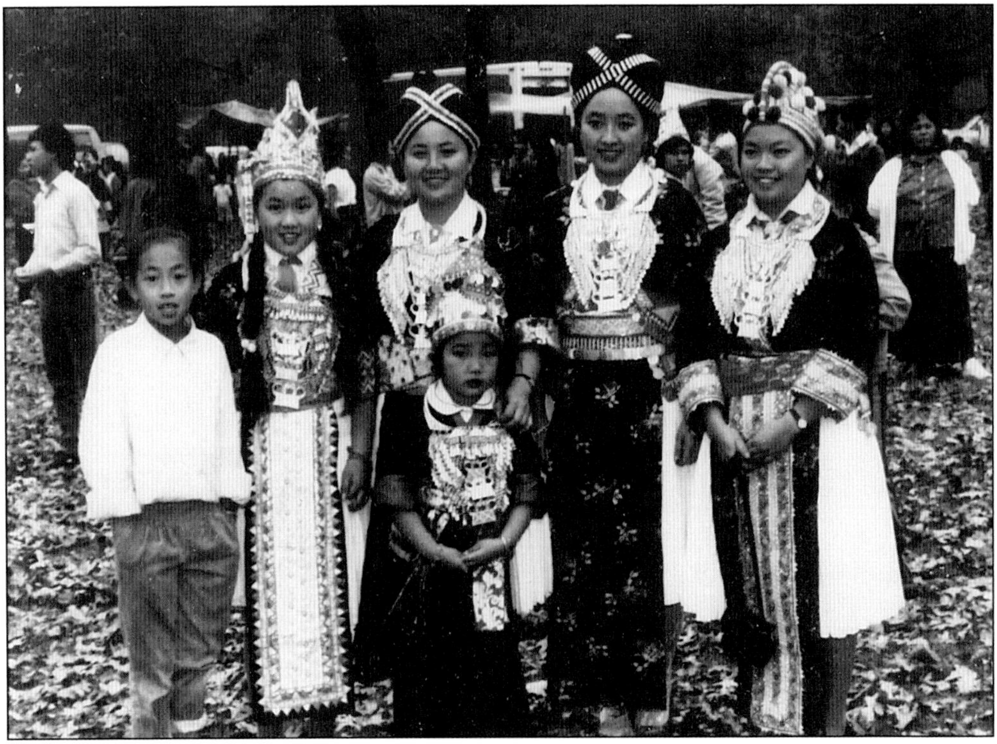

Following the Vietnam War, the latest group of immigrants to make La Crosse their home were refugees from Southeast Asia. Dressed in traditional costume, these young ladies participated in Hmong New Year's celebrations.

Four

Civil Servants

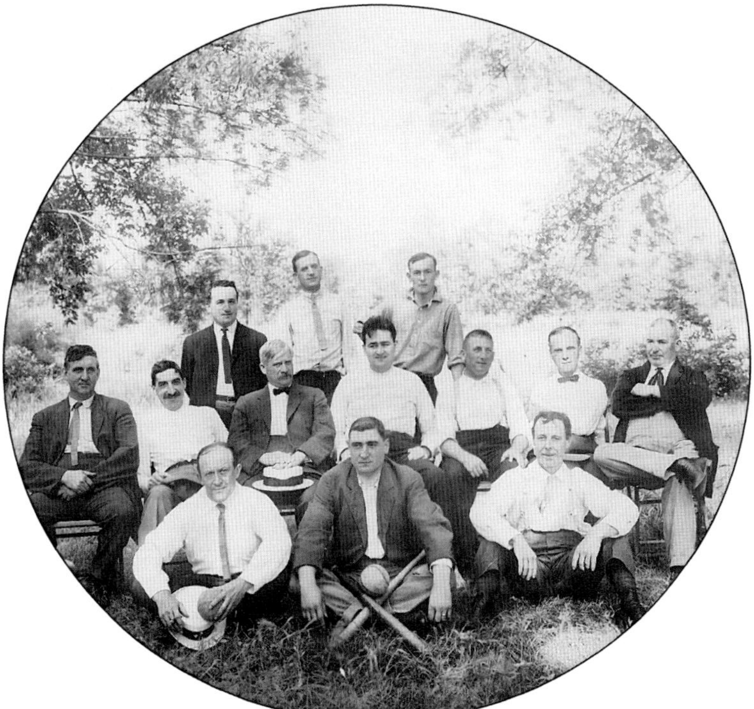

The 1907 city employee's baseball team apparently had a few "ringers" who were not strictly city workers. The men in this photo are identified, from left to right, as follows: (first row) William Roelling, common council member from the 11th Ward; John Schneeberger, proprietor of the Union Hotel; and A.J. Roth, architect; (second row) B.C. Smith, secretary/treasurer of Smith Manufacturing Company; Frank Roth, realtor; Mayor William Torrence; Joseph Bartl, brewer; Otto Granke, owner of a meat market; Justice of the Peace George B. Marvin Jr.; and City Attorney Paul Mahoney; (third row) C.A. Worth, reporter for the *La Crosse Leader-Press*; unidentified; and Jake Padesky, student.

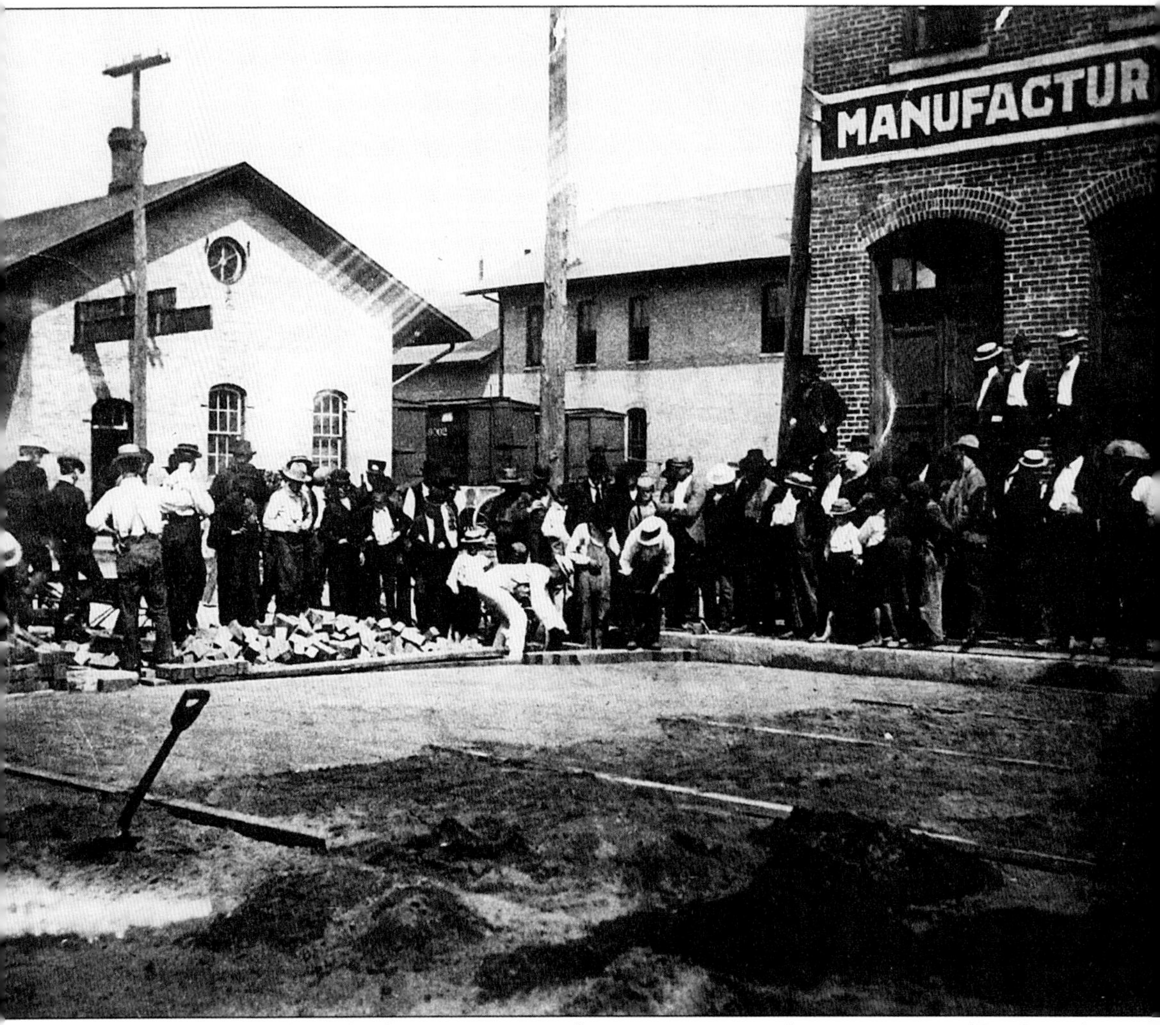

The new century brought about progressive ideas in many areas of government, and La Crosse's mayor, Wendell Anderson, led the drive for brick paving of the muddy downtown area. Seen in this photo, the first brick street was laid out at Front and Vine Streets on July 5, 1900.

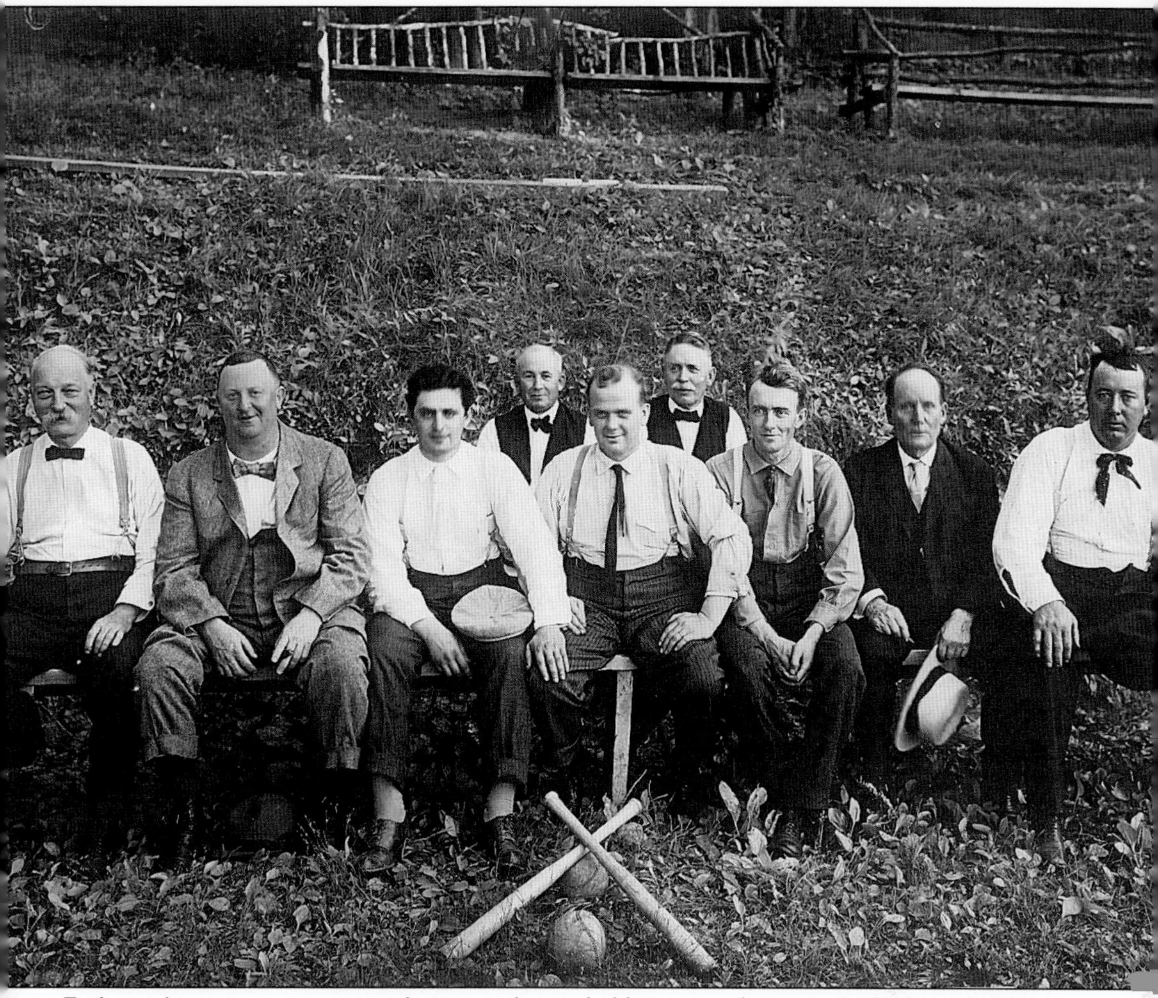

Early in the century, county and city employees held an annual picnic. Each group fielded a battling baseball team, and the competition for the honor of winning the annual game was fierce. The 1907 county worker's "Baseball Nine" were James Lang, jailer at the county jail; Morgan Evans, rural mail clerk from Bangor; Louie Omerberg, constable; Leonard Kleeber, coroner; E.A. Thompson; George P. Bradish, county surveyor; Charles Rawlinson, county clerk; J.L. Pettingill, Notary Public and abstractor; and Sheriff Chris J. Burns, who had had a brilliant local career 20 years earlier as a member of the La Crosse team that was sponsored by his father's business, the Burns Wholesale Fruit House.

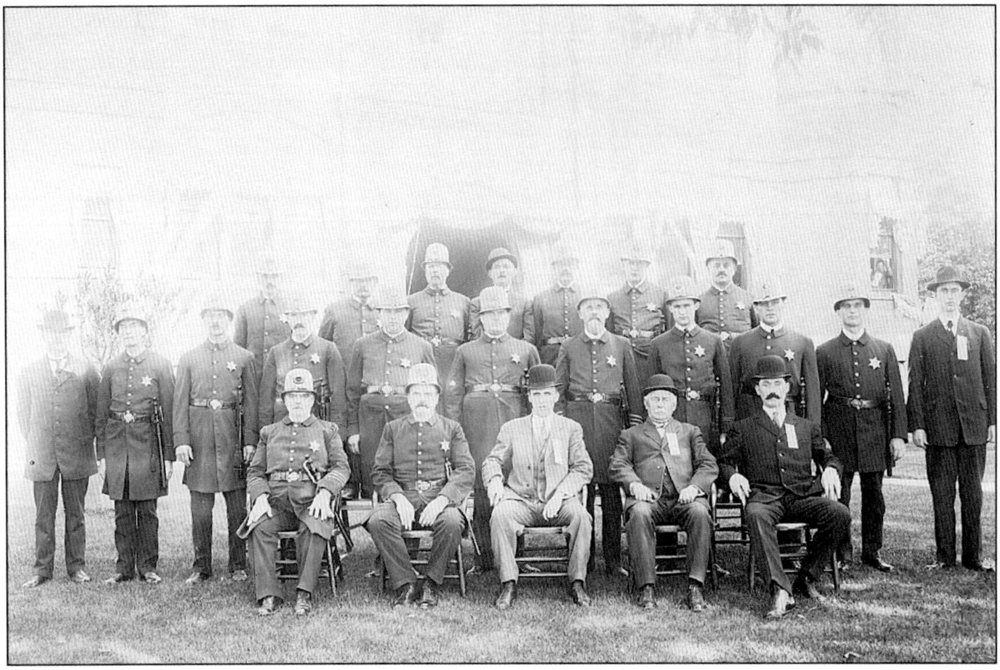

The La Crosse Police Department, complete with frock coats, bobby sticks, star badges, and helmets posed for this snapshot on September 17, 1909, "Taft Day" in the city.

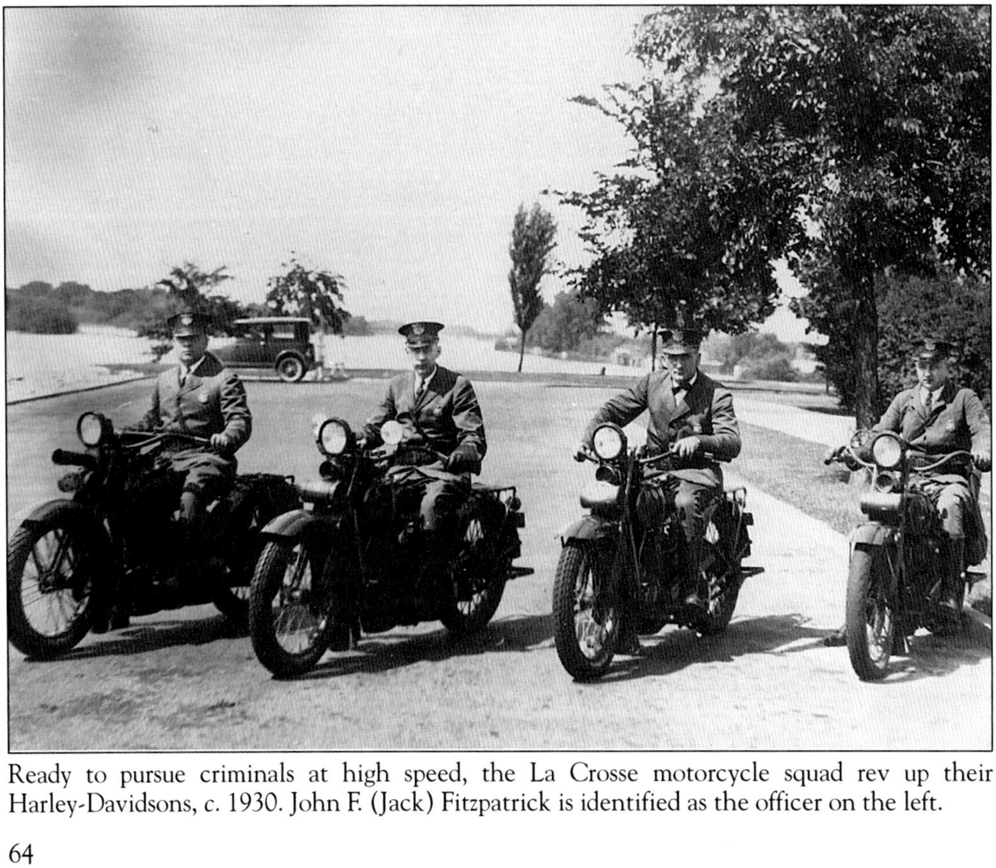

Ready to pursue criminals at high speed, the La Crosse motorcycle squad rev up their Harley-Davidsons, c. 1930. John F. (Jack) Fitzpatrick is identified as the officer on the left.

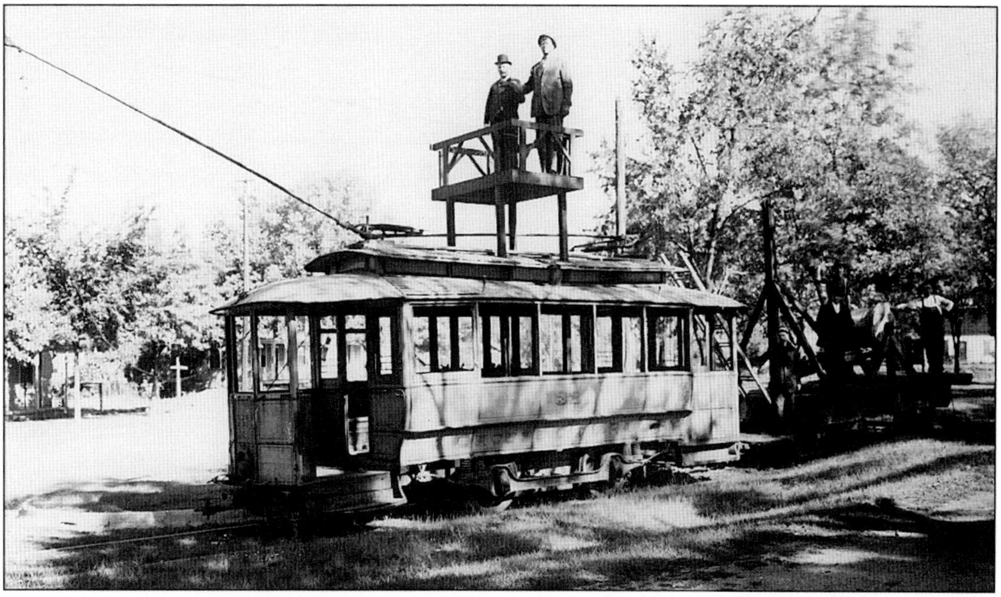

Shown in this *c.* 1893 view is the first electric trolley car in La Crosse. The trolley cars were originally pulled by horses, but technology demanded that city rail systems be updated to stay modern. This trolley pulled a trailer laden with a roll of copper wire for electrifying the system.

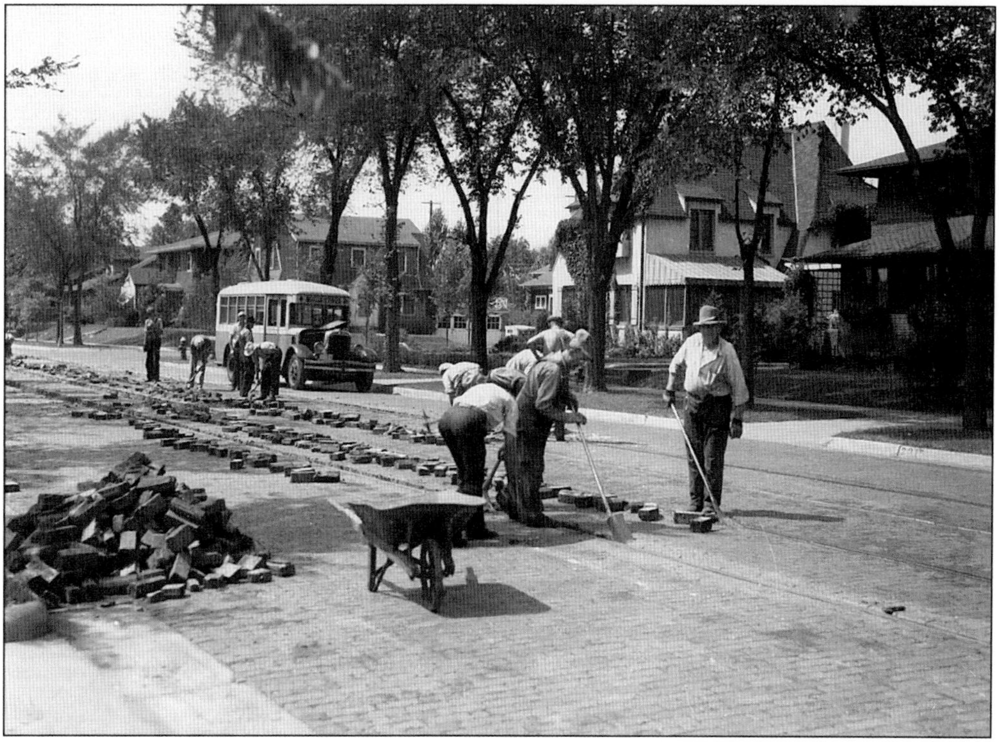

What is one year considered the latest in cutting-edge technology is old-fashioned only a few years later. This 1934 scene shows the removal of the streetcar tracks at Twenty-Second and Main Streets in La Crosse. Automobiles replaced the trolley systems as the transportation method of choice, and soon, brick streets would be replaced by asphalt.

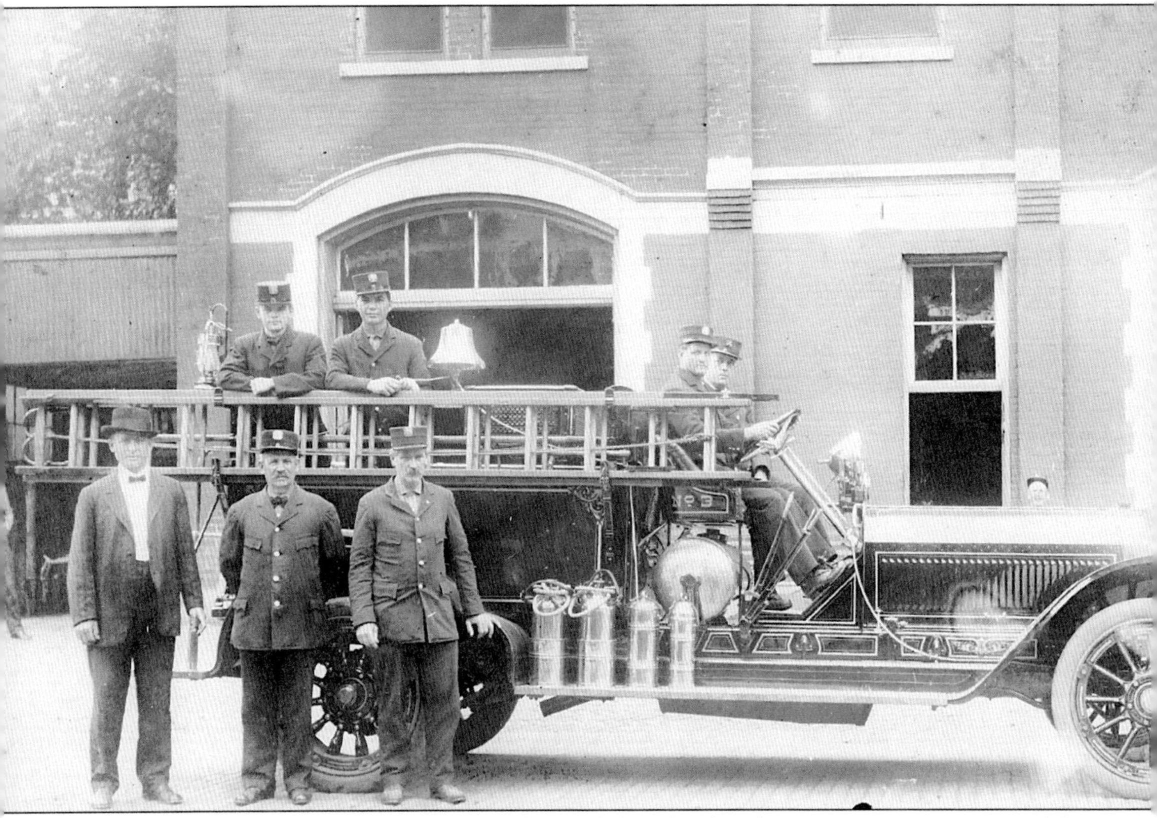

Taken on July 10, 1915, this photograph highlights the fire department's new motorized fire engine. Everything is shiny and new, from the bell to the fire extinguishers.

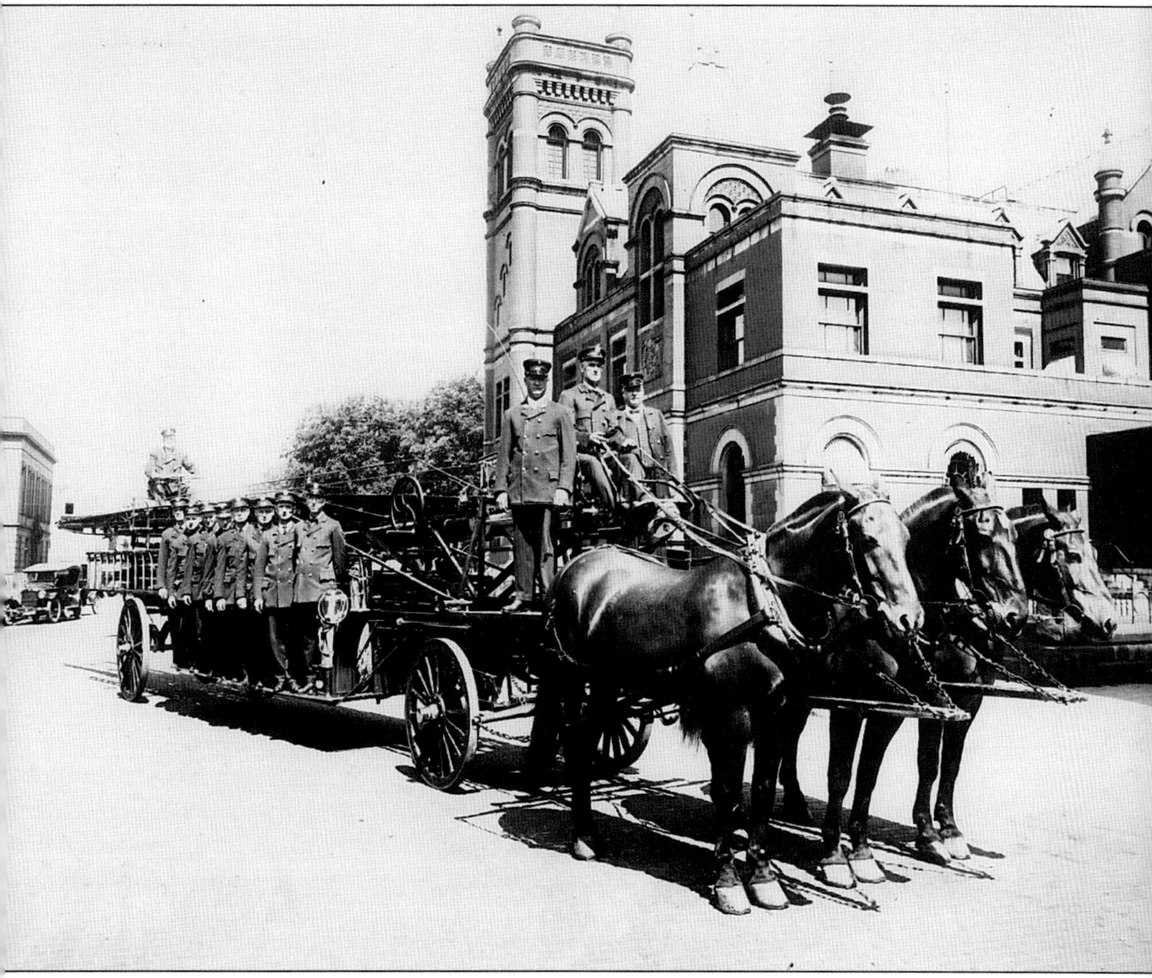

The fire department's horses were retired in April 1926. Gathered on the extension ladder wagon, the firemen pay final homage to their equine colleagues.

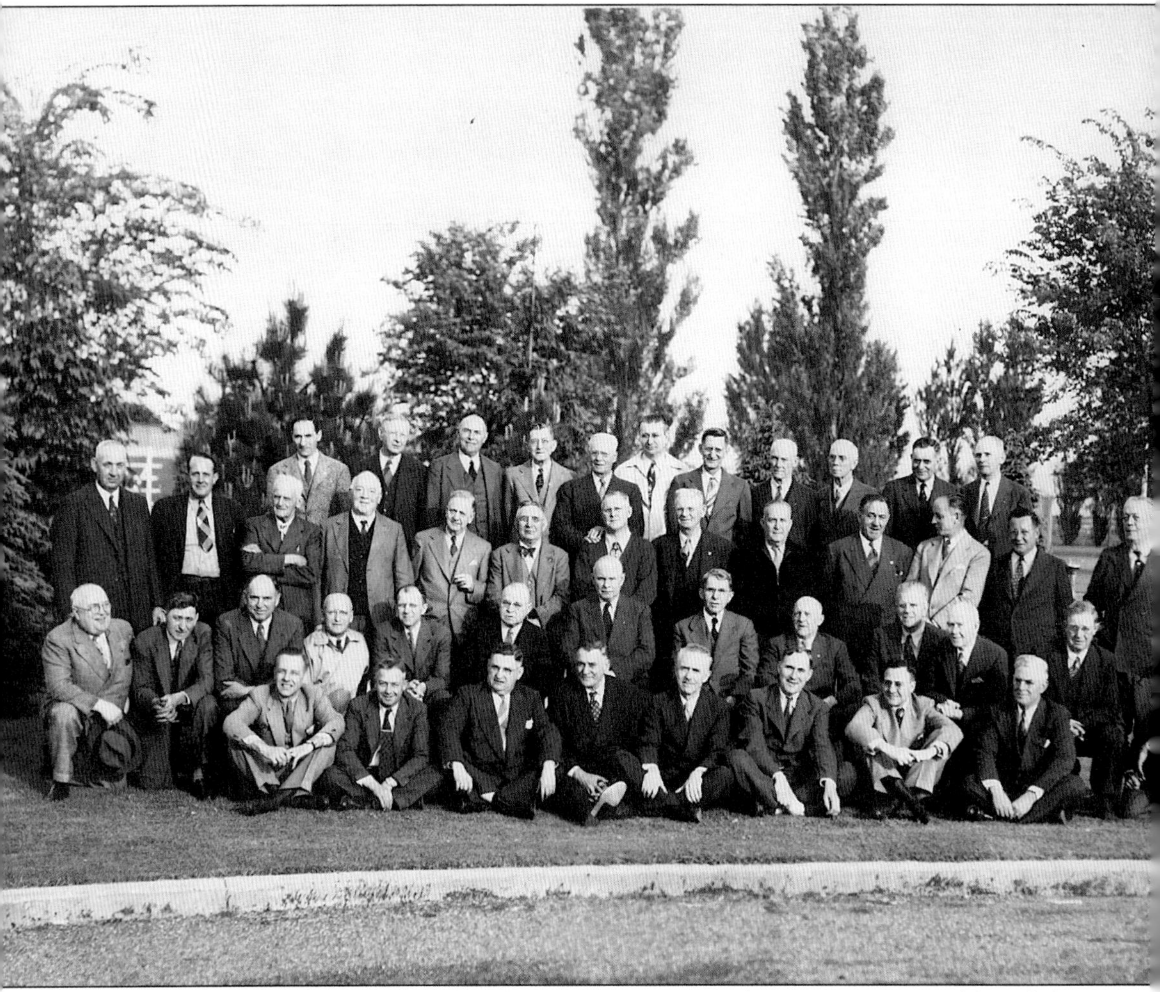

La Crosse city officials posed for this photo on a sunny June day in 1945. Pictured from left to right are, (front row) E.P. Hartl, Carl Wahlstrom, George Hanson, Jack Roop, R.S. Mitchell, Fred Steele, Quincy Hale, and Ed Conghlin; (second row) Harry Newberg, Charles Beranek, John Barth, John Colman, Franklin Pamperin, J.J. Verchota (mayor), Archie Downey, J.C. Houska, W.P. Roellig, R.W. Bardwell, A.M. Murphy, Warren Smigh, and Melvin Knutson; (third row) H.F. Rick, Grant Thrune, E.H. Derr, Edward Lueth, Walter Bigelow, Henry Mayer, Harold Eeg, J.G. Becker, R.D. Stewart, Nordahl Nustad, Alf Gundersen, R.H. Anderegg, and F.C. McGlachlin; (fourth row) Walter Roth, Lambert Keizer, A.R. Kempter, Otto Zielke, James Durland, Fred Kramer, J.J. Domahoski, A.G. Jamesson, William Strauss, Henry Streicher, and Peter Sieger.

Five

EARNING OUR BREAD AND BUTTER

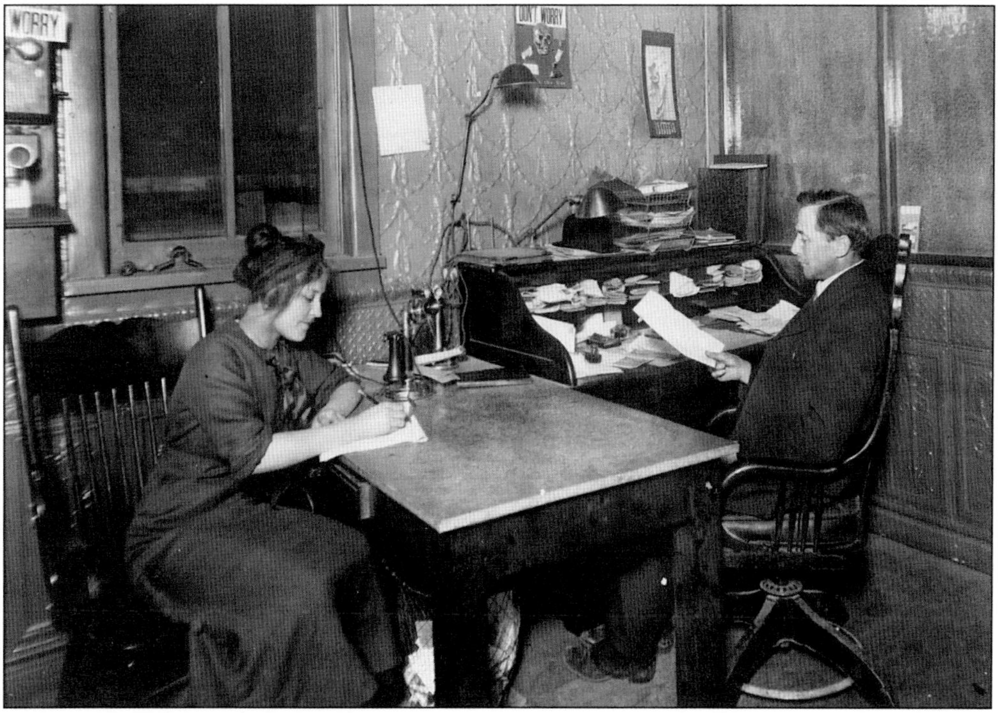

This is the office of the Arenz Shoe Company, located at 323 Pearl Street, *c.* 1915. Joseph S. Arenz was the owner. Notice the pressed-tin wall covering, telephone, the mass of electric wires, and the secretary's "modern" hair style.

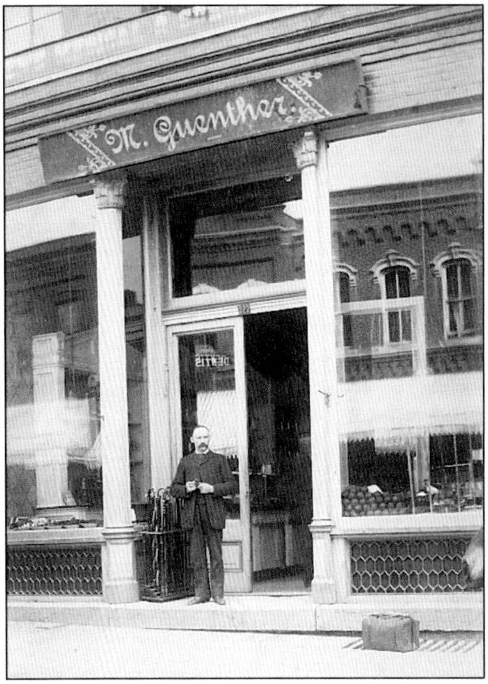

Moritz Guenther came to La Crosse in 1864 and opened his shop in 1878. This c. 1900 photograph shows him outside his 322 Main Street shop, which was advertised as being a bakery, candy shop, ice cream, and oyster parlor.

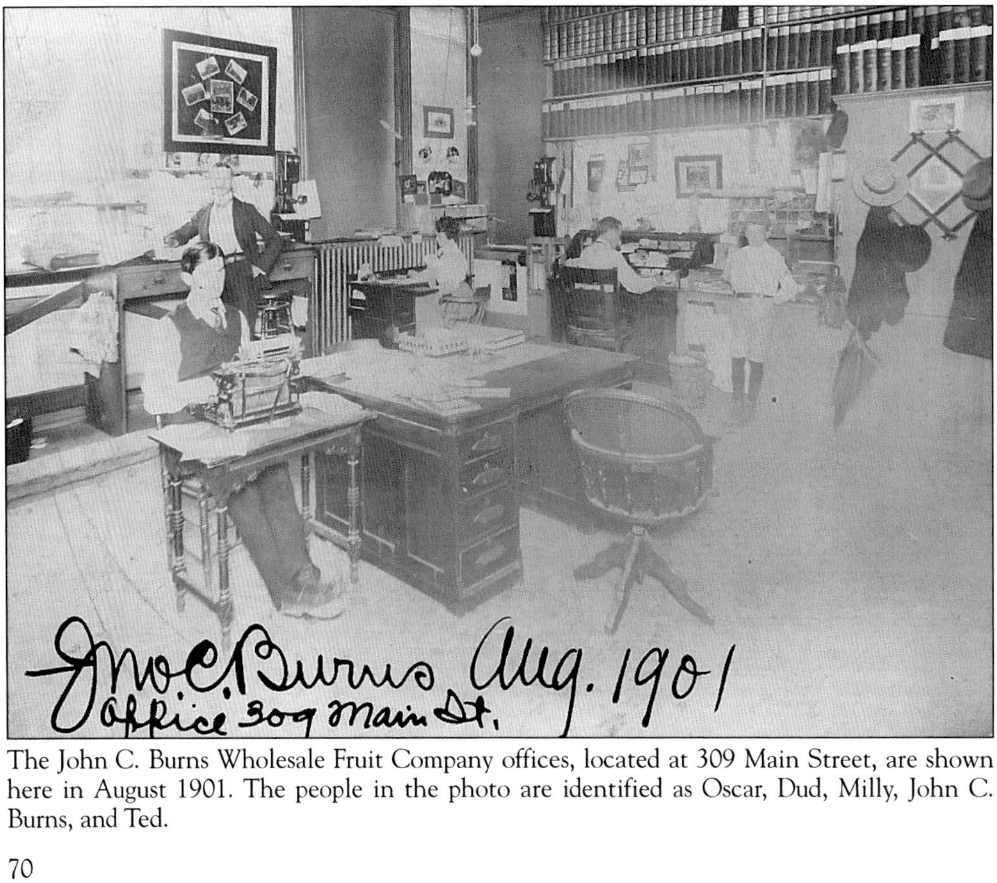

The John C. Burns Wholesale Fruit Company offices, located at 309 Main Street, are shown here in August 1901. The people in the photo are identified as Oscar, Dud, Milly, John C. Burns, and Ted.

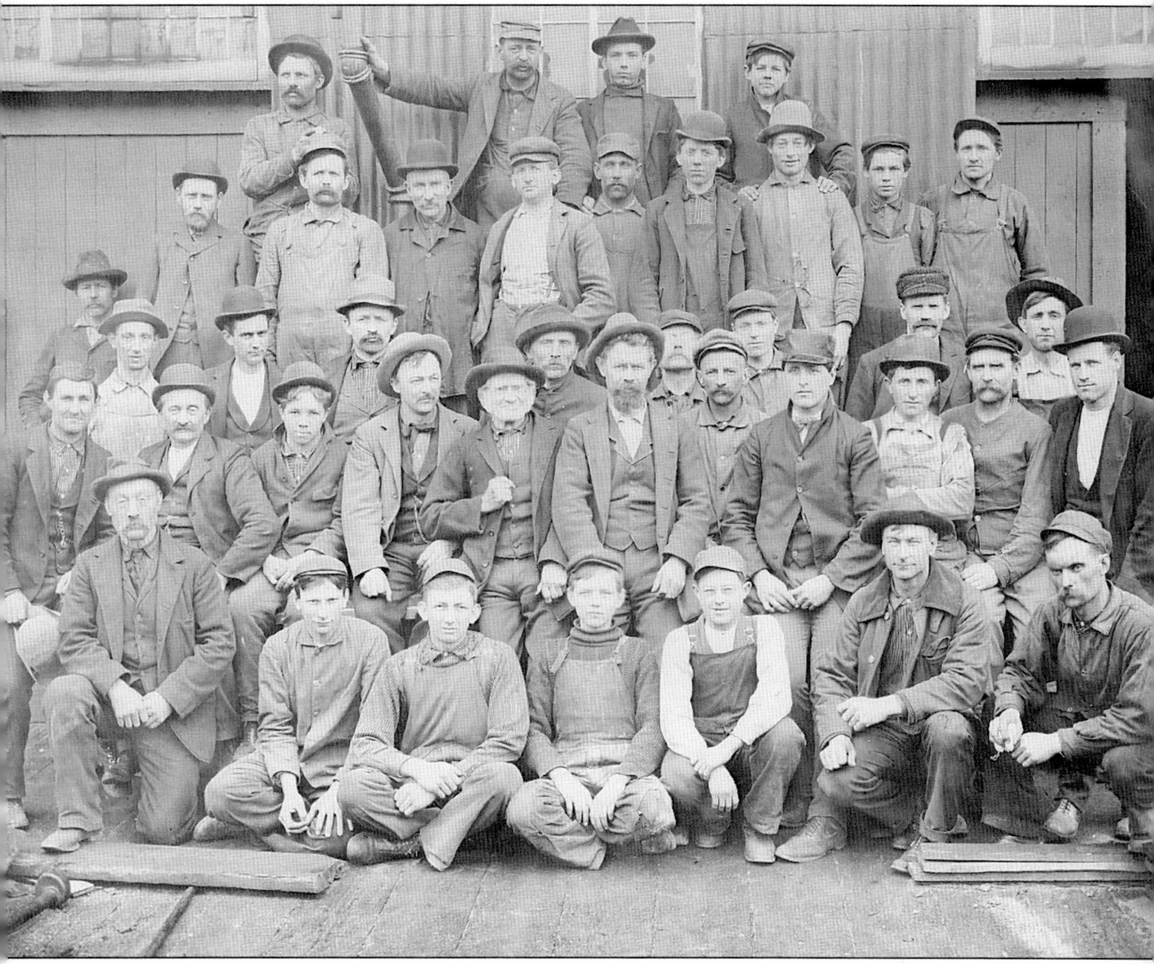

The R.C. Kuhn Sash and Door Company, located at the corner of Second and Jay Streets, also made Mission-style furniture. The employees in this 1903 photograph are unidentified and range in age from young boys to elderly men. Notice the many styles of hats worn by the workers.

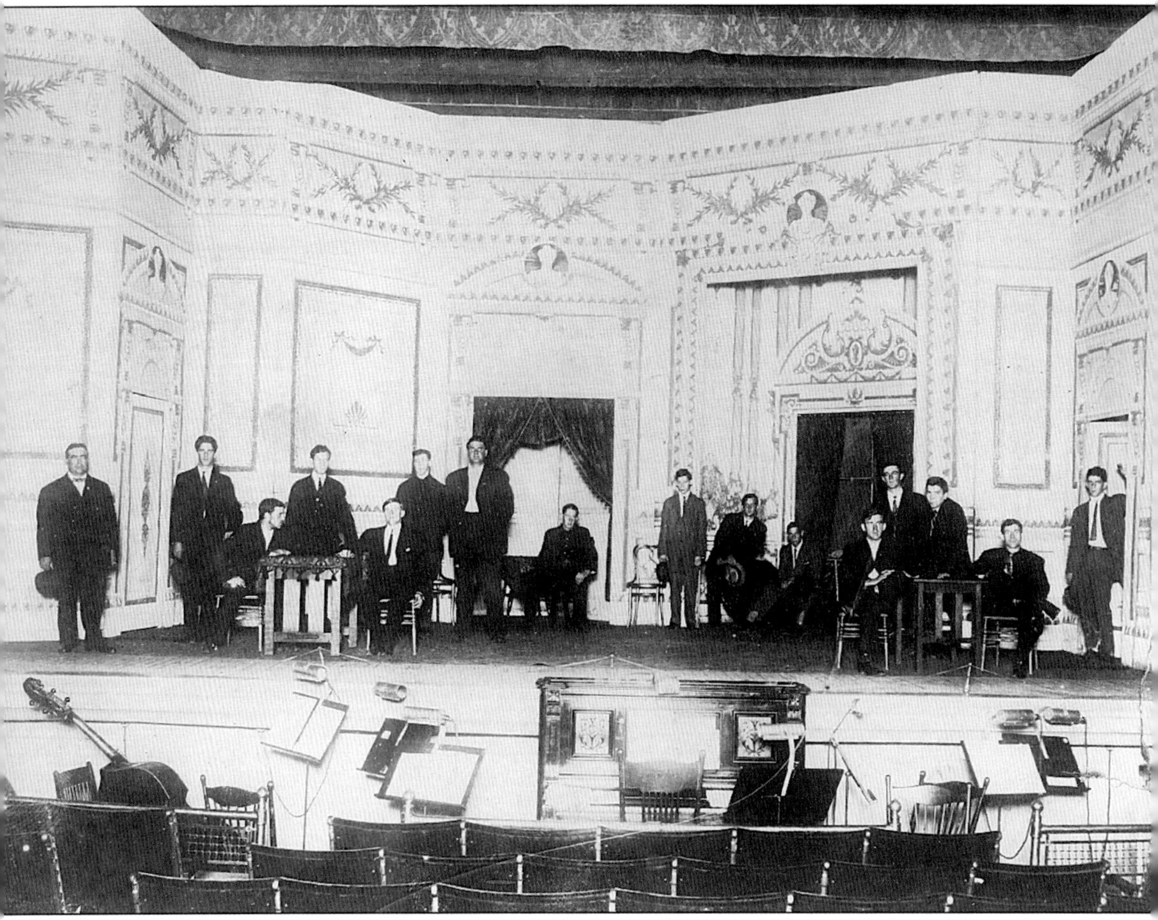

The stage crew of the old La Crosse Theatre, located on Fifth between Main and Jay Streets, pose in front of the "center door fancy set" in this photo from 1903. According to the identification on the photograph, they are as follows: Jim Jarvis, T. Heinitze, William Freise, Buff Thompson, John Zimmerer, Bill Robey, William Kriesel, Charles Conrad, Charles Larson, J. Johnson, Red Drake, L. Weber, ? Weber, John Simke, ? Fritag, and W. MacKenzie.

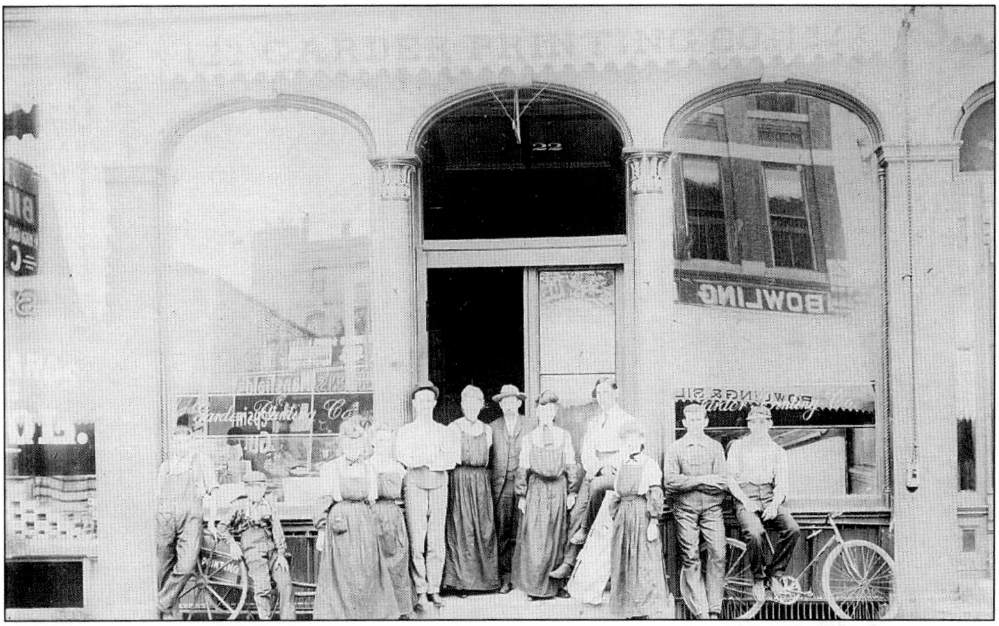

The employees at Garder Printing Company, located at 122 North Third Street in La Crosse, are shown here c. 1904. From left to right, they are as follows: Tom Kubal, unidentified, Ida Liesenfeld, Pearl Schlutter, D.F. Schlutter, Agnes Lindberg, John Garder, Annie Lourie, Charles Baumann, ? Burrows, Joe Kotnour, and Adolph Liesenfeld.

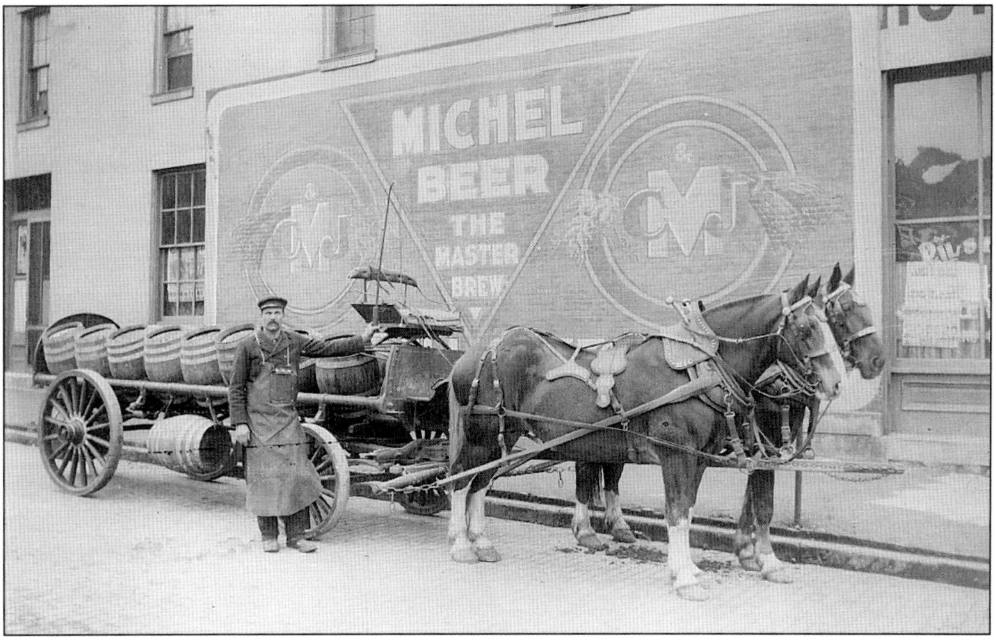

Draft horses Chief and Fred stand patiently with teamster Sam Erickson ready to pull their wagon laden with barrels of Michel beer in 1904.

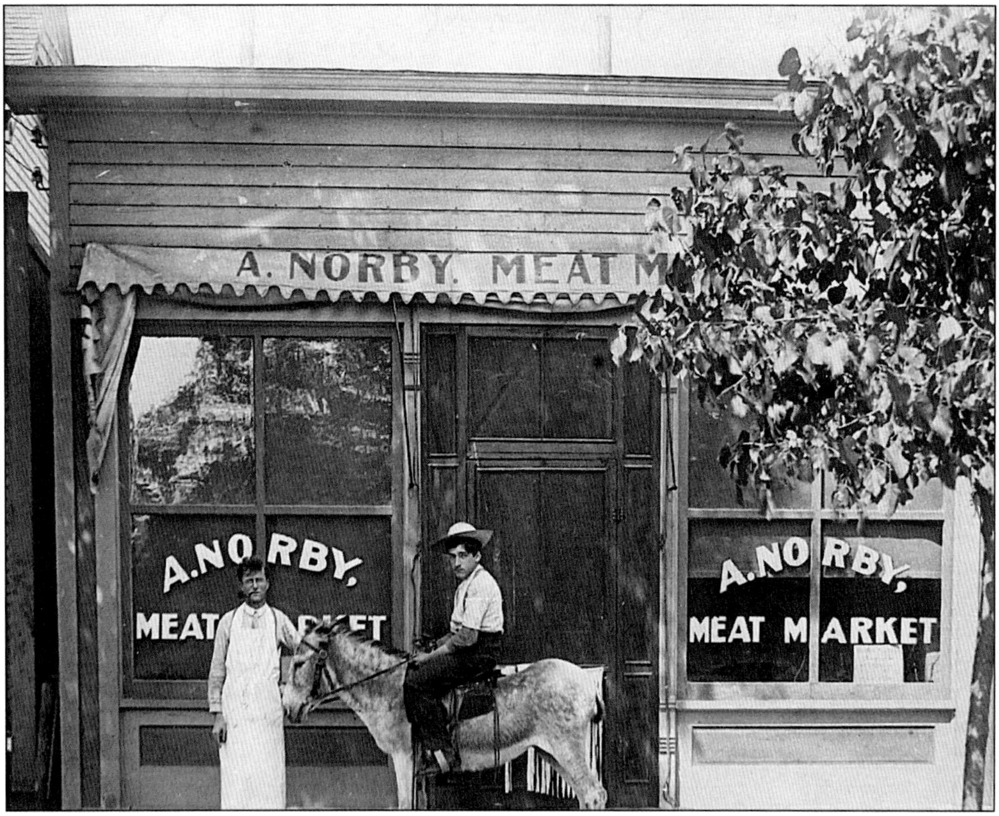

After having worked as a butcher for several years, Albert Norby opened his own meat market at 929 Mississippi Street, *c.* 1903. Mr. Norby is seen in this photo with his young neighbor, John Bezpaletz, whose father owned a market on Ninth Street.

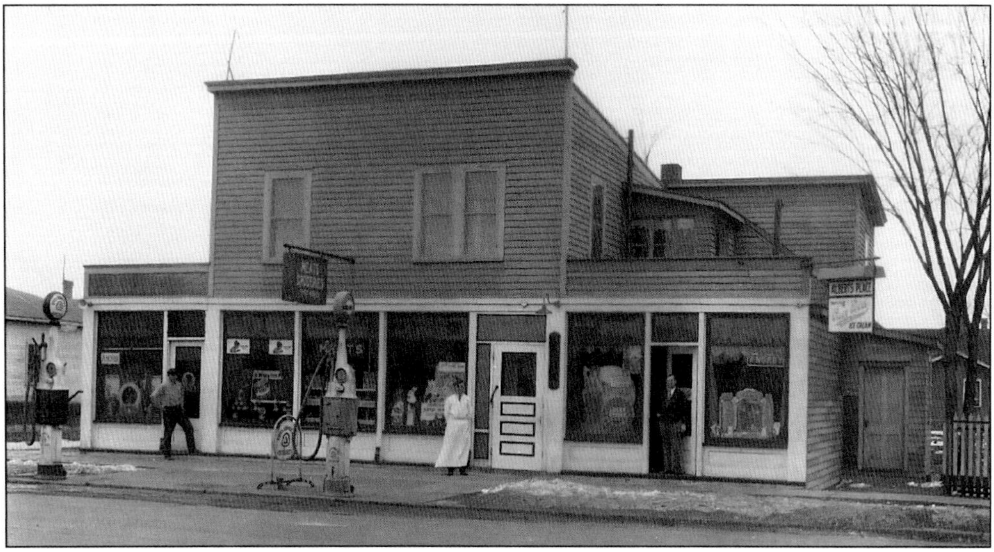

Norby's Market moved to 1804 Jackson Street *c.* 1919, where it was a fixture for many years. This *c.* 1936 photo shows that Albert's son Theo had taken over the running of the store, gas pumps had been installed, and Albert had his own business called "Albert's Place."

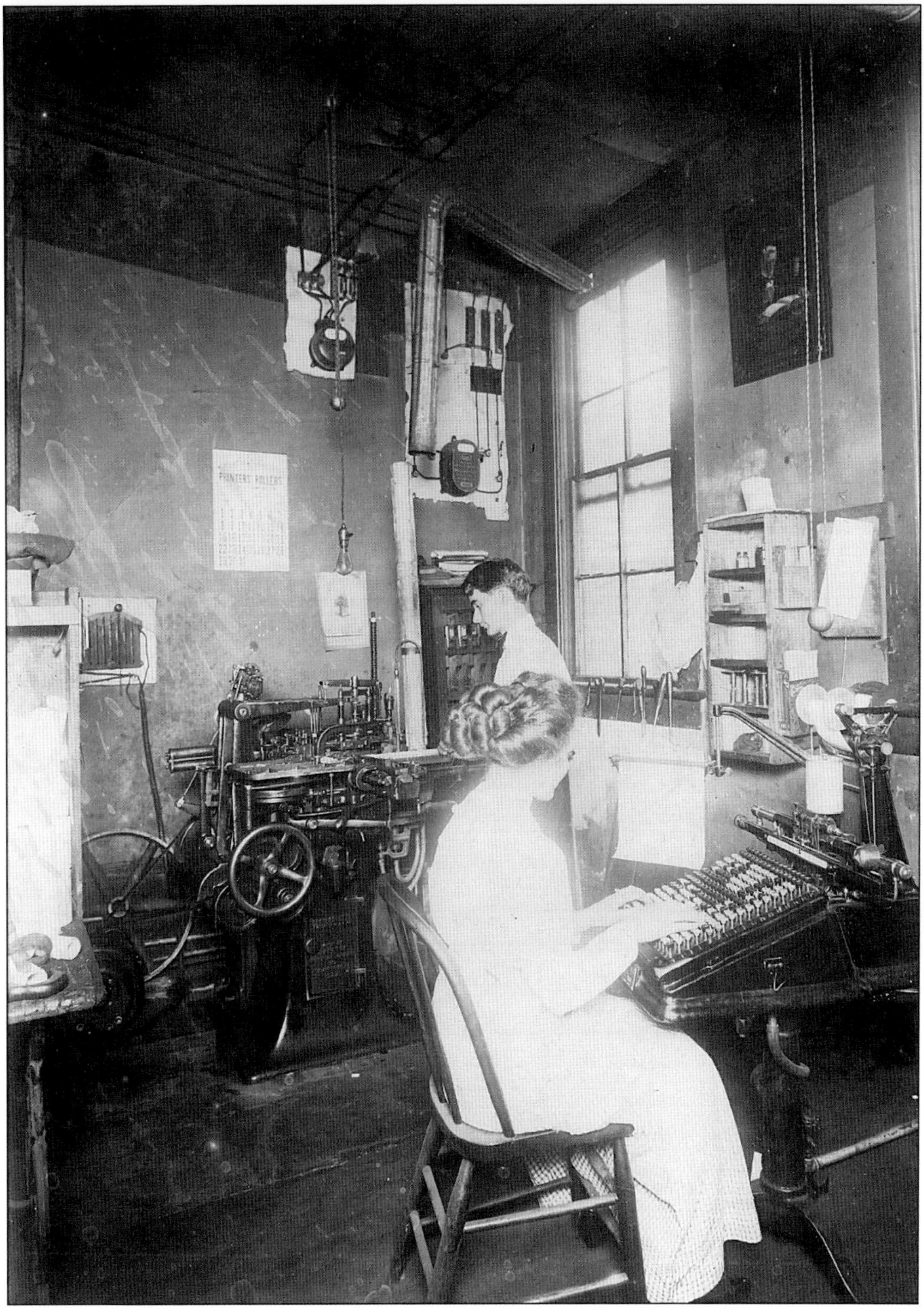

G.A. and Marcella Keller are shown in their shop, Keller Printing, at 110 Pearl Street c. 1905.

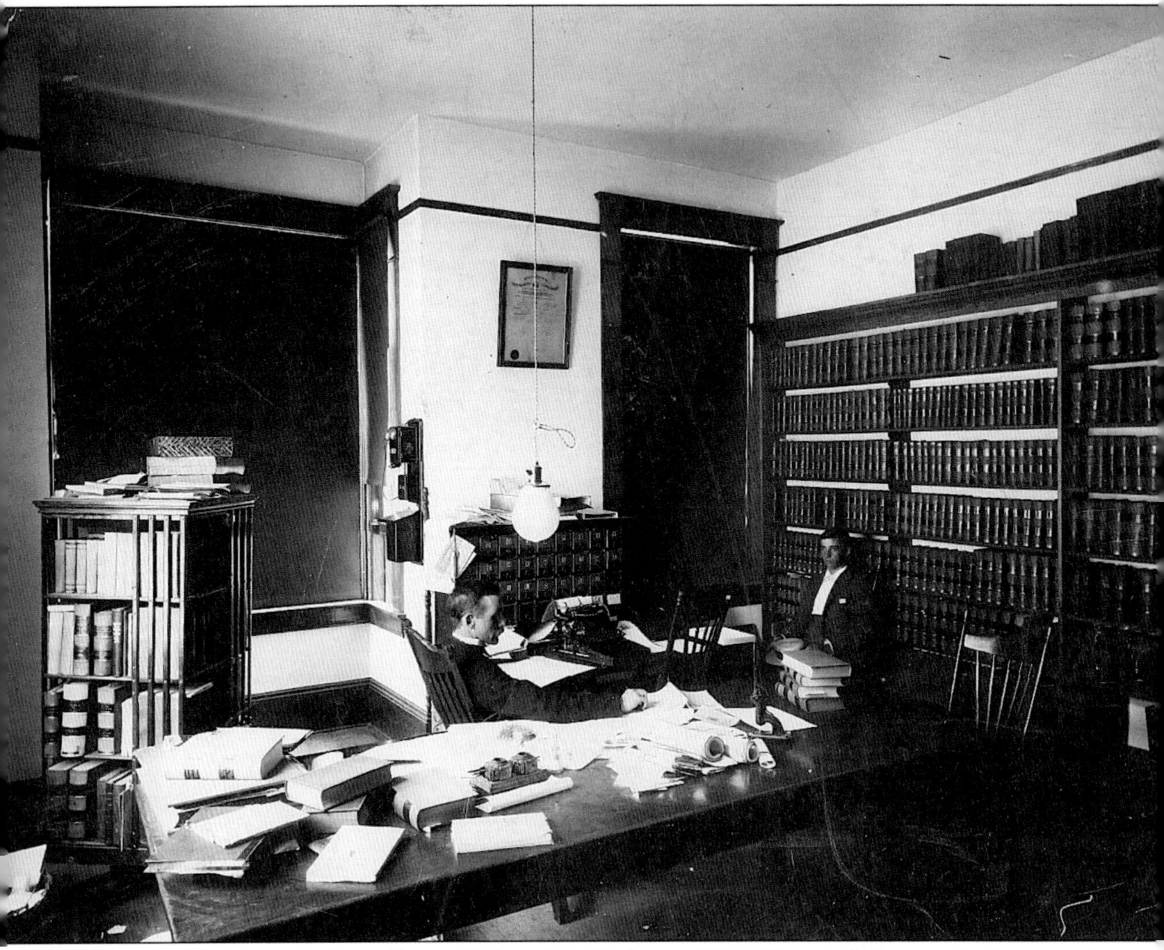

Pictured here are the law offices of Edward C. Higbee *c.* 1905. Electric lights, a telephone, and typewriter denote a "modern" office. Edward, who became a Circuit Court Judge, is seated on the left, and on the right, holding his straw hat, is a young Jesse E. Higbee.

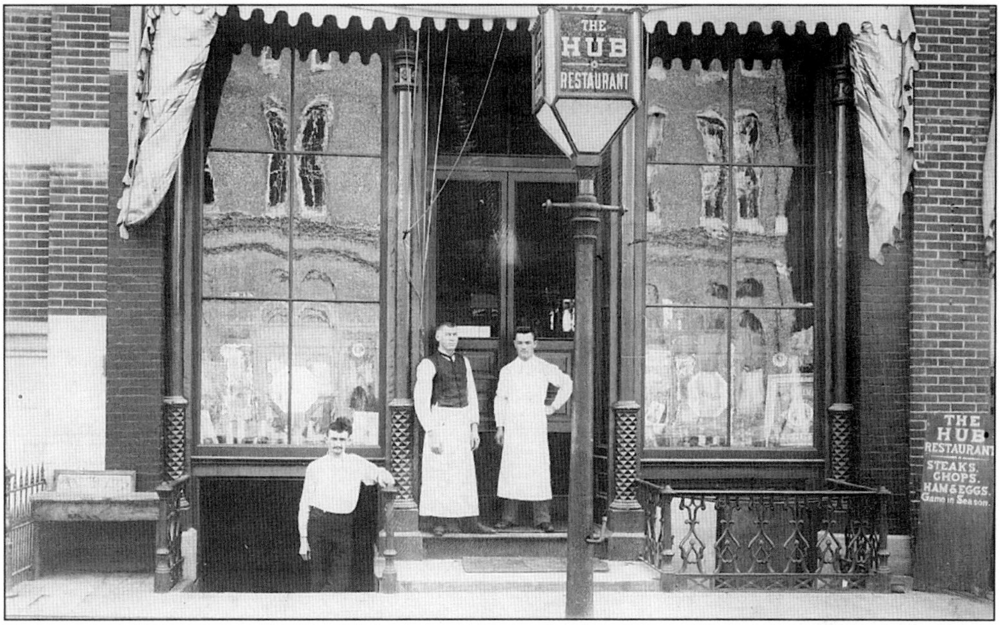

Harry H. Miller ran the Hub Restaurant at 105 South Third Street from 1900 until 1907. These c. 1905 exterior and interior photos show the diner, which carried the following advertisement in the City Directory: "Harry Miller, the man who made La Crosse famous, serves the finest 25¢ dinners in America."

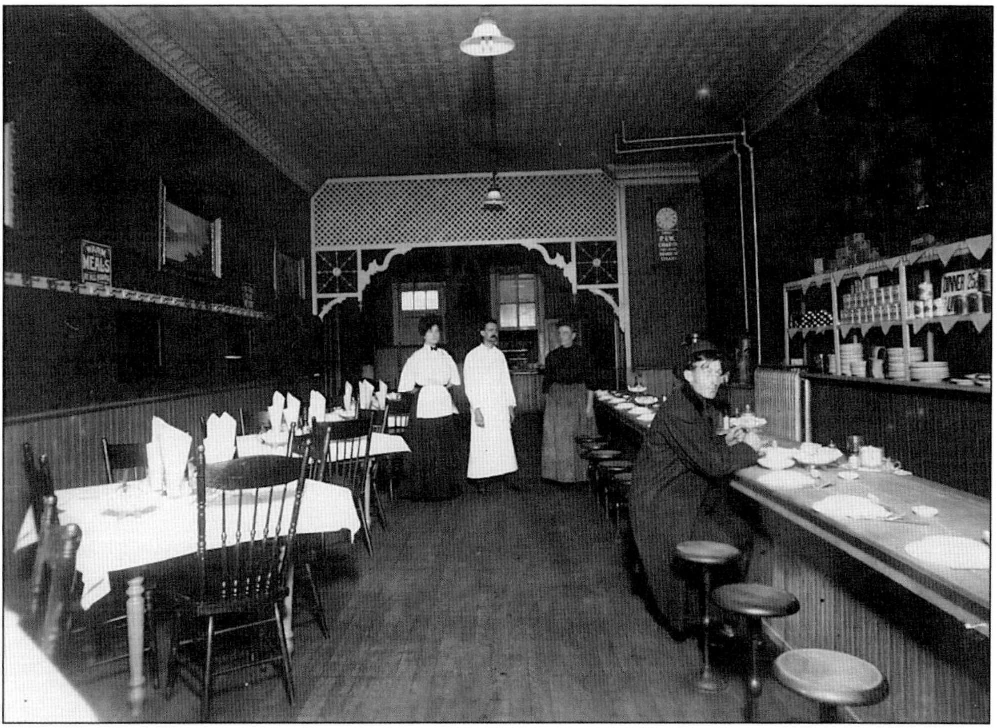

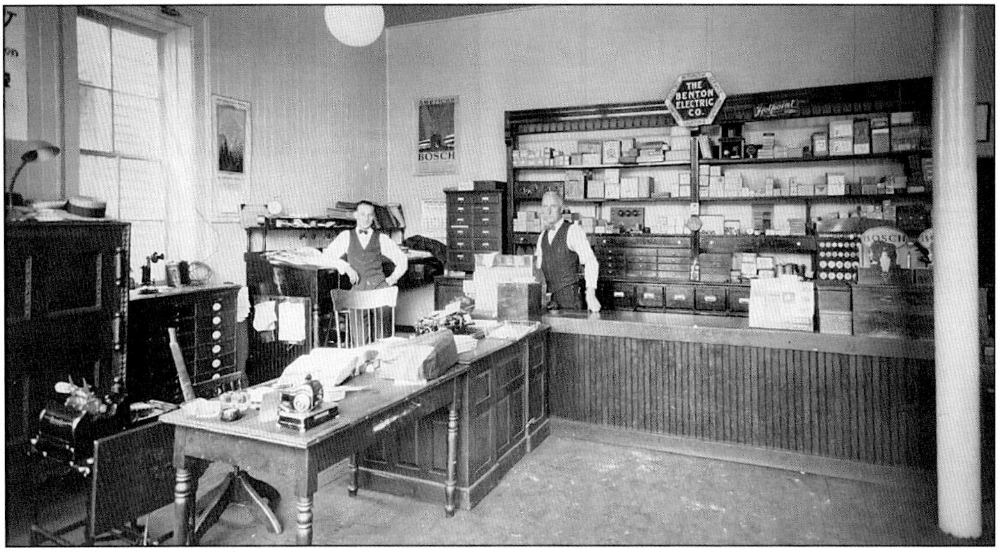

Located on the corner of Front and Pearl Streets, Benton Electric Company was operated by Thomas P. Benton and his son, W.F. Benton. In this *c.* 1905 photo, the younger Benton is standing on the left, with his father behind the cash register.

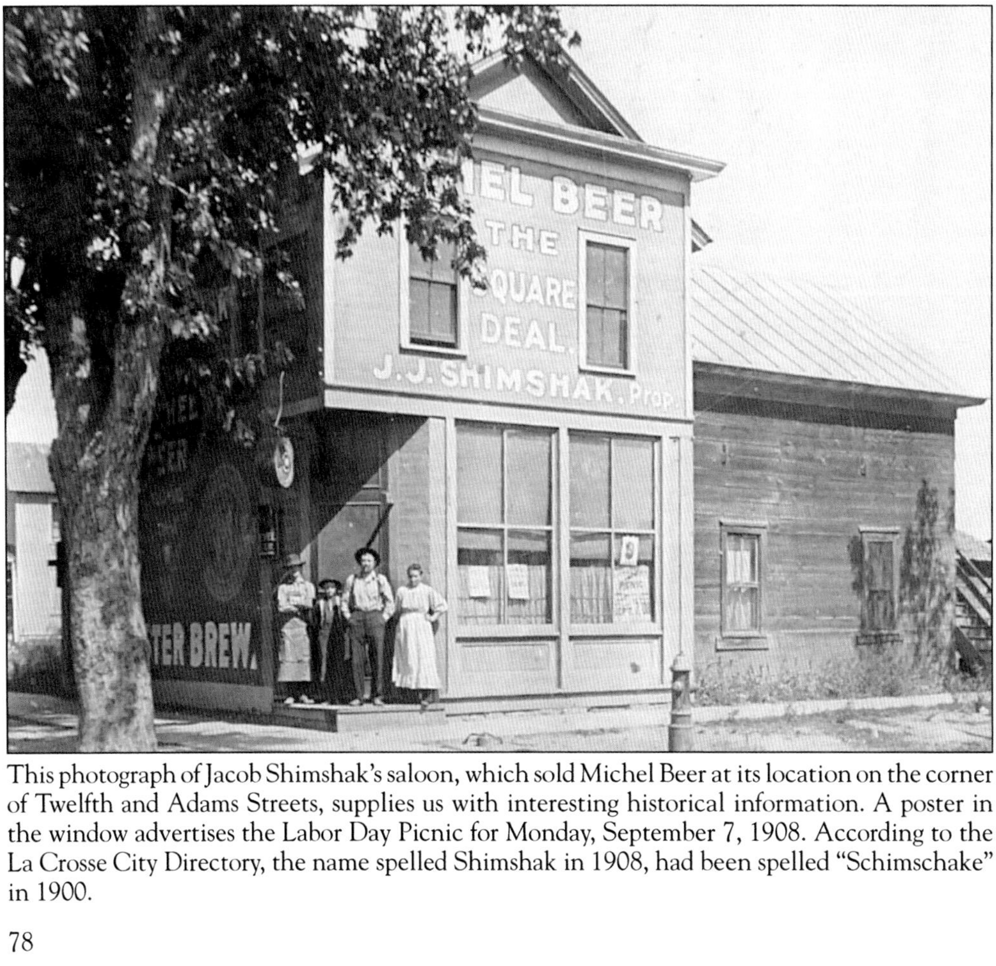

This photograph of Jacob Shimshak's saloon, which sold Michel Beer at its location on the corner of Twelfth and Adams Streets, supplies us with interesting historical information. A poster in the window advertises the Labor Day Picnic for Monday, September 7, 1908. According to the La Crosse City Directory, the name spelled Shimshak in 1908, had been spelled "Schimschake" in 1900.

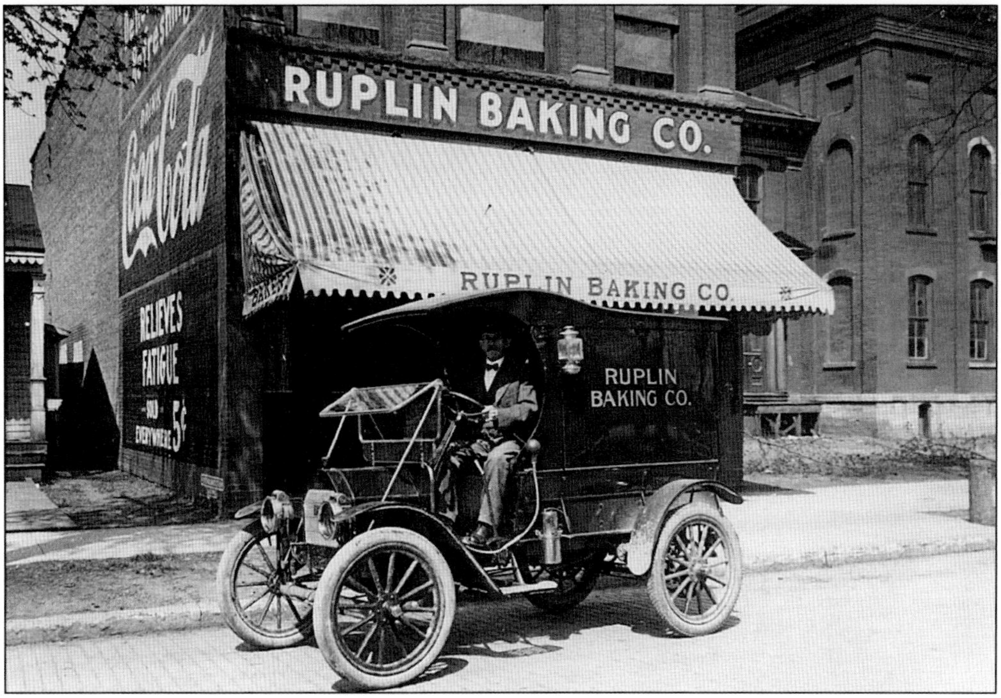

Jacob and Mary Ruplin's employed their own children through the years at their bakery, which was located at 412 South Fourth Street. Arthur, Carl, Fred, Emma, Walter, and William all worked at the bakery in one capacity or another. New to La Crosse in 1895, Ruplin opened his bakery the same year. This *c.* 1910 photo shows the most up-to-date delivery truck used for transporting baked goods to weddings, balls, and parties.

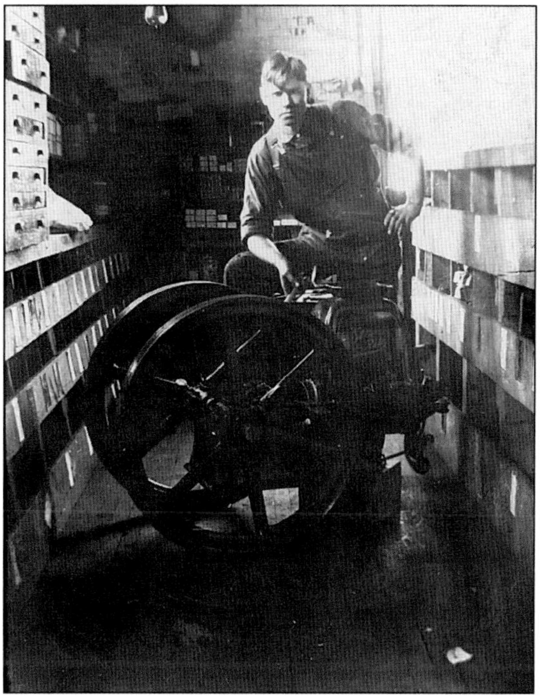

The Sta-Rite Engine Company manufactured gasoline engines at its plant on Front Street. Immortalized here in 1912, and striking a manly pose, is Arza R. McVey, one of Sta-Rite's workers.

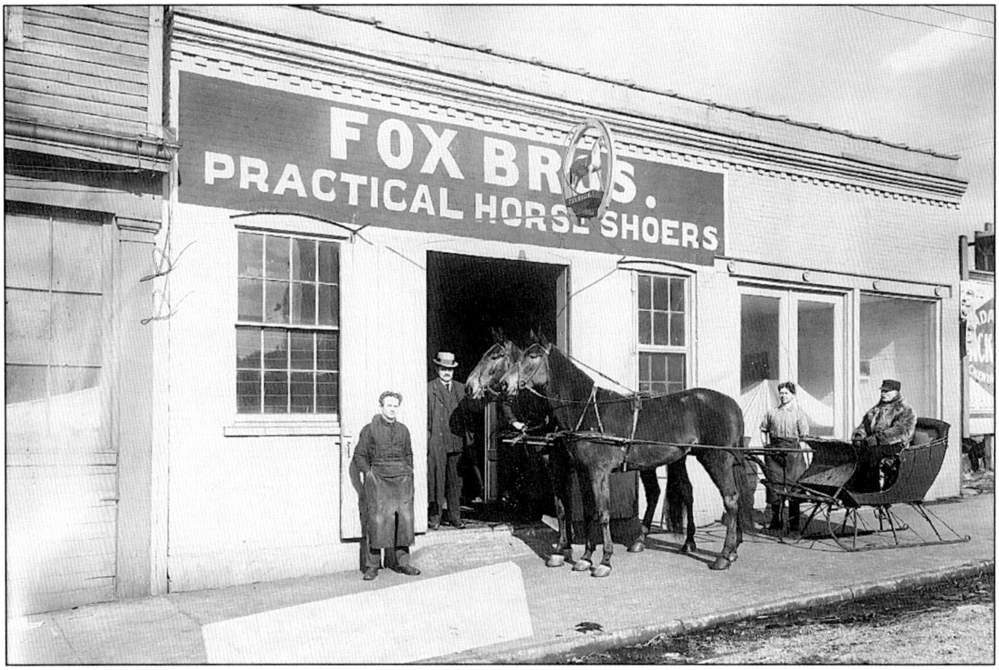

The Fox Brothers opened their "Practical Horse Shoers" shop at 205 State Street in 1909, perhaps not fully aware of the automobile's future impact in drastically changing the world of transportation.

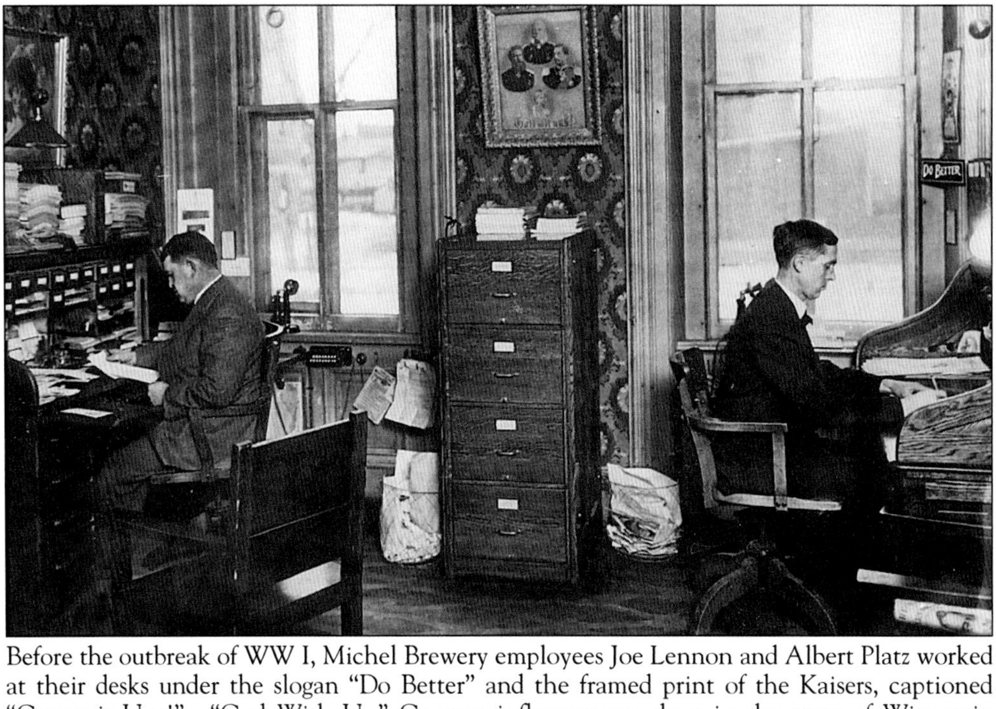

Before the outbreak of WW I, Michel Brewery employees Joe Lennon and Albert Platz worked at their desks under the slogan "Do Better" and the framed print of the Kaisers, captioned "Gott mit Uns!"—"God With Us." German influence ran deep in the state of Wisconsin and especially in La Crosse's brewing industry. The folded newspaper carries a drawing of Woodrow Wilson.

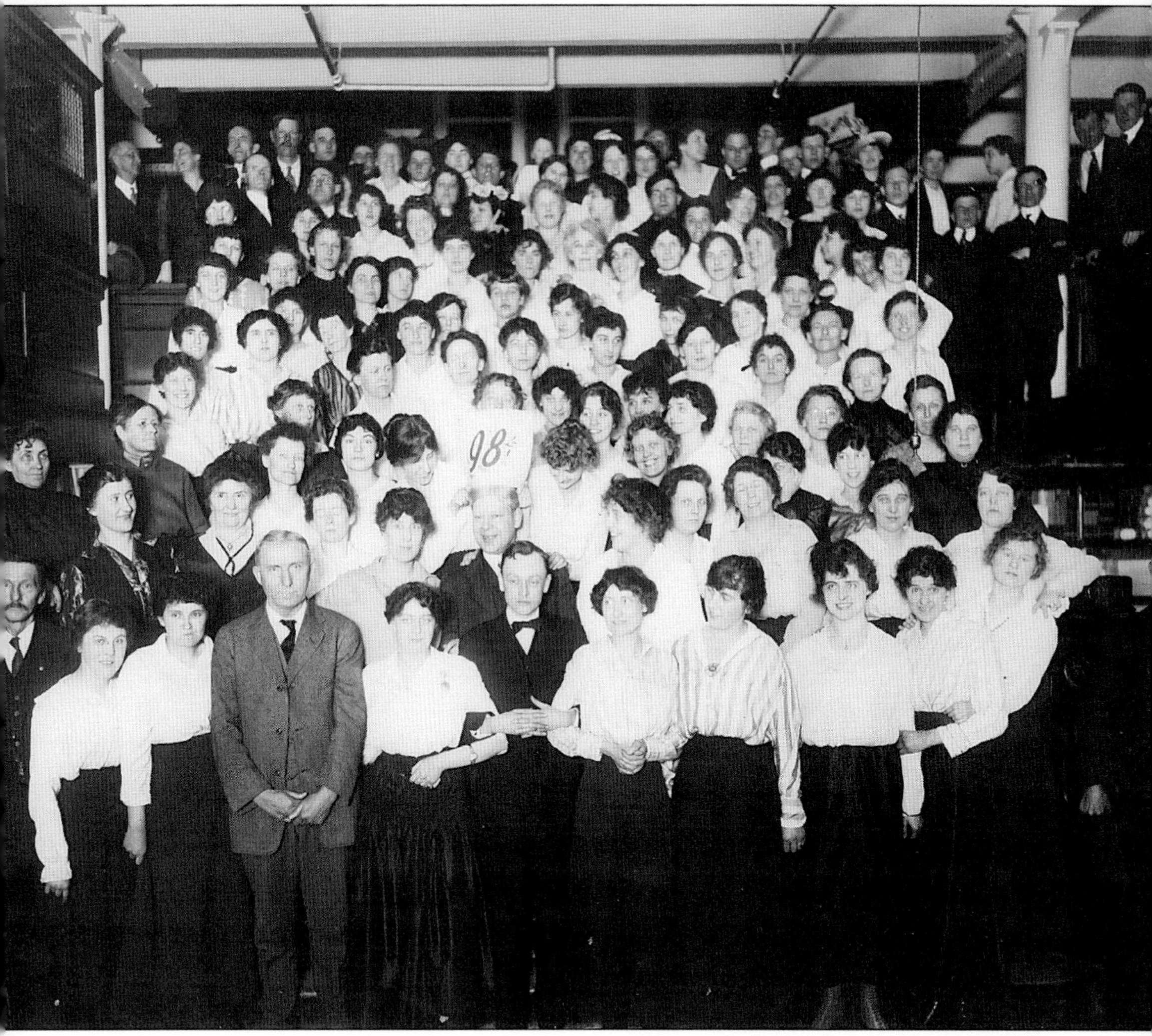

Posing in about 1910, Doerflinger's Department Store employees gathered for a group photograph. A female associate playfully placed a sign reading "98¢" on the head of Mr. Dorflinger himself.

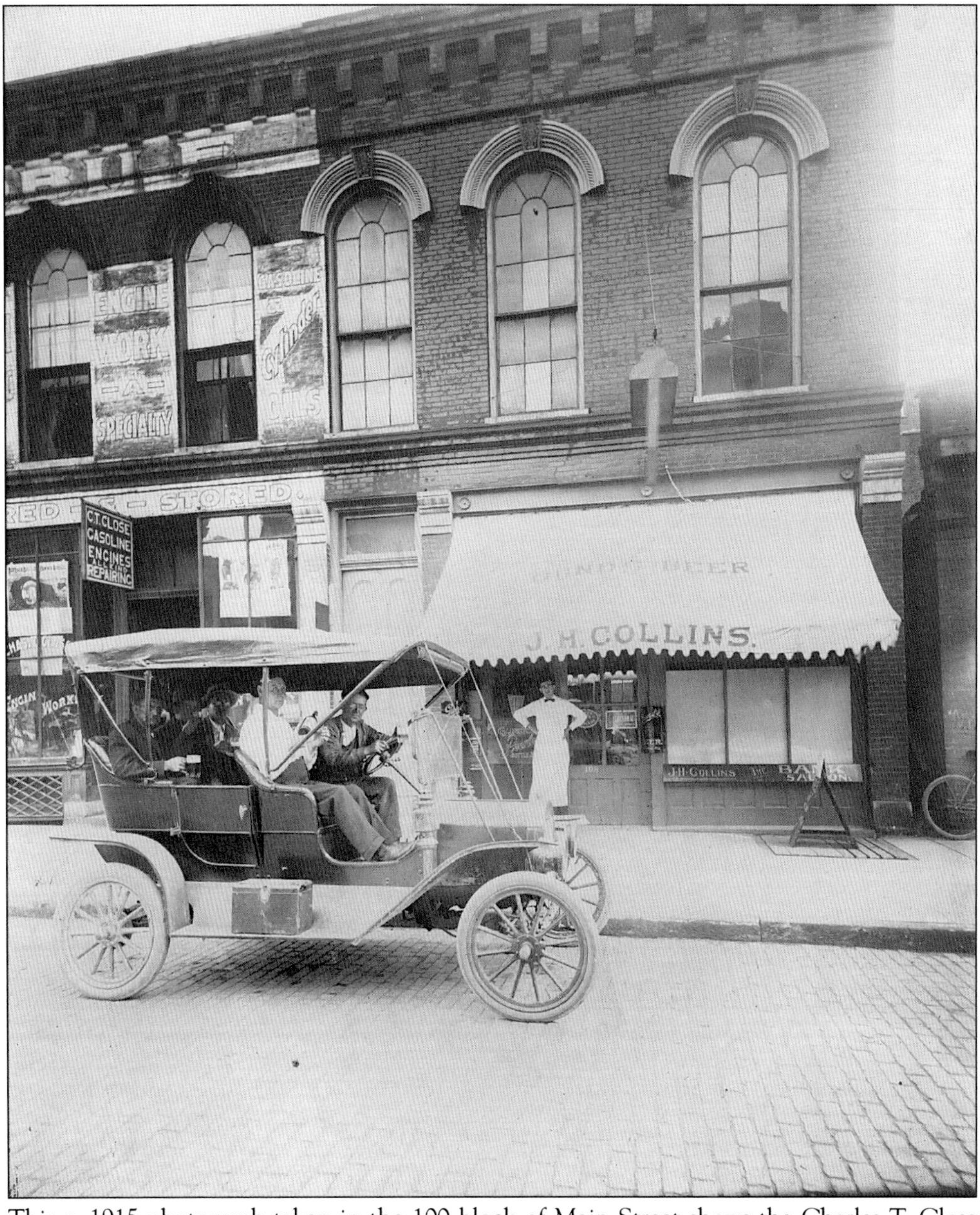

This c. 1915 photograph taken in the 100 block of Main Street shows the Charles T. Close machine shop and engine repair business and J.H. Collins' tavern. Perhaps the "horseless carriage" and its occupants had visited both establishments, since the car seems in good running order and the men are enjoying some "liquid refreshment."

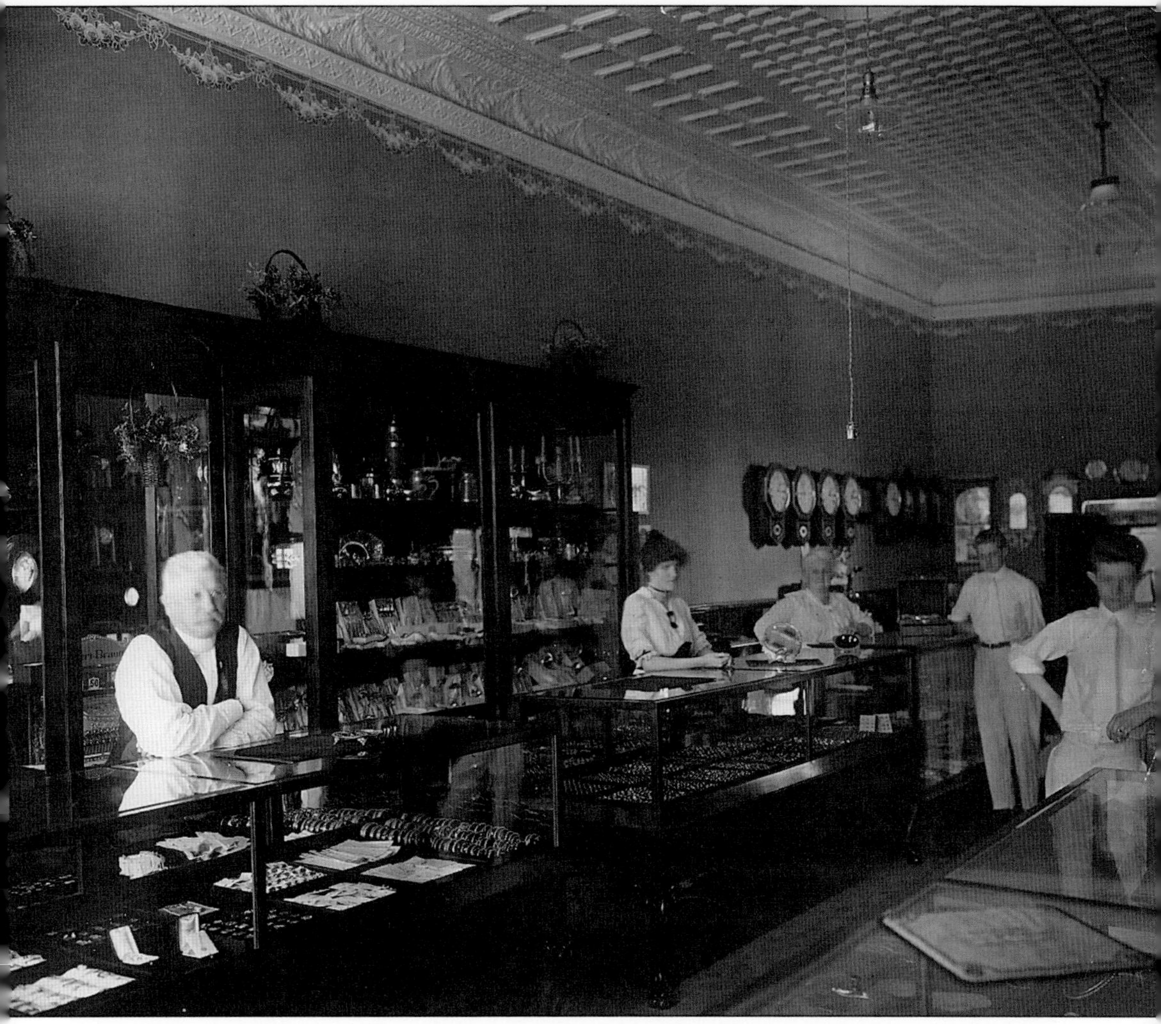

Robert Braun owned a jewelry and fine gift shop at 318 Pearl Street in La Crosse. Shown in this c. 1915 photograph are Robert Braun, his daughter Erna (an optician who examined eyes and fitted spectacles at the store), his wife, Phoebe Braun, and sons Adolph and Edwin, who were apprentices to their father at the time of this photo. Both boys went on to become watchmakers.

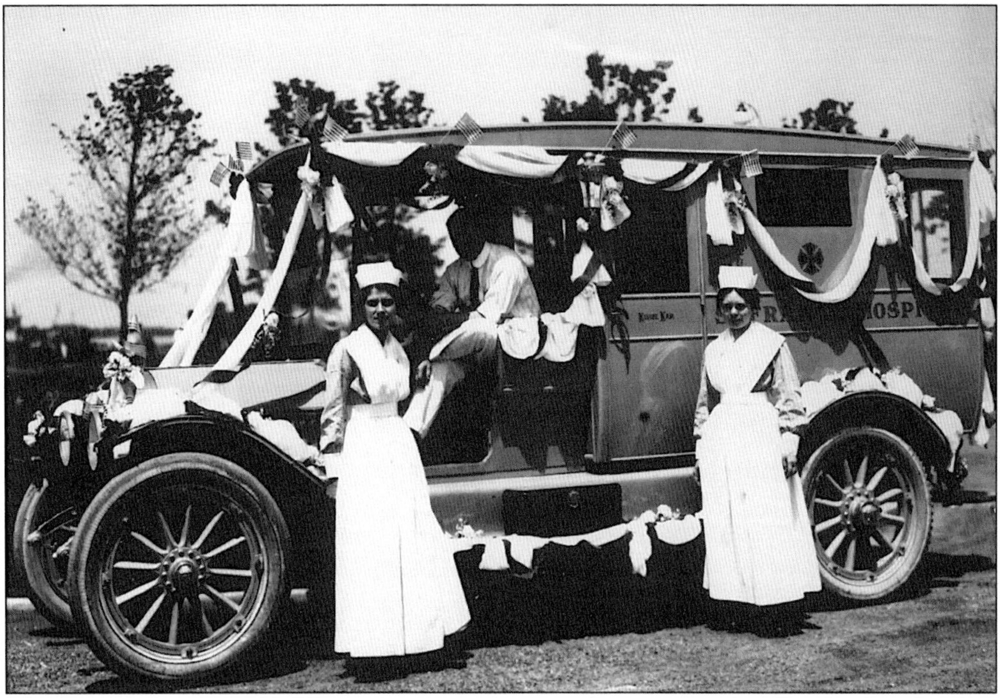

The St. Francis Hospital ambulance is shown here, decked out for a parade c. 1920. The nurses and driver stand in front of a shiny "Kissel Kar" that is draped in bunting, flags, and flowers.

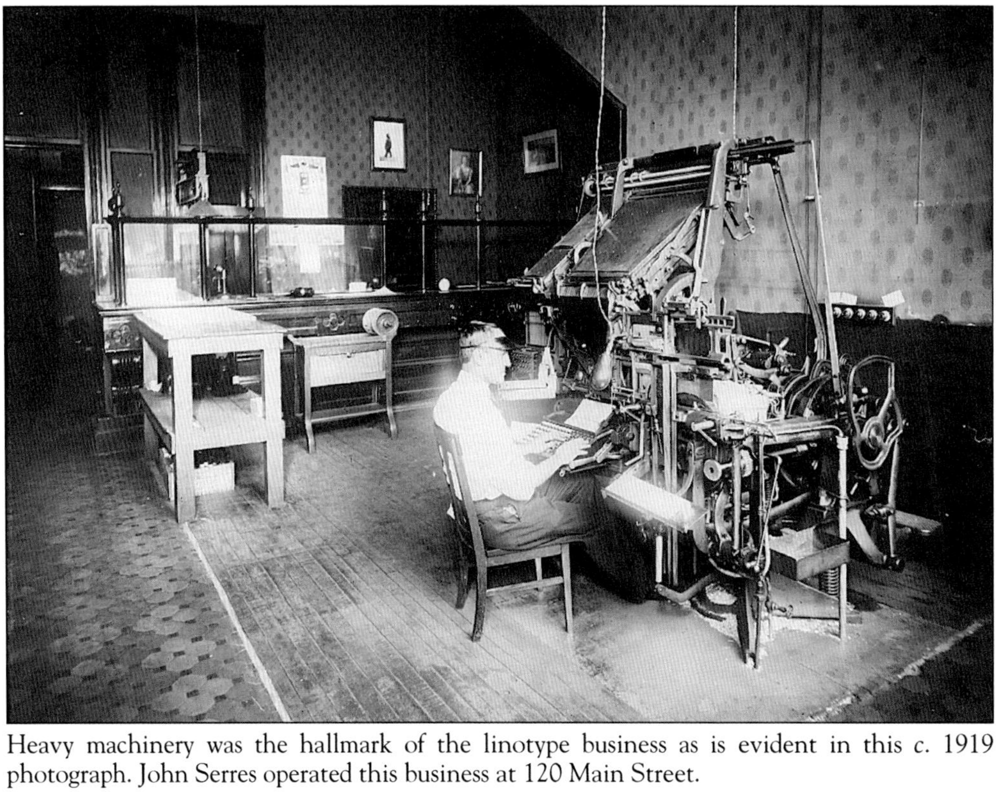

Heavy machinery was the hallmark of the linotype business as is evident in this c. 1919 photograph. John Serres operated this business at 120 Main Street.

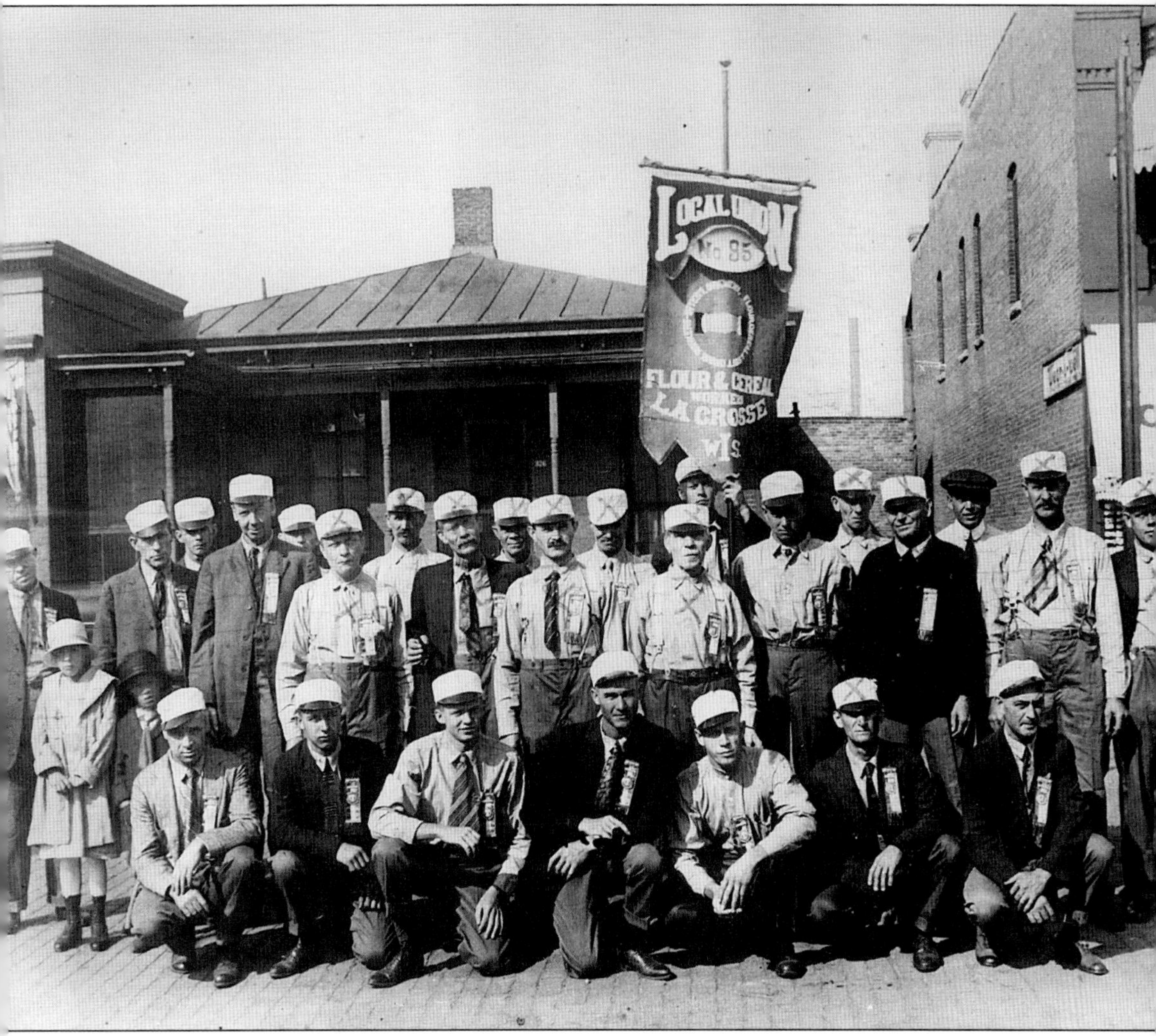

Workers at Listman Mills, the makers of Marvel Flour, are gathered near the Trades and Union Hall at 415 Jay Street *c.* 1921. Members of Local 95 of the Flour and Cereal Workers Union, these men wear their badges and caps proudly. Herman L. Schultz & Son clothing store can be seen in the background.

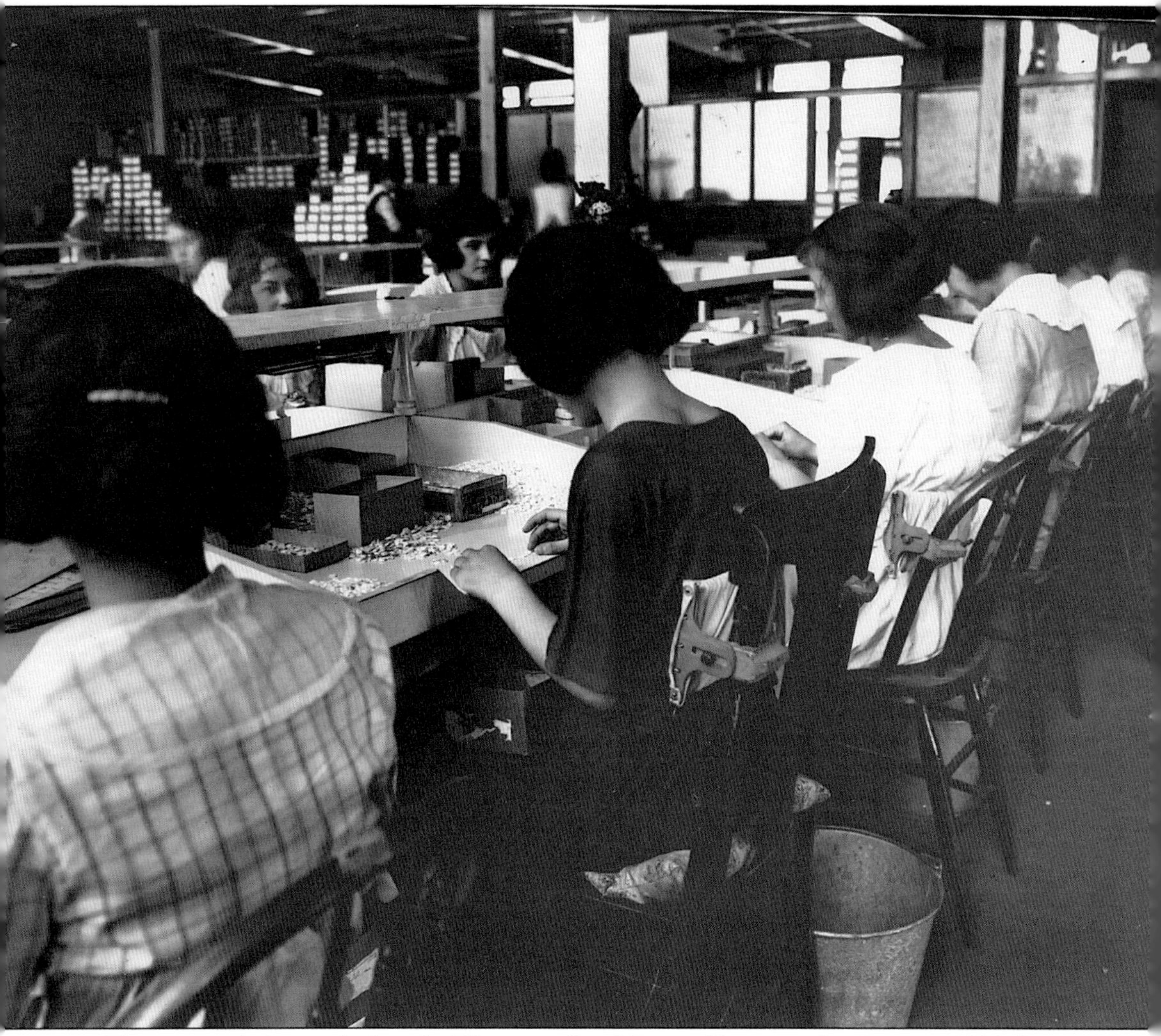

These young ladies worked in the Wisconsin Pearl Button Factory in La Crosse *c.* 1920. Button sorters constituted only a few of the over 200 workers at the factory, which opened in 1901 to manufacture buttons from clam and mussel shells.

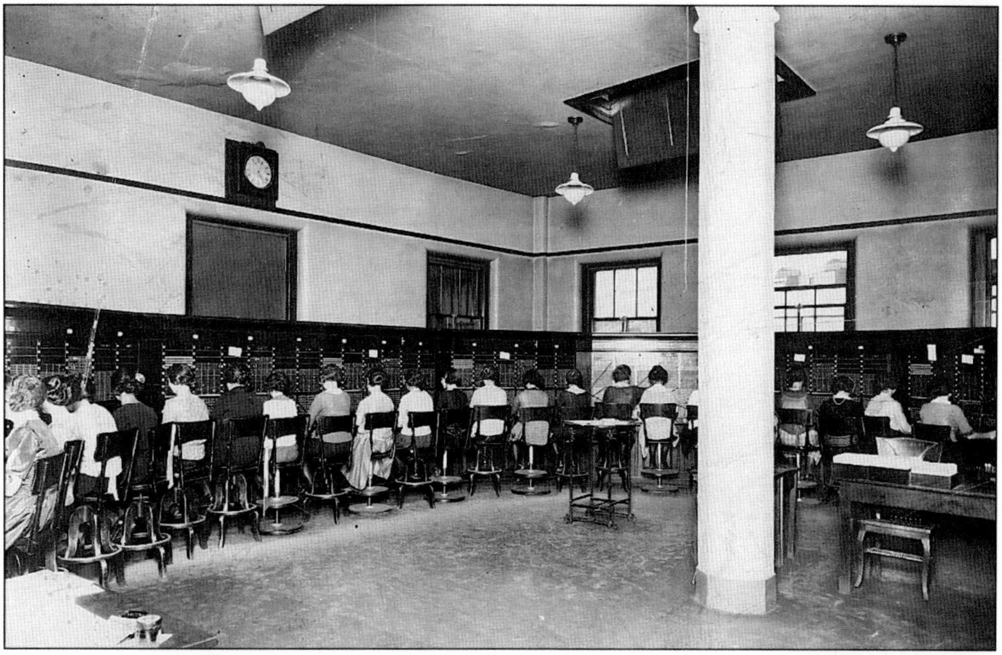

This candid shot of the operators employed by the La Crosse Telephone Company was taken in September 1922. Pictured from left to right are, Alma Johnson, Florence Heileman, Edna Oakes, Ida Cohen, Mildred Edwards Granke, Stell Manning, Ruth Bramwell Clace, Wanda Fahler, Evelyn Moe, Rose Shedesky, Mildred Wodzynski, Florence Pieper Schubert, Margaret Latterman, Clara Schultz, Helen Bruring, Myrtle Klaber, Marie Johnson, Anna Roth, Gertrude Larson, Elsie Woelke Staples, and Eileen Blum.

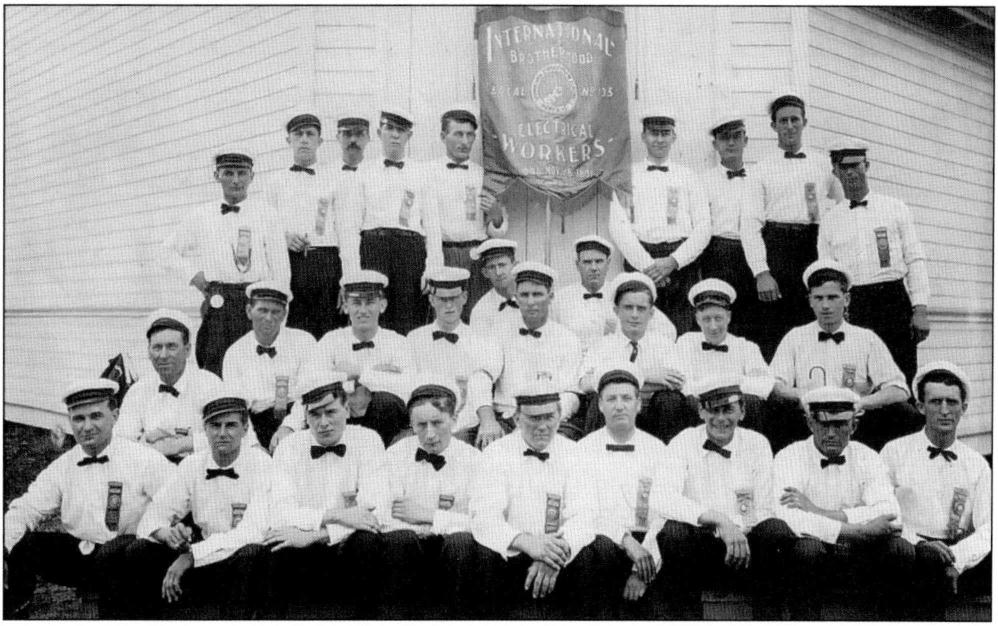

According to the banner in this undated photograph, the International Brotherhood of Electrical Workers was organized on November 18, 1891. La Crosse's Local 135 are shown wearing their bow ties, caps, and badges.

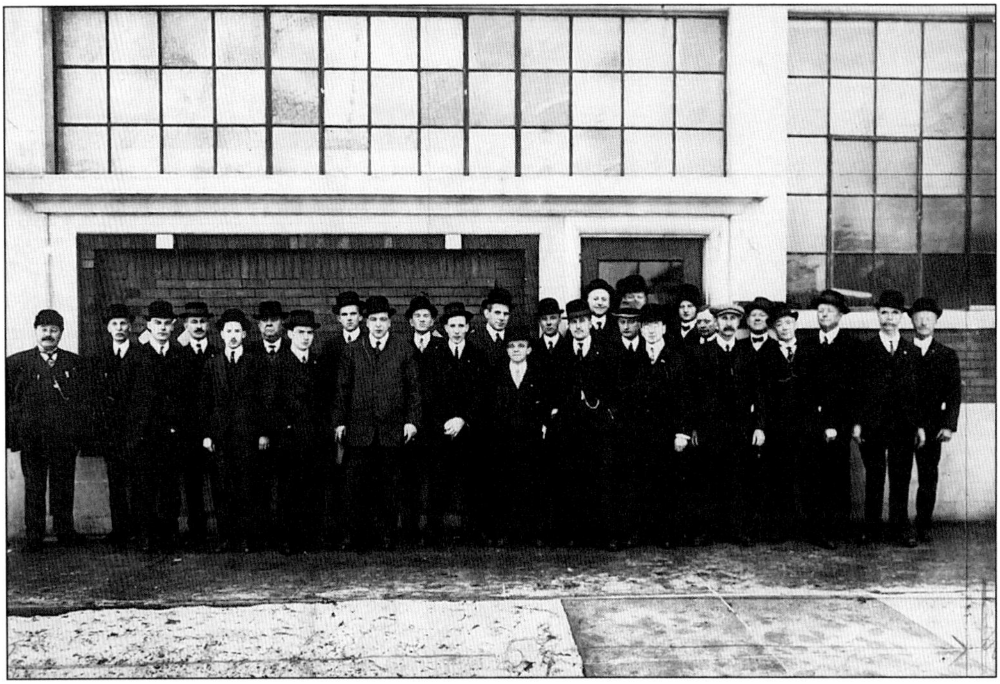

Gathered for a meeting during the 1920s, the sales force employed by La Crosse Rubber Mills stood outside the factory for this group photograph.

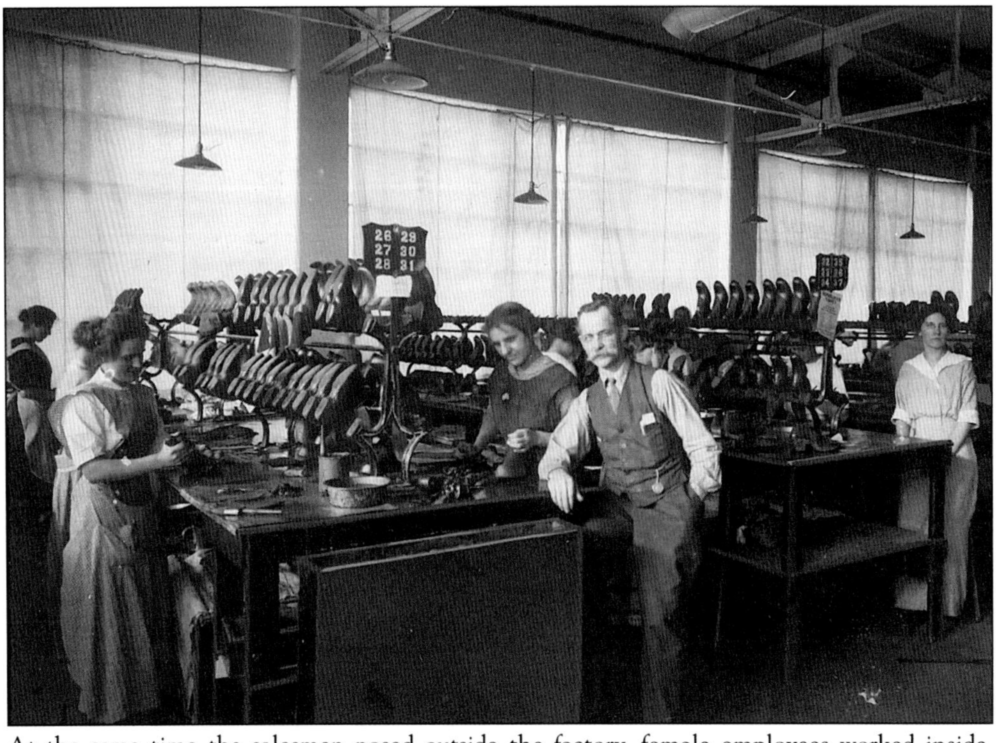

At the same time the salesmen posed outside the factory, female employees worked inside, assembling rubber shoes.

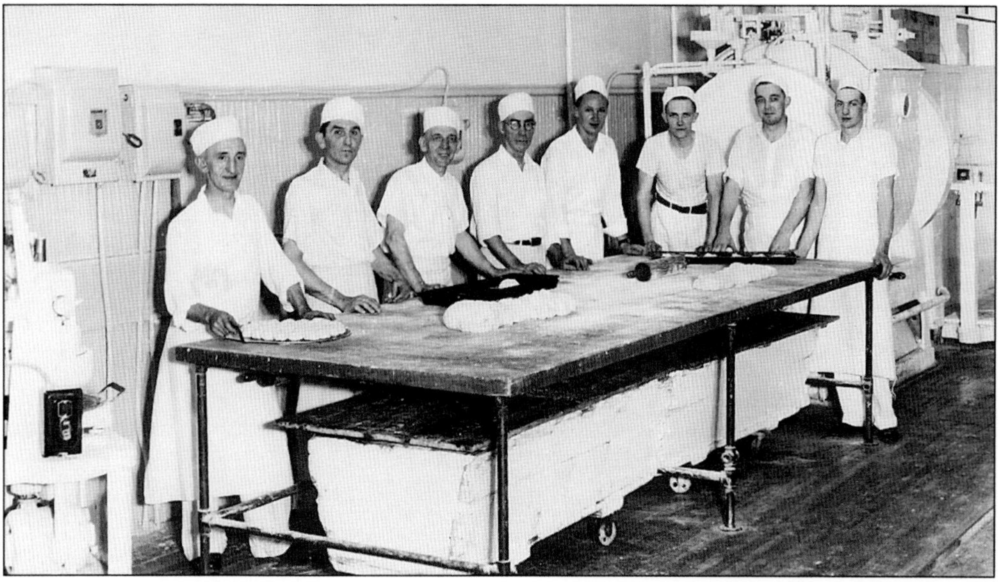

In the late 1940s, Federal Bakery at 522 Main Street employed eight bakers. Those identified are, from left to right, Paul Leuck, Robert Marx, unidentified, and Percy Rochester. The remainder of the men are unidentified.

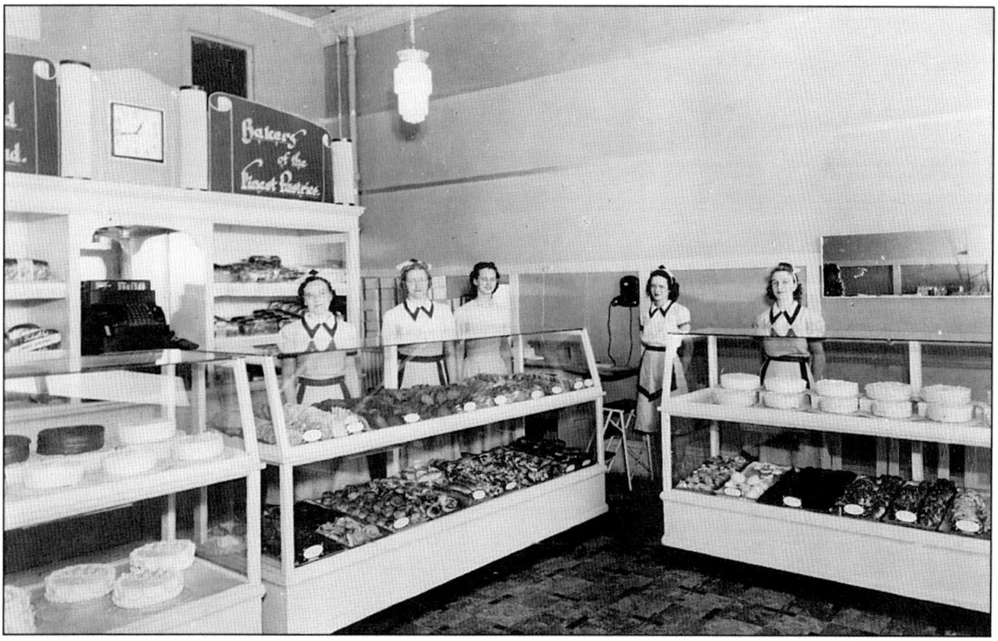

The women who worked at the Federal Bakery c. 1946 included Selma Schorch, Mabel Olson, and Dorothy Foster French, the office secretary. The other women in the photograph are unidentified.

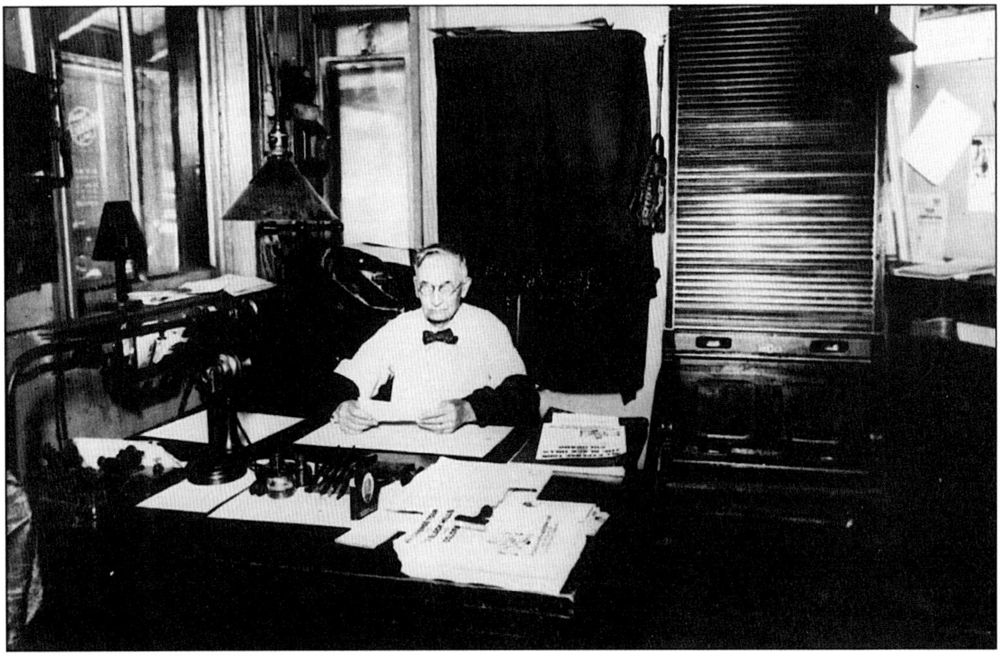

In this photograph taken June 4, 1932, William E. Sparling is shown behind his desk at the Chicago and North Western Railway ticket office in La Crosse. Mr. Sparling served as a telegraph operator and ticket agent.

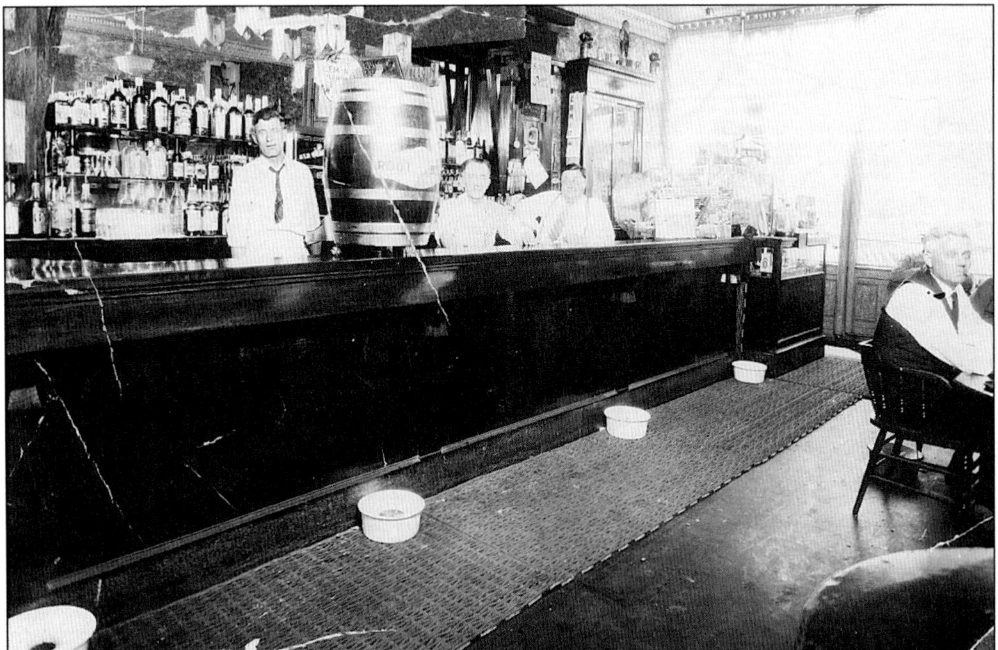

The Milwaukee Road Bar, located at 424 Copeland Avenue, was photographed in May 1936. Charles Schwertfage (left) was the bartender.

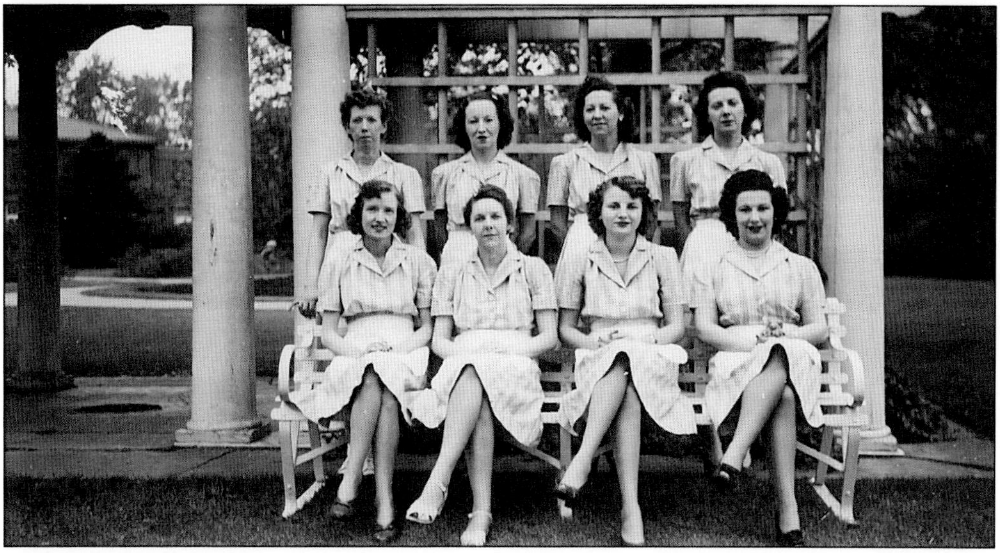

Only two of the women in this photo of the La Crosse Mutual Loan and Building Association employees have been identified. They are Eva Frisch (front row, on the left) and beside her, Wilma Sampson Johnston. These ladies, dressed in identical uniforms, posed c. 1954.

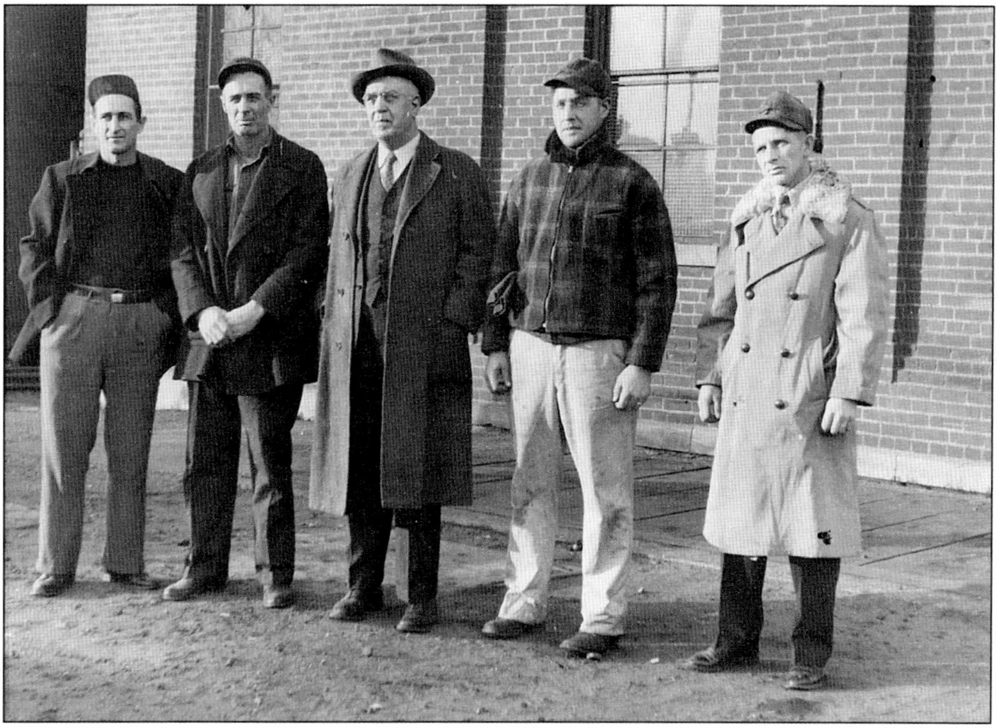

Edgar Johnson, Art Ames, Frank Wilkenson, John Minor, and Walton Minor are pictured in this 1948 view outside the Northern States Power Company building. The power company is located on Fifth Avenue North.

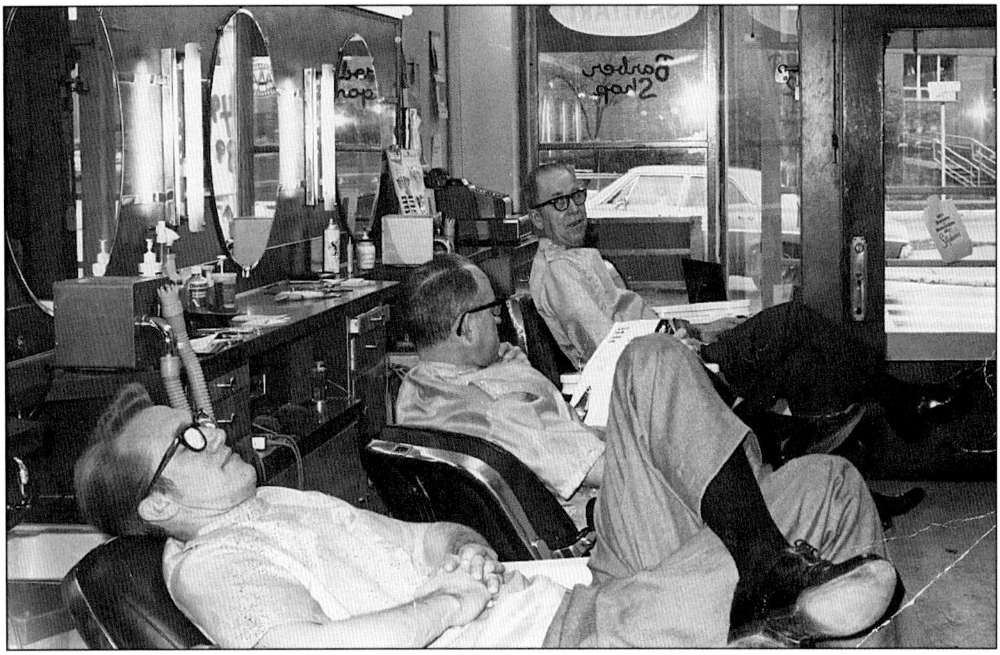

The Sanitary Barber Shop was a local fixture for over 50 years. Located across from the University of Wisconsin-La Crosse campus at 1804 State Street, the shop served both the student and neighborhood populations until it closed in 1998. This photo from the early 1970s shows barbers Jerry Sanford, Dick Brown, and Len Bennett taking a break between customers.

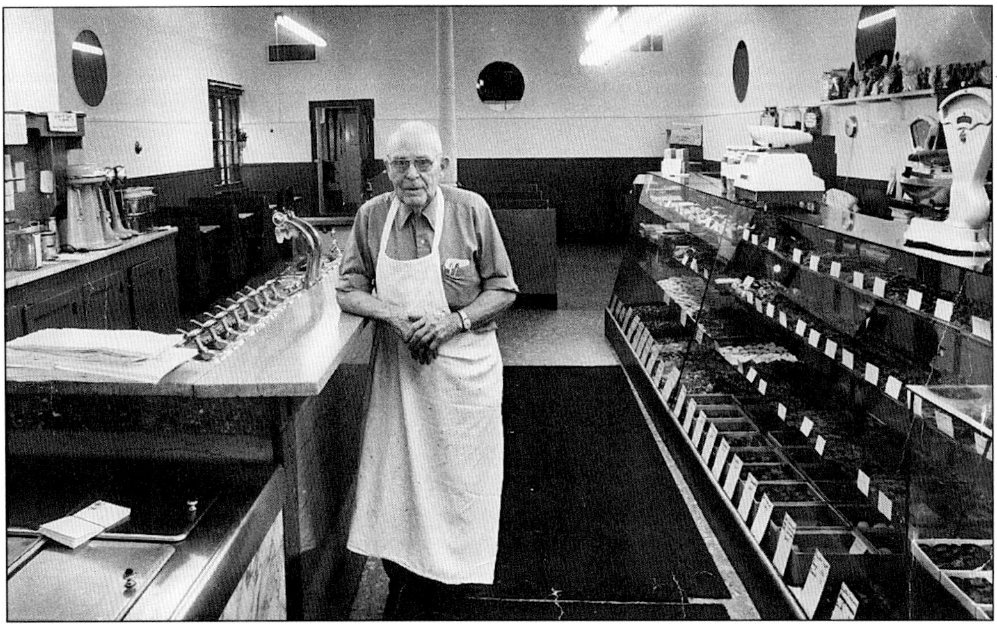

Cecil Allen bought North La Crosse's Sweet Shop in 1921. In this photo taken in 1981, Mr. Allen poses amid the chocolates and ice cream confections.

Six

EVERYDAY LIVING

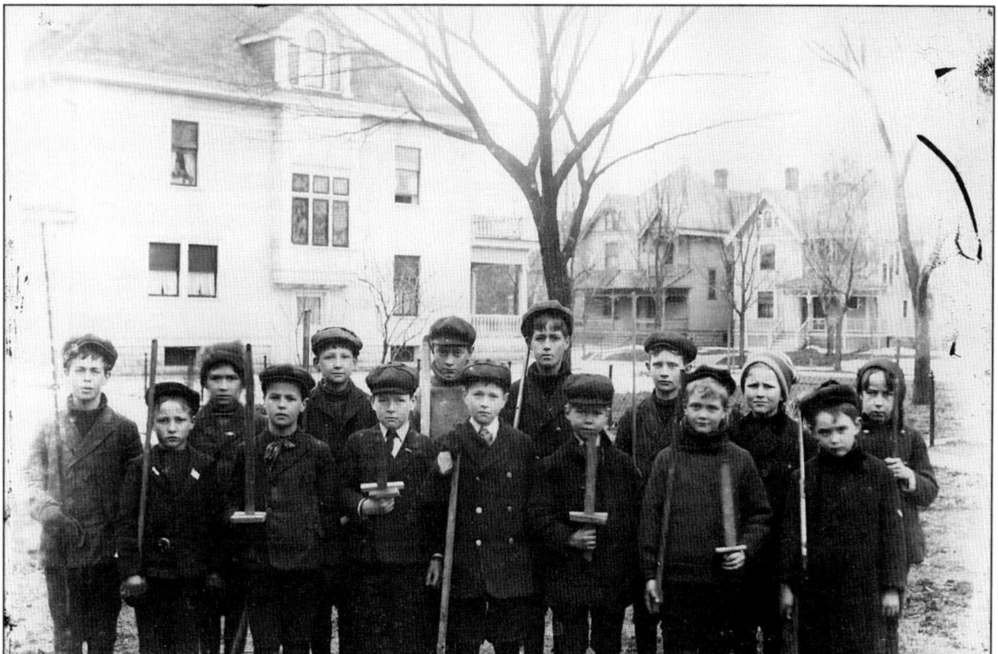

"Holway's Army" assembled on Dr. Edward Evans's lawn in the 100 block of South Thirteenth Street for this picture c. 1905. From left to right are William Holway, Otto Werner, Parker Boynton, Gordon Holway, Stanley Harrison, Arthur Evans, William Cargill, James Evans, Orlando Holway, Lester Bangsberg, Frank Funke, George Cargill, Joseph Colman, ? Thompson, and Sam Anderson. The Holway boys' father was Orlando Holway, Spanish-American War veteran and adjutant general of the Wisconsin National Guard from 1913 until his death in 1923.

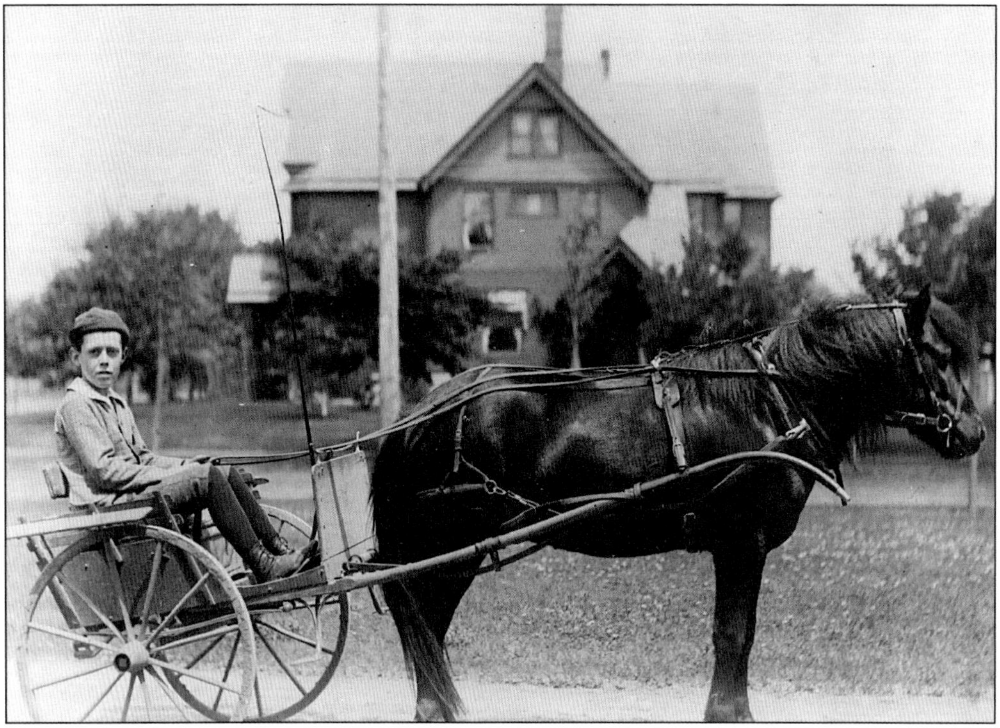

L.C. Colman was the vice-president of the Spence-McCord Drug Company, and his wife, Geneva, was an avid and creative photographer. Mrs. Colman, one of the first female amateur photographers in La Crosse, put together a fascinating album of candid shots taken at the turn of the century. This image captured Bert Spence, the son of T.H. Spence, who was Colman's partner in the drugstore business.

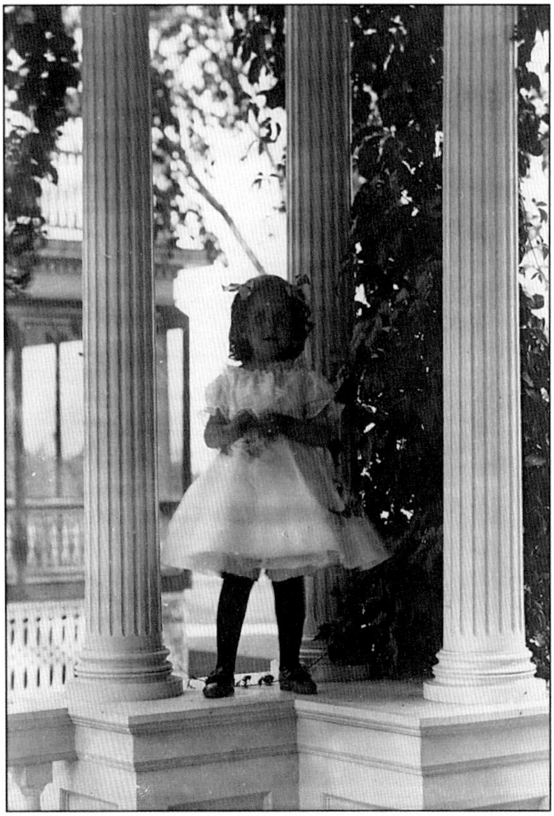

At the dawn of the new century, lovely little Charlotte Colman is seen posing for her aunt Geneva Colman amid the impressive pillars of her home on Fifteenth Street.

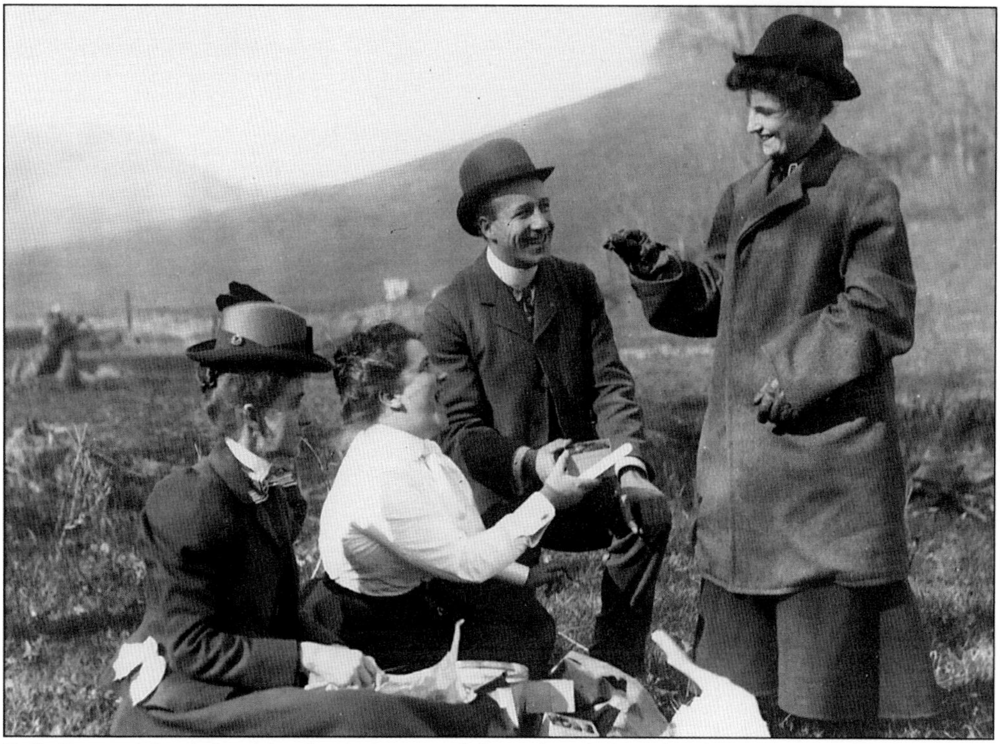

Belle Burton's birthday, May 5, 1900, was celebrated with friends. The caption under this photo in the Colman album reads, "Picking over strawberries." Jessie James, Belle Burton, Charles Cone, and Jane Cone are pictured.

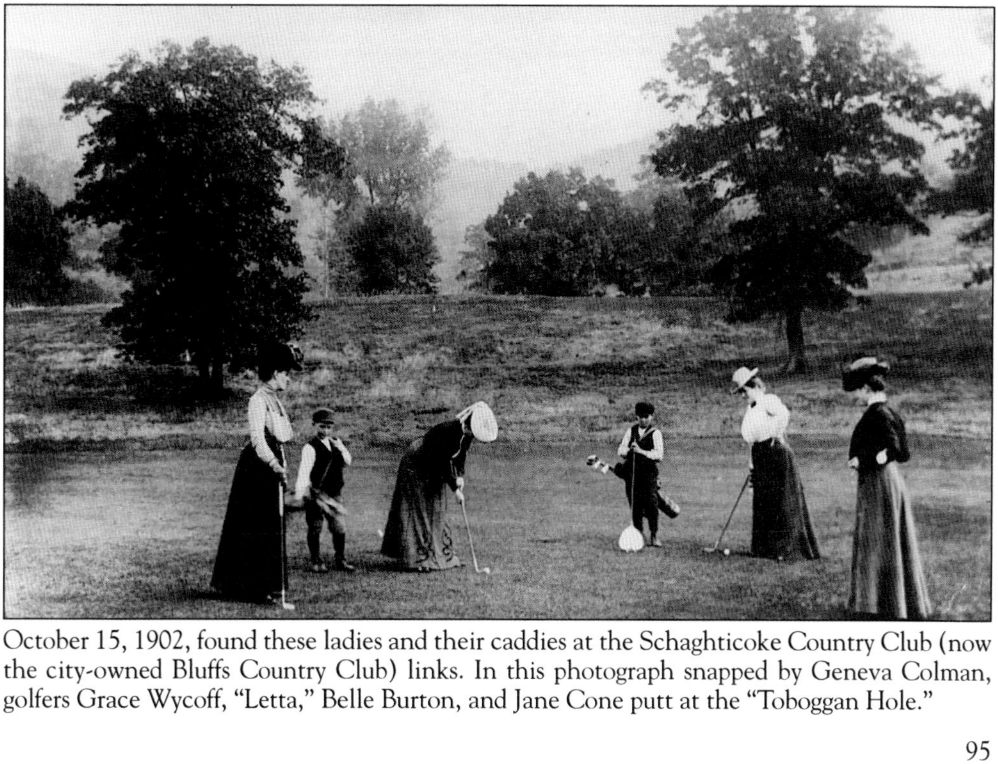

October 15, 1902, found these ladies and their caddies at the Schaghticoke Country Club (now the city-owned Bluffs Country Club) links. In this photograph snapped by Geneva Colman, golfers Grace Wycoff, "Letta," Belle Burton, and Jane Cone putt at the "Toboggan Hole."

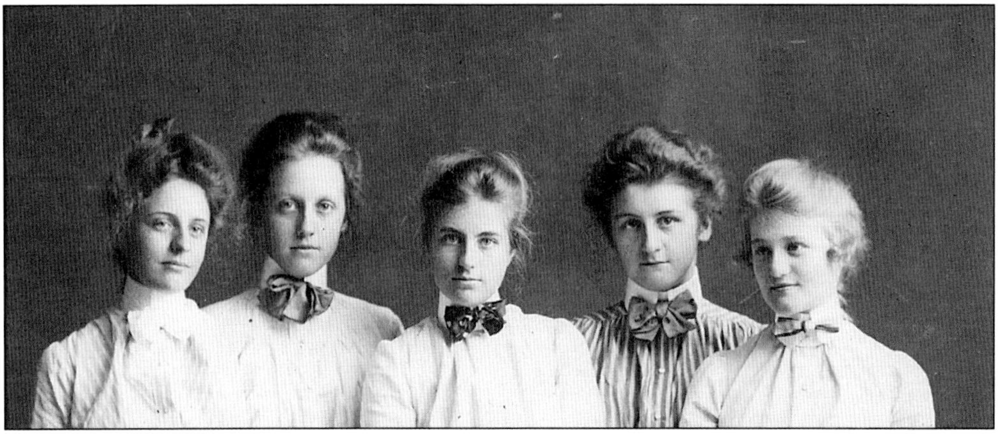

On October 2, 1900, these five friends posed for the photographer at Pryor studios in La Crosse. The young ladies pictured are Edna Coren, Agnes McCord, Gert Norbeck, Melinda Funk, and Freda Michel.

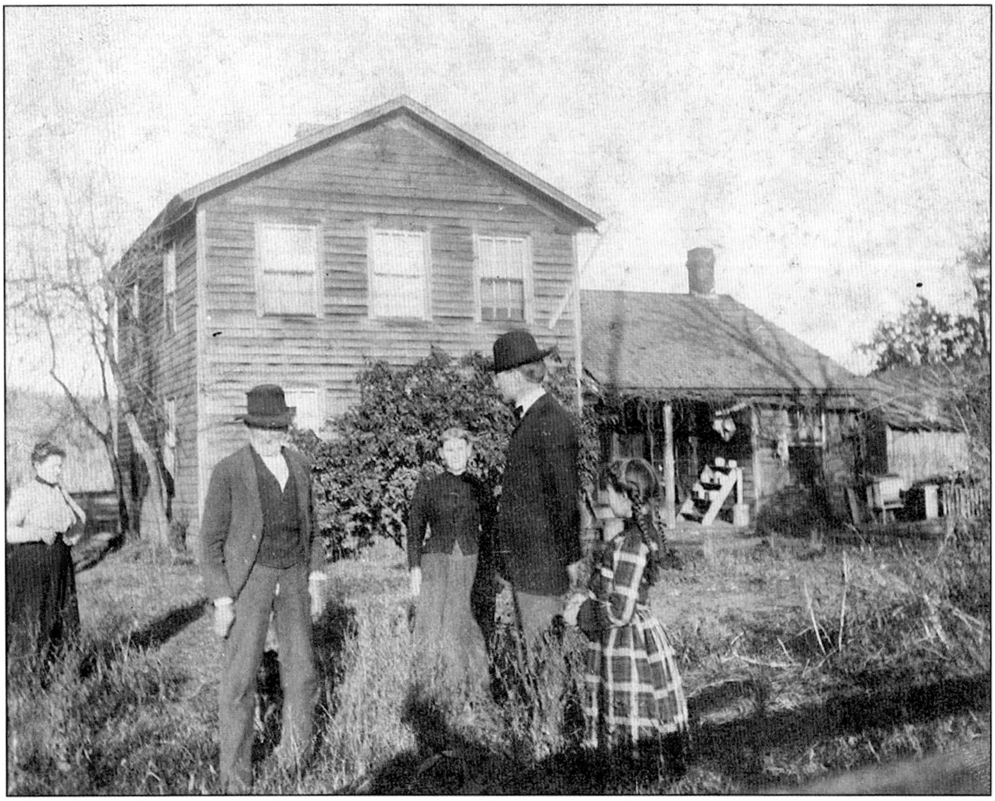

This photograph is labeled "Grandpa Miller's old homestead, 1901. Township of Midway, north of Onalaska." The Swarthout family owned the farm.

Five children of Hattie M. and George H. Ray pose in this c. 1901Pryor Studio photograph. Harriet, Robert, Anne, George, and Richard's father was a lumberman, president of the State Bank of La Crosse, and assemblyman. The Rays lived at 928 King Street. A younger brother, John, was soon added to the family.

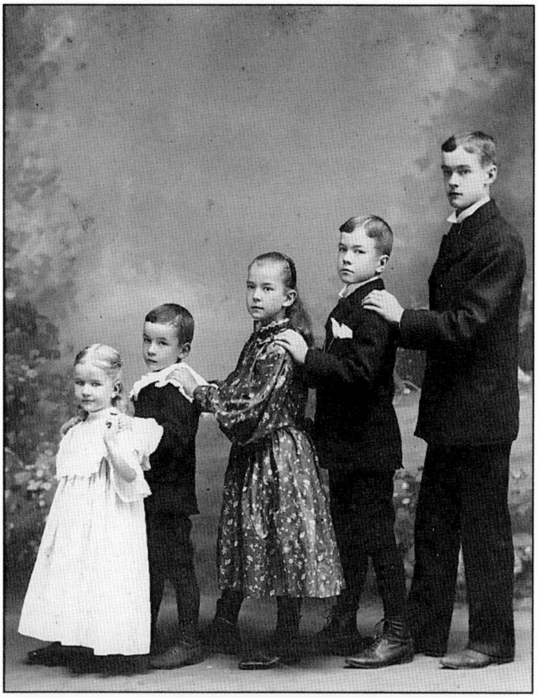

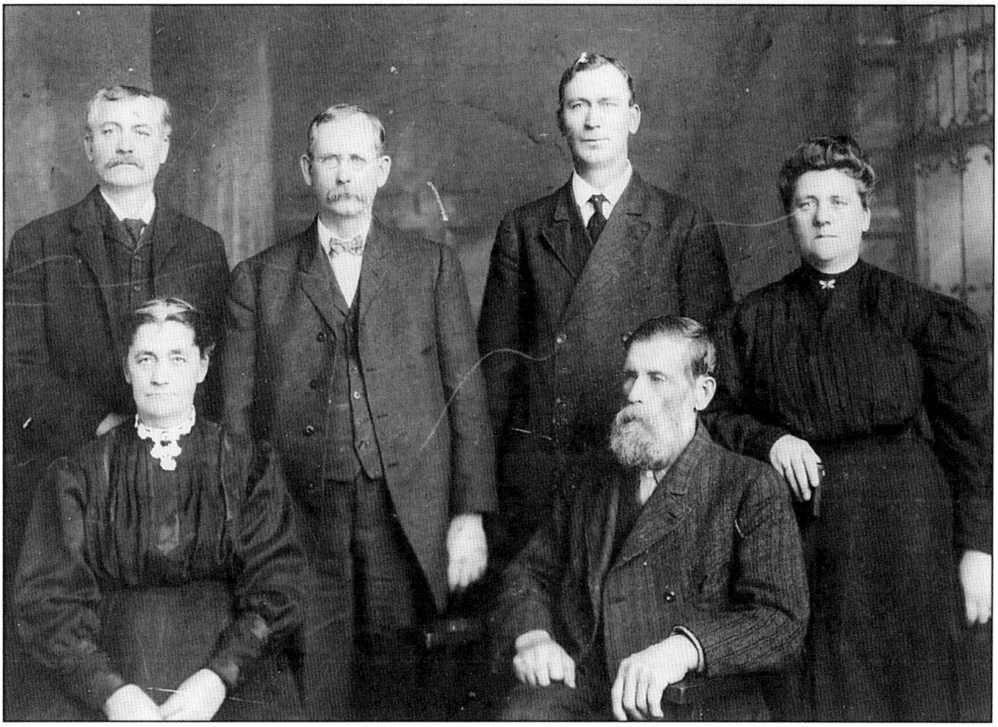

The Nelson siblings were photographed in La Crosse *c.* 1905. They are, from left to right, (standing) John Gustave Nelson, Peter Nelson, Bernt Nelson, and Ellen Nelson Ulven; (seated) Berthe Nelson Larson and Johannes Nelson. All the men in the family were carpenters.

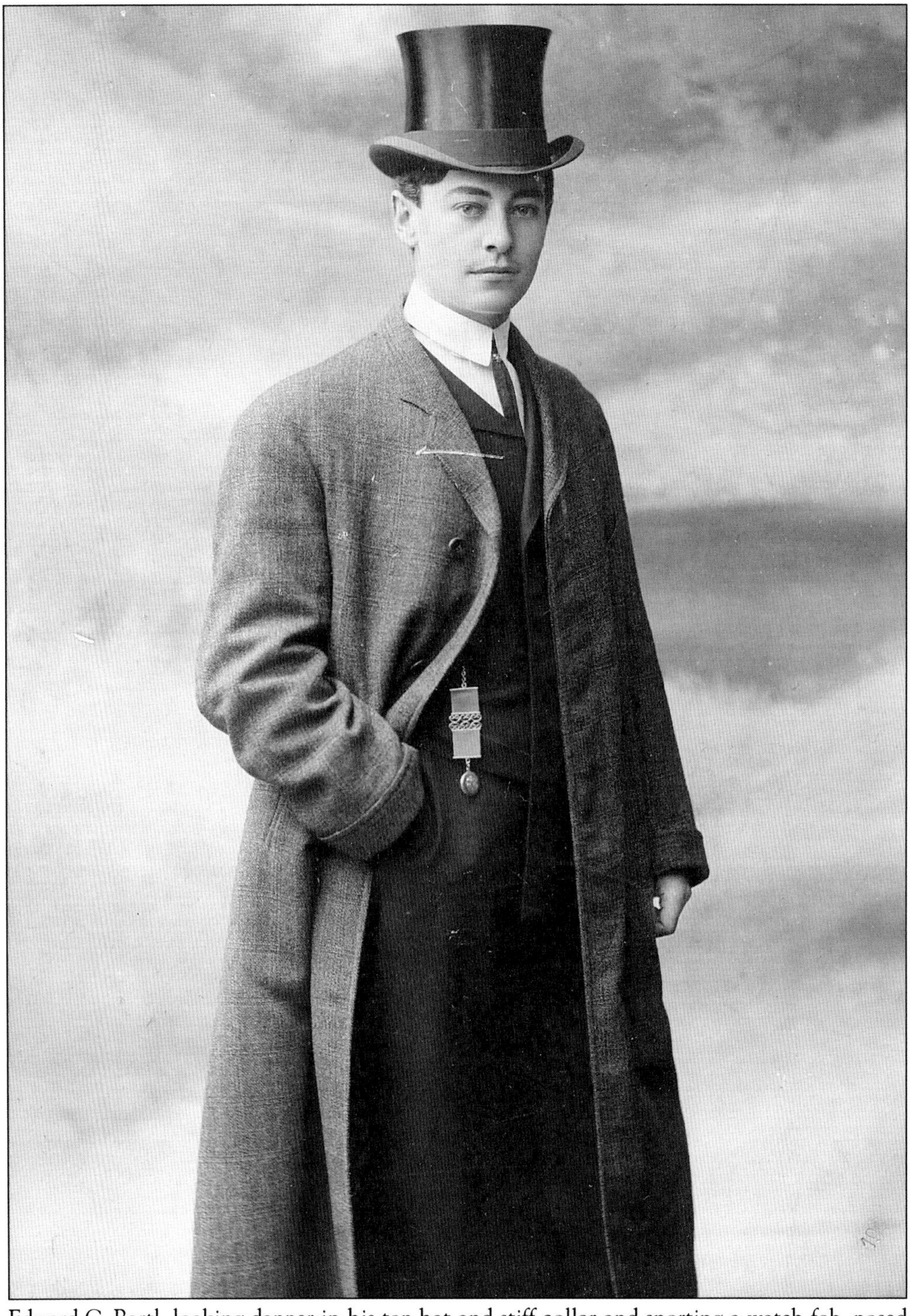

Edward C. Bartl, looking dapper in his top hat and stiff collar and sporting a watch fob, posed in a photographer's studio in Pilsen, Bohemia, on August 26, 1903. The youngest son of Frank Bartl, a La Crosse brewer whose family came to America from Bohemia, Edward retraced his father's journey and returned to his family's homeland.

Elizabeth Rose Schnell modeled for this c. 1904 portrait at Bosshard Studios to commemorate her confirmation at the German Evangelical Lutheran Church. The church, now called First Evangelical Lutheran Church, is located at the corner of Cameron and West Avenues.

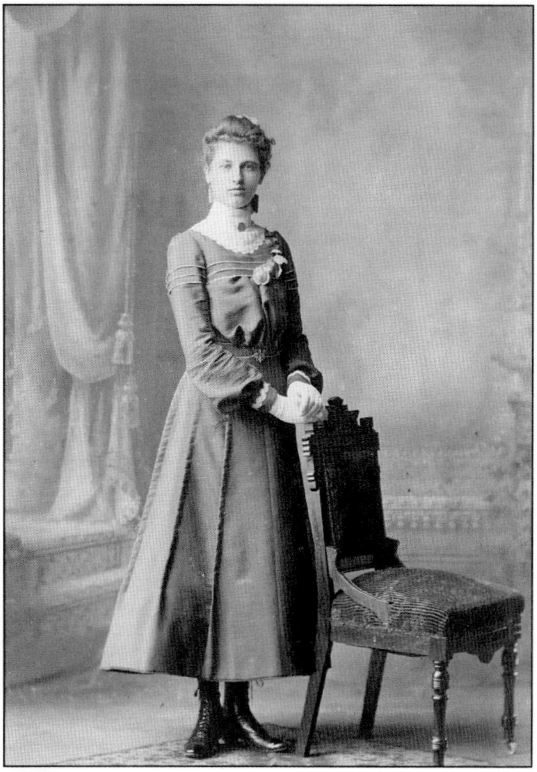

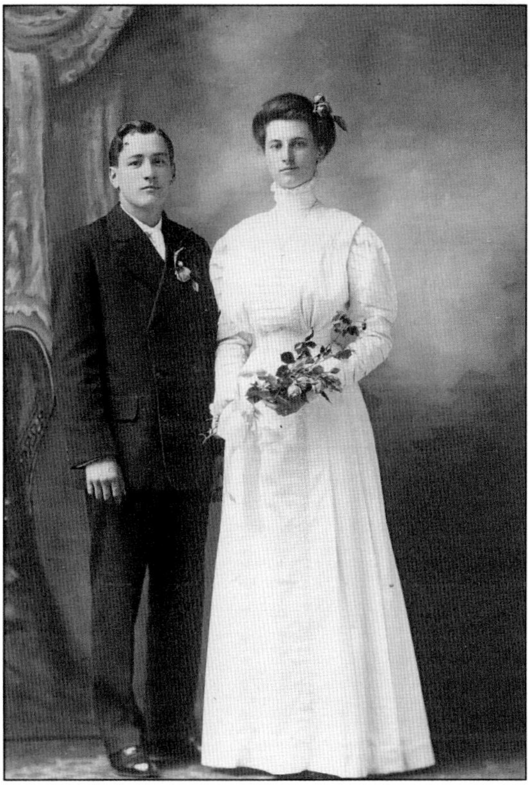

Moss Studios of La Crosse, which advertised its "Electric Light Studio," photographed Elizabeth Schnell and Joseph Raith's wedding portrait in 1909.

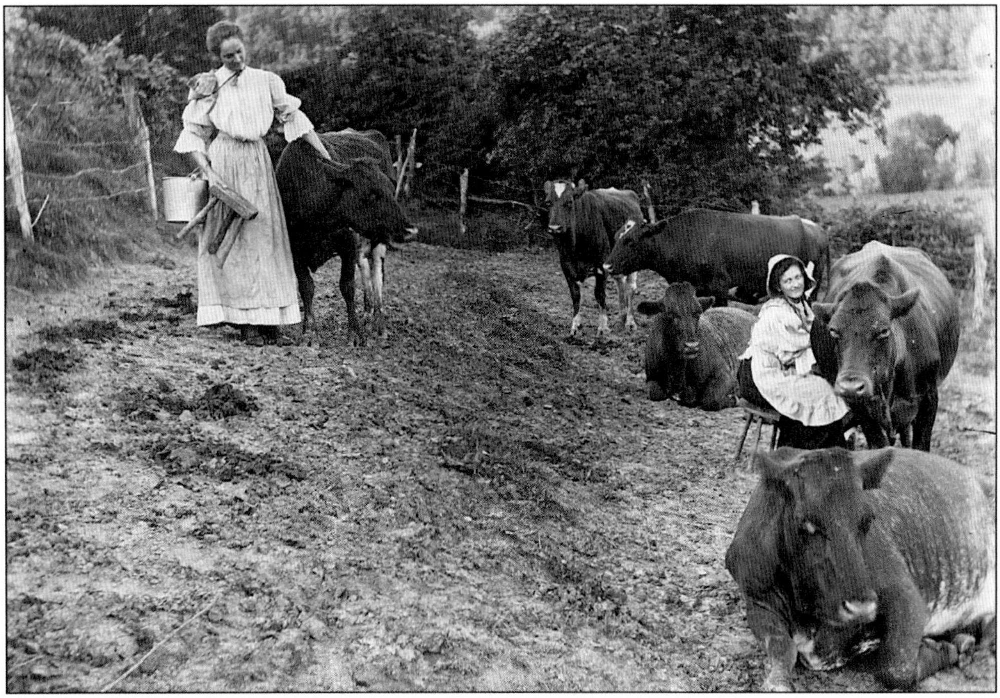

The great majority of land surrounding La Crosse has been used for agricultural purposes since settlers first arrived. This photograph of milkmaids, taken "at 6 p.m. on Jake Fetzner's pasture in Brownsville, Minn., July 1, 1906" is a print from a glass-plate negative.

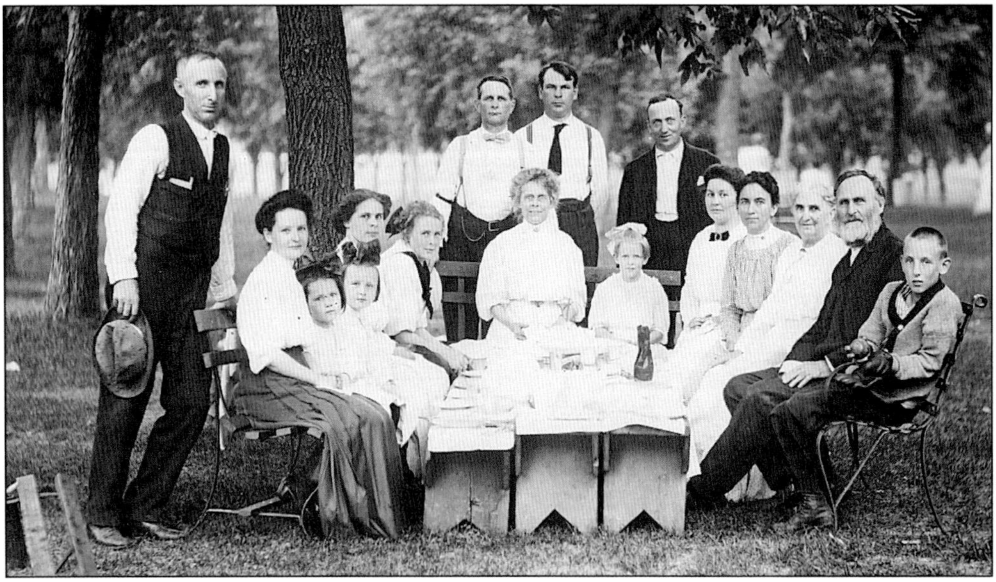

The reverse of this picture postcard reads, "Myrick Park, La Crosse, Wisconsin. Taken at 6:30 p.m., August 25, 1909. Birthday Picnic for Will F. Benton. Names of those on the right: Edwin L. Benton, Thomas P. Benton, Mary D. Benton, Marian L. Benton, Mrs. J.L. Lowe; Sitting on end: Minnie and Margaret Pryor. On the left: Will F. Benton, Mrs. J. Langdon, Dorothy Langdon, Isabel Langdon, Edith C. Pryor, Alice R. Pryor. Standing: Will A. Pryor, Rev. J.L.Lowe, John Langdon."

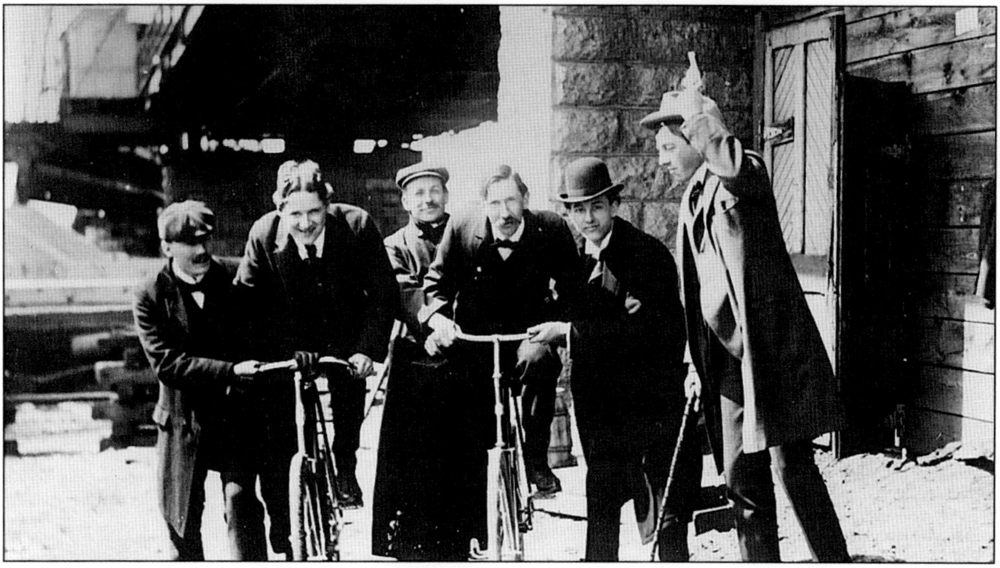

This action shot was snapped on Front Street at the base of the Wagon Bridge *c.* 1910. The bicycle race involved Archie Morse (president and manager of the La Crosse Can Company) on the left bicycle, and Gilbert Woodward (an attorney) on the right bicycle.

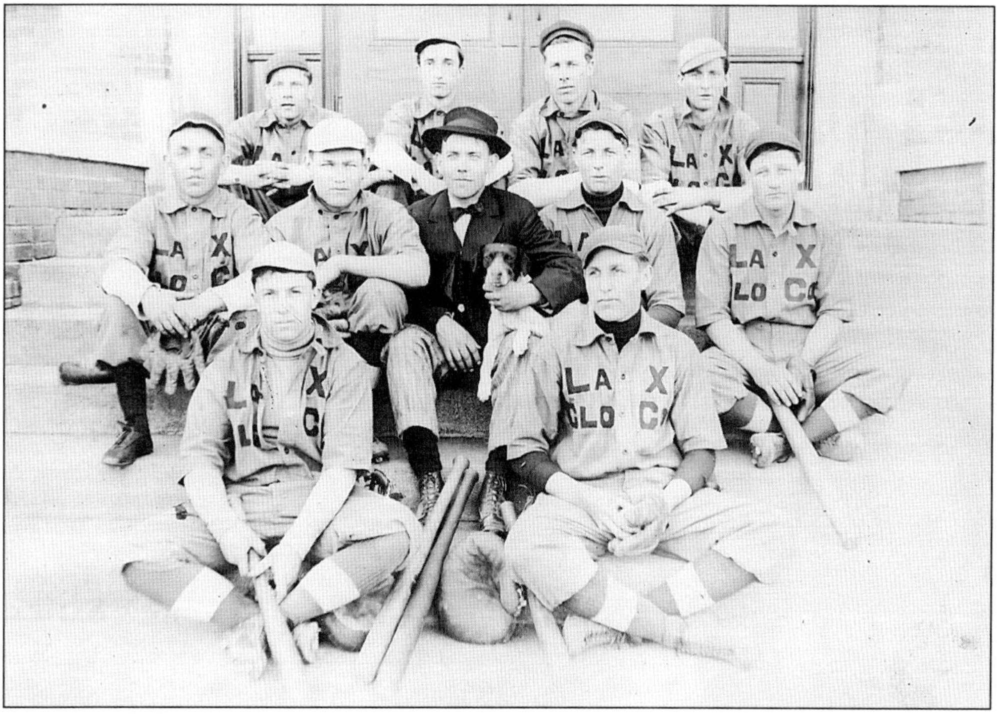

La Crosse Clothing Company's baseball team was caught on film in this 1910 team photo. The manager, Ted Solie Sr., is the only identified and non-uniformed person. Even the mascot's name is unknown.

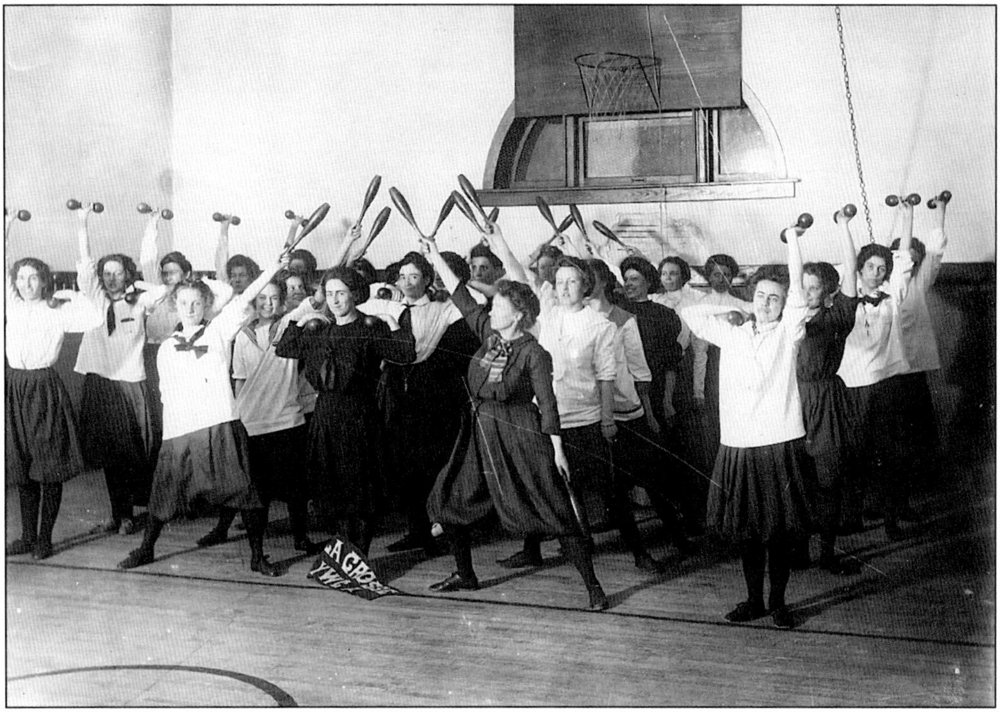

La Crosse's Young Women's Christian Association building was a popular meeting place for young ladies in 1911. The newest craze of physical fitness and healthful lifestyles was aided by flat-heeled shoes, bloomers, and middy blouses. Exercising without the constraints of corsets and the prying eyes of men gave women a new sense of freedom.

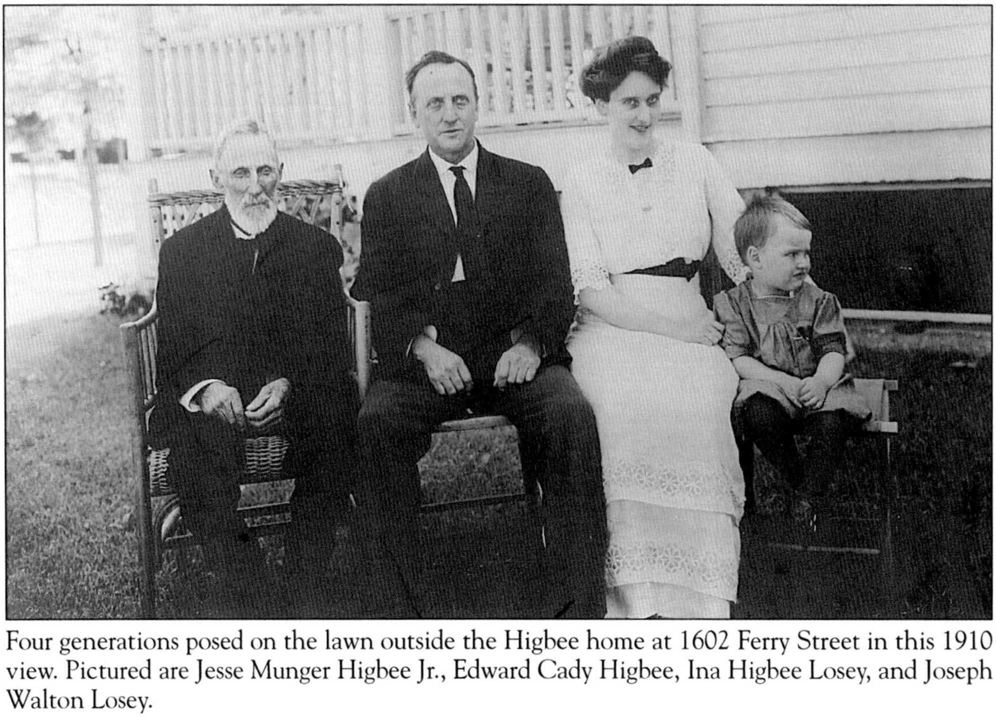

Four generations posed on the lawn outside the Higbee home at 1602 Ferry Street in this 1910 view. Pictured are Jesse Munger Higbee Jr., Edward Cady Higbee, Ina Higbee Losey, and Joseph Walton Losey.

Daring young Kathryn Arenz took a spin on the Indian motorcycle, which belonged to her husband, Albert, sometime after the turn of the century.

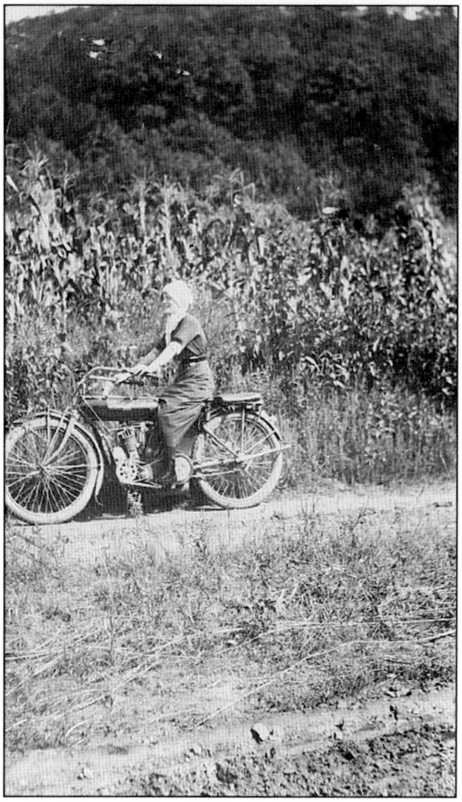

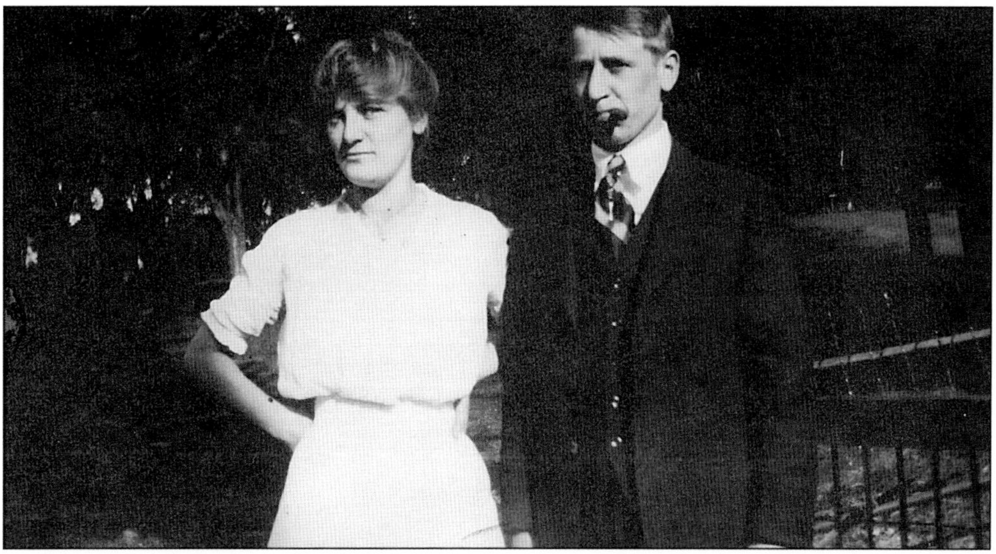

Kathryn and Albert Arenz lived at 2501 Cass Street in 1915, the date of this photo. Having worked in the family business, Arenz Shoe Store at 323 Pearl Street, since he was a young man, Albert became president of the business after the death of his father, Joseph, in 1934.

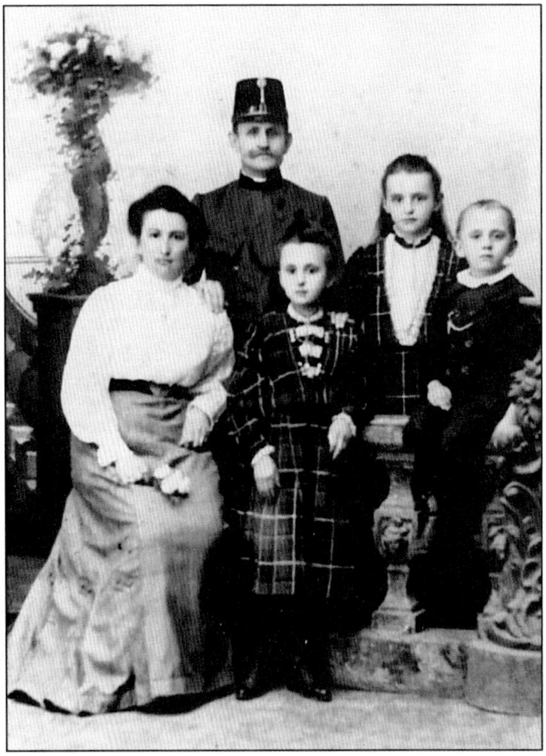

Anna, Bahumil, Betty, Ann, and Godfrey Schedivy are shown here c. 1912. The family came to La Crosse that year and lived in a Bohemian neighborhood called "Hungry Point." Bahumil married Anna, his second wife, in 1908, and together they had two more daughters, one of whom died in infancy.

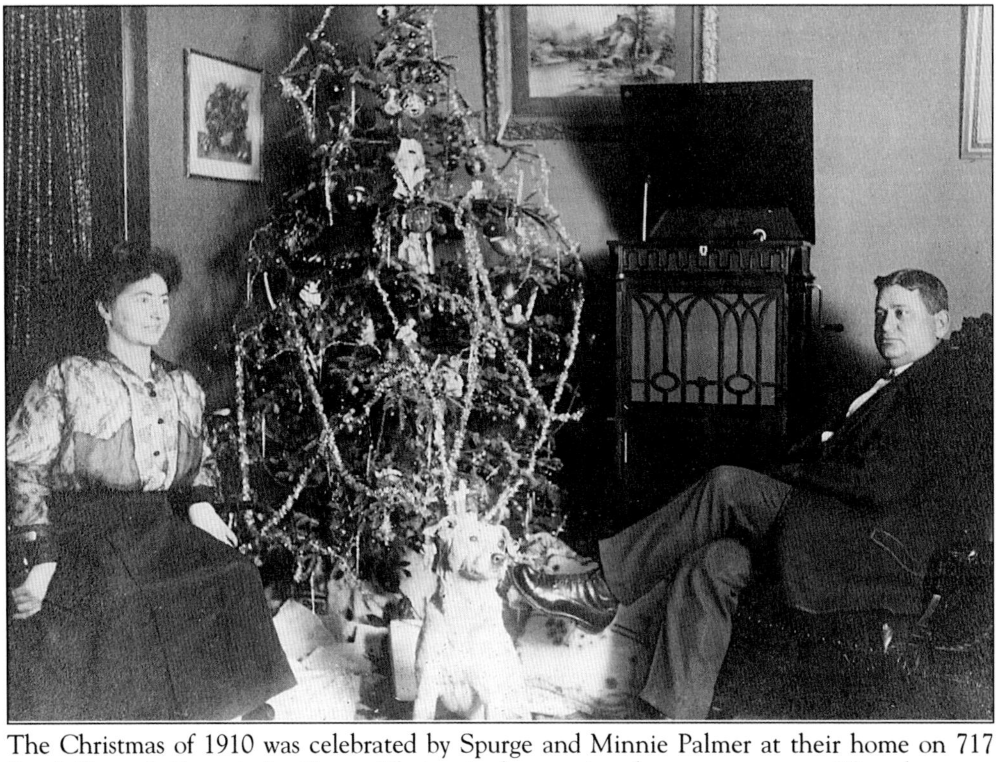

The Christmas of 1910 was celebrated by Spurge and Minnie Palmer at their home on 717 South Seventh Street in La Crosse. Their prized possession that year was a new Victrola.

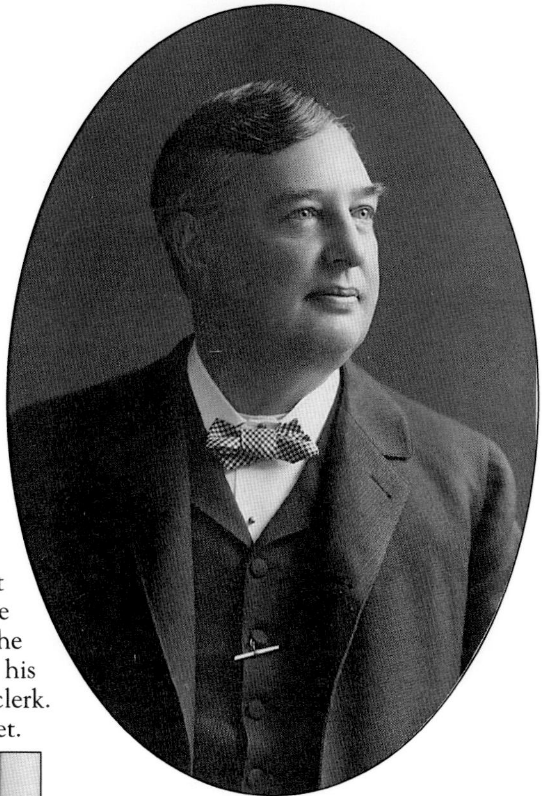

Alfred Harrison began his career as a court reporter and eventually became clerk of the U.S. District and Circuit Courts, a post he held from 1895 to 1925. Upon his death, his daughter Miriam took over his duties as clerk. Their home was located at 1333 Main Street.

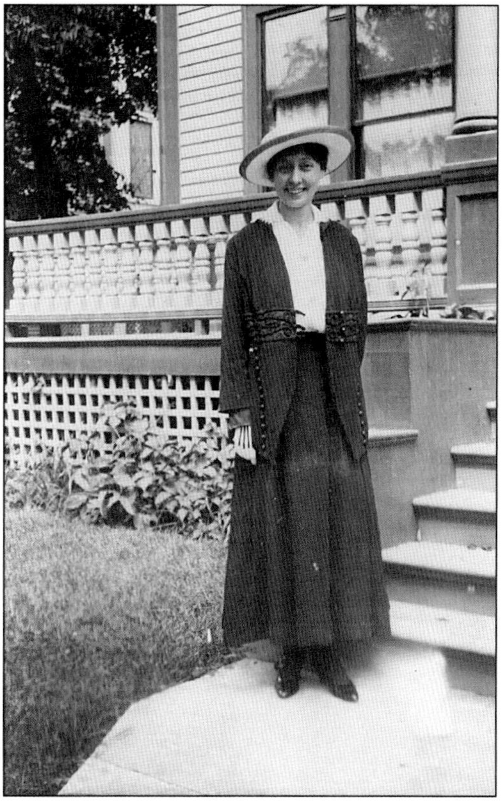

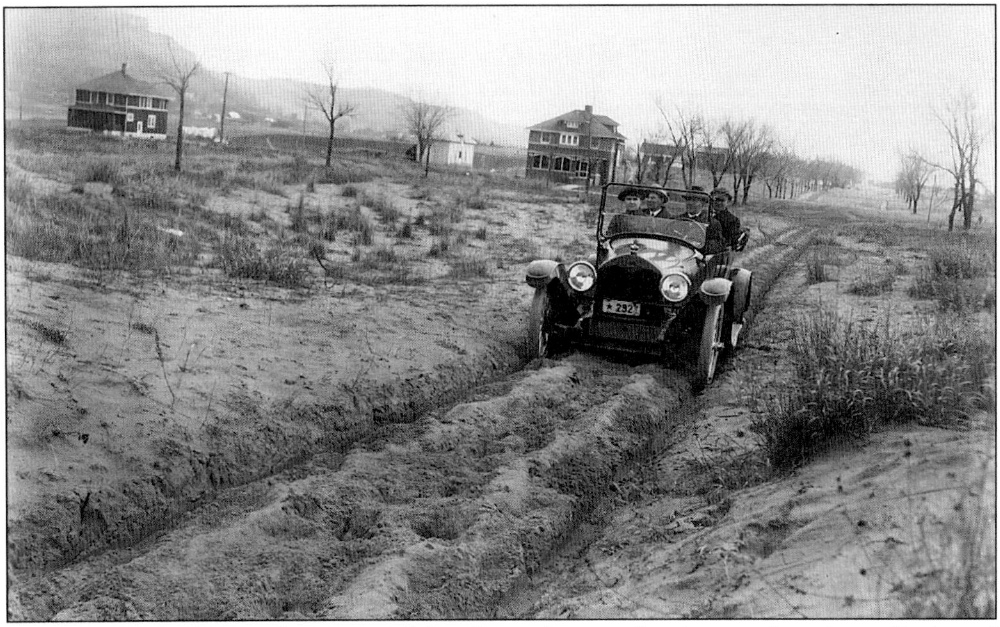

According to the data on the reverse of this photo, the car is heading north on Losey Boulevard at the corner of King Street. The adventurous people are unidentified, but the car's license tag is a 1916 Wisconsin plate, setting the date for the muddy drive.

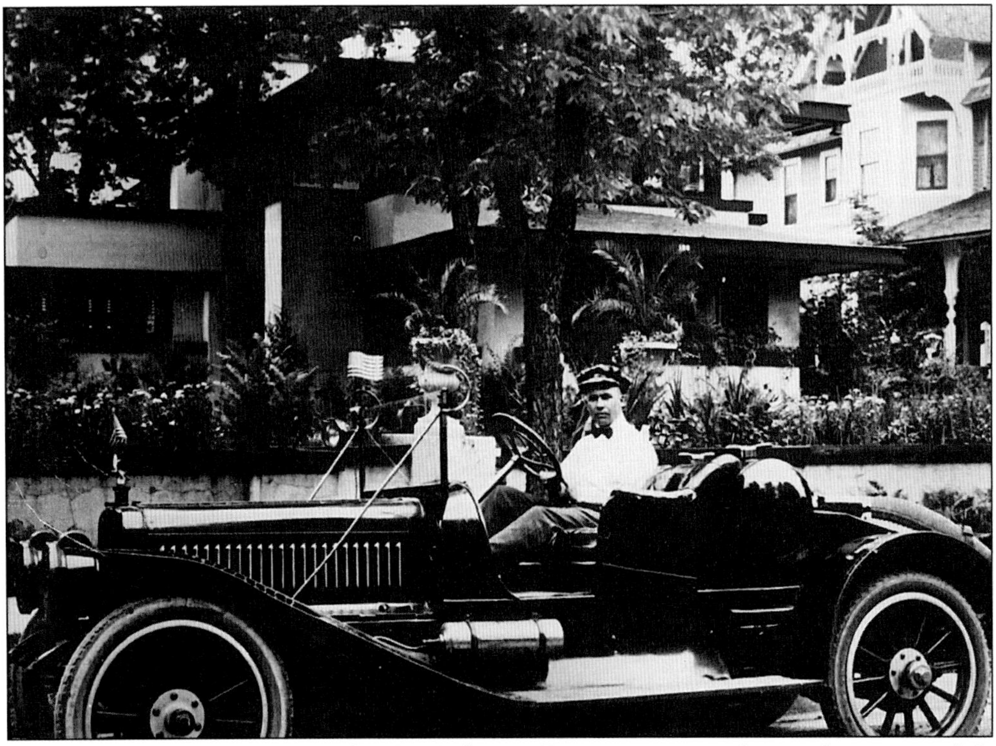

Otto Mueller, the brewmeister for G. Heileman Brewery, poses in his modern automobile in front of his modern Prairie-style home c. 1919. The house was located at 128 South Fourteenth Street.

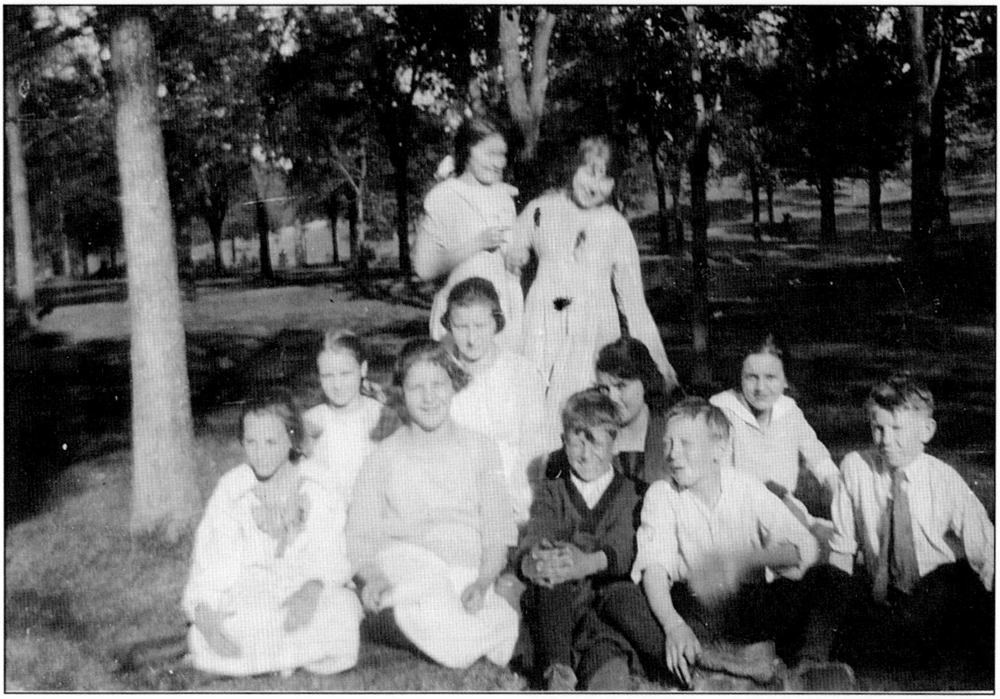

In the summer of *c.* 1917, these children from a Bohemian neighborhood were photographed playing at the park. Pictured from left to right are Roz Kubal, Elsie Shaker, M. Neuverth, France Bina, Rose Slovak, Lill Bell, Helen Prucha, Julia Neuverth, Joe Fried, J. Bruha, and G. Speha.

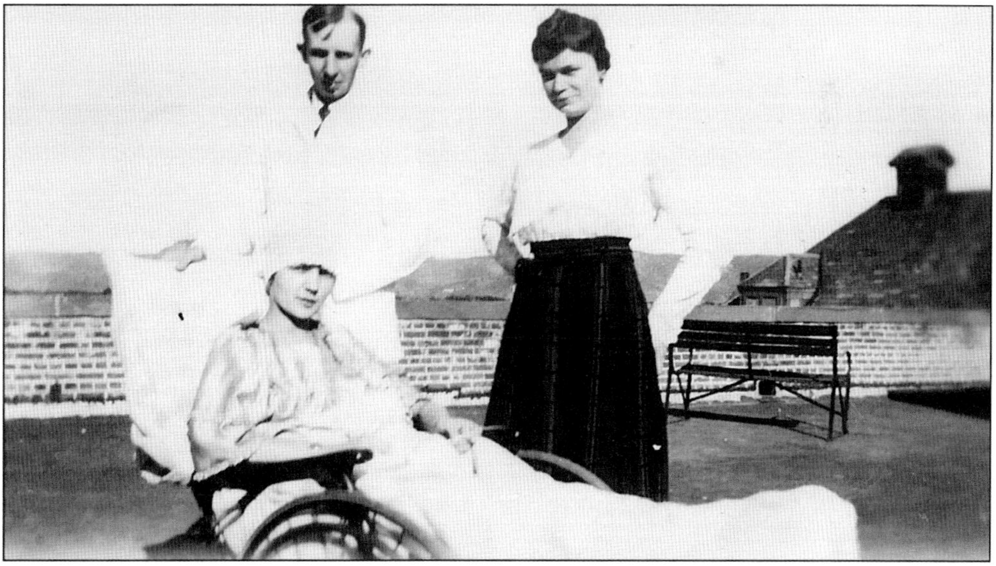

Grace Forbes suffered a hip injury while playing basketball at La Crosse High School in 1918 and endured a long recovery period. As part of her treatment, Grace spent time on the roof of Lutheran Hospital for fresh air. The identification on the photo reads, "Dr. (Edward S.) Carlsson and Johnny, with Grace in the invalid chair."

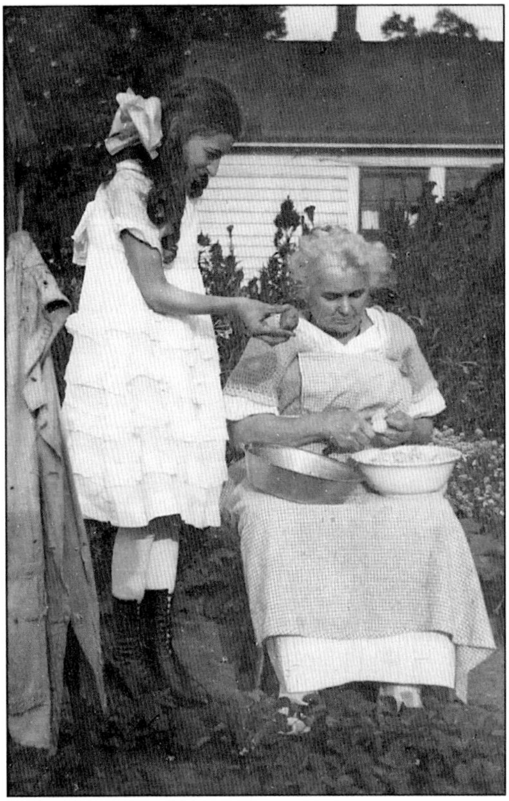

In this c. 1919 photograph, Lucile M. Euler helps an older woman who may be her grandmother with potato peeling. Lucile's father, Charles, owned a drugstore at Eleventh and State Streets. Her mother was Ida Koch Euler.

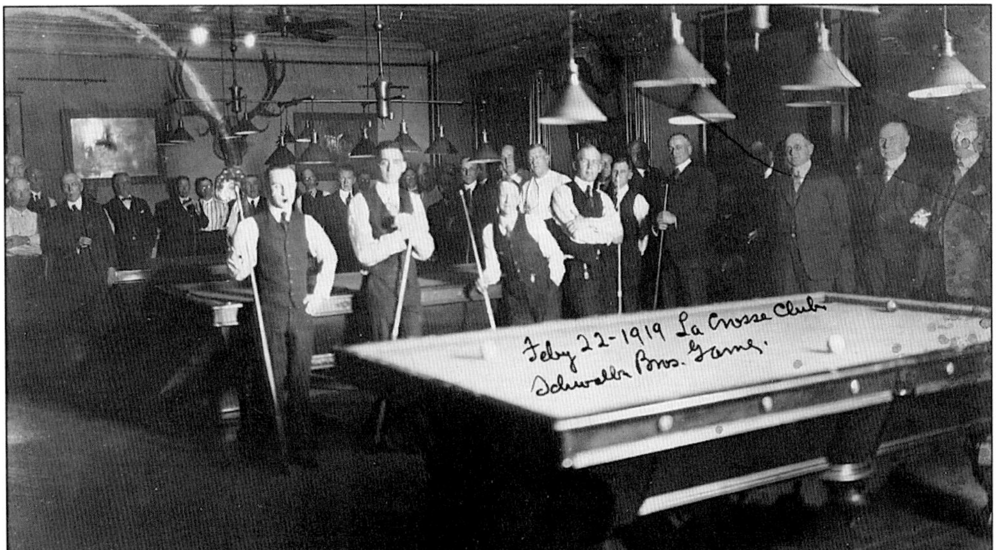

The La Crosse Club drew quite a crowd for the Schwalbe brothers' billiards game in 1919. Arthur, Frank Jr., and Edwin worked in the firm of Frank R. Schwalbe and Sons, builders and contractors.

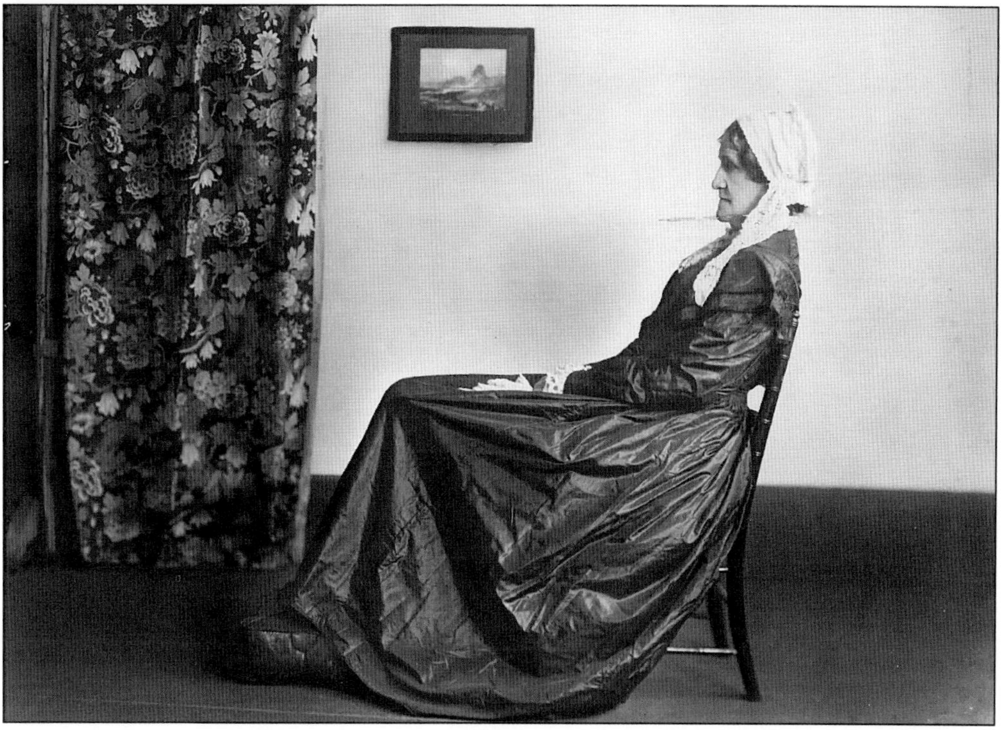

Nannie Hammer Colwell Dorset posed as "Whistler's Mother" for a 1920 La Crosse Charity Ball. Mrs. Dorset's first husband, Wilson Colwell, led La Crosse troops into the Civil War and was killed in battle in 1862. Her second husband was the Reverend Charles Palmer Dorset, one-time rector of Christ Church, Episcopal.

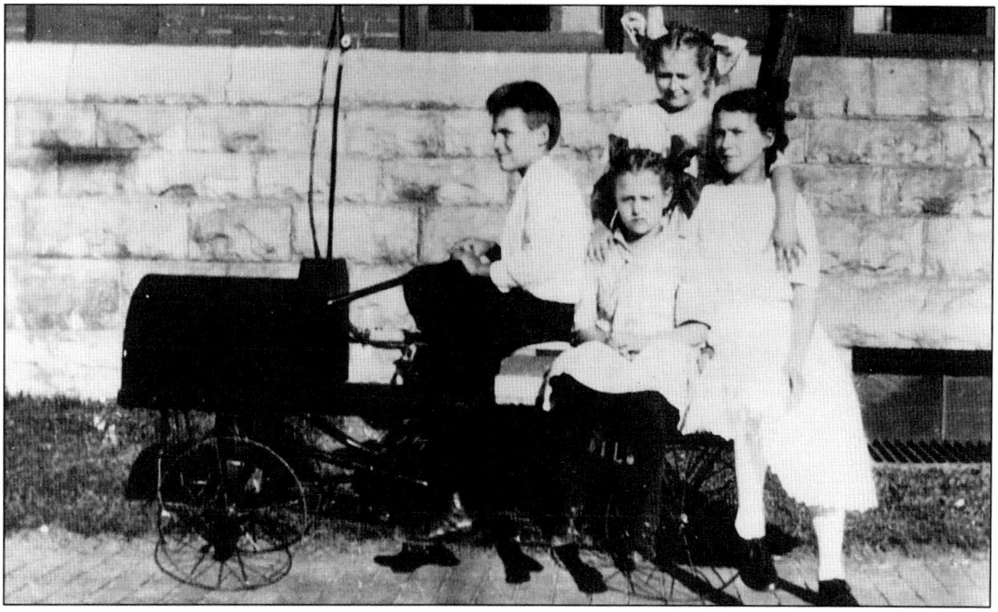

Henry and Doris Ahrens, their cousin Maria Kable, and Marie Ahrens posed for this photo in 1915 at Third and Vine Streets in La Crosse. Their homemade "kiddy car," complete with a steering device and wire wheels, was their preferred mode of transportation.

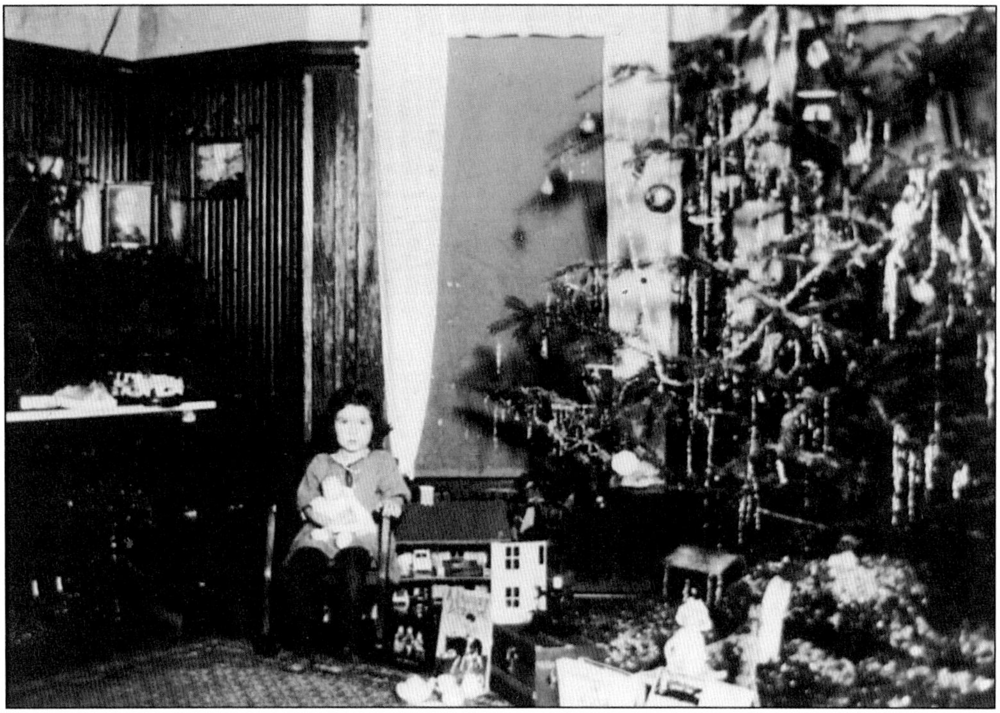

Little Elizabeth Canfield was showered with gifts at Christmas in 1926. Her presents included a doll house, books, tea set, paper dolls, a child-sized chair, and a baby doll. Elizabeth's father, Harry, was superintendent of the U.S. Bureau of Fisheries. The family resided at 226 South Sixteenth Street.

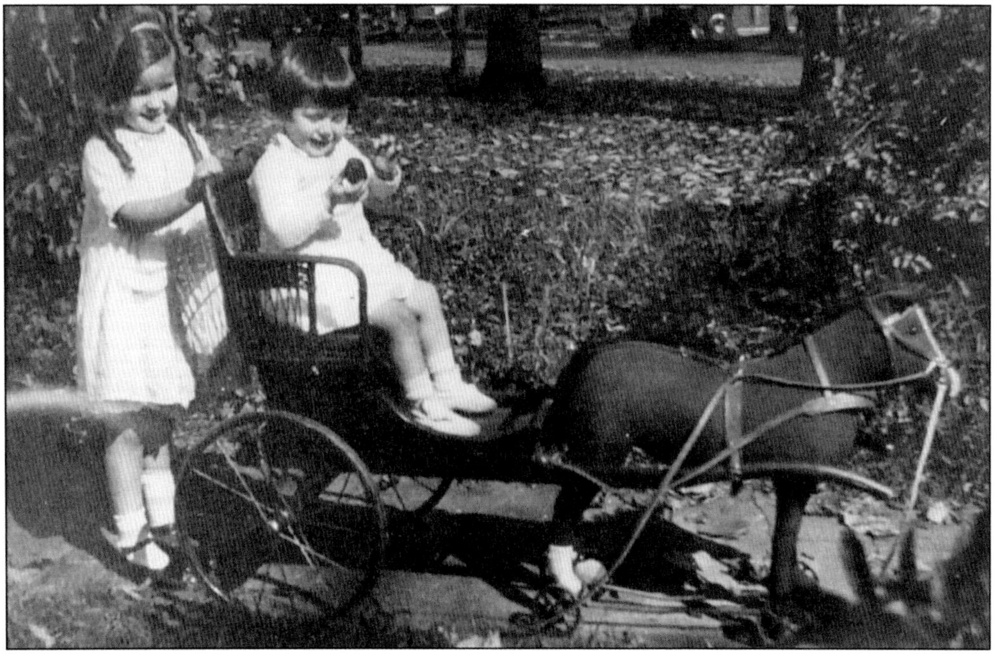

Sally and Nancy Hyde play with their toy pony cart c. 1934. The stuffed pony and wicker-seated cart are presently part of the La Crosse County Historical Society collection.

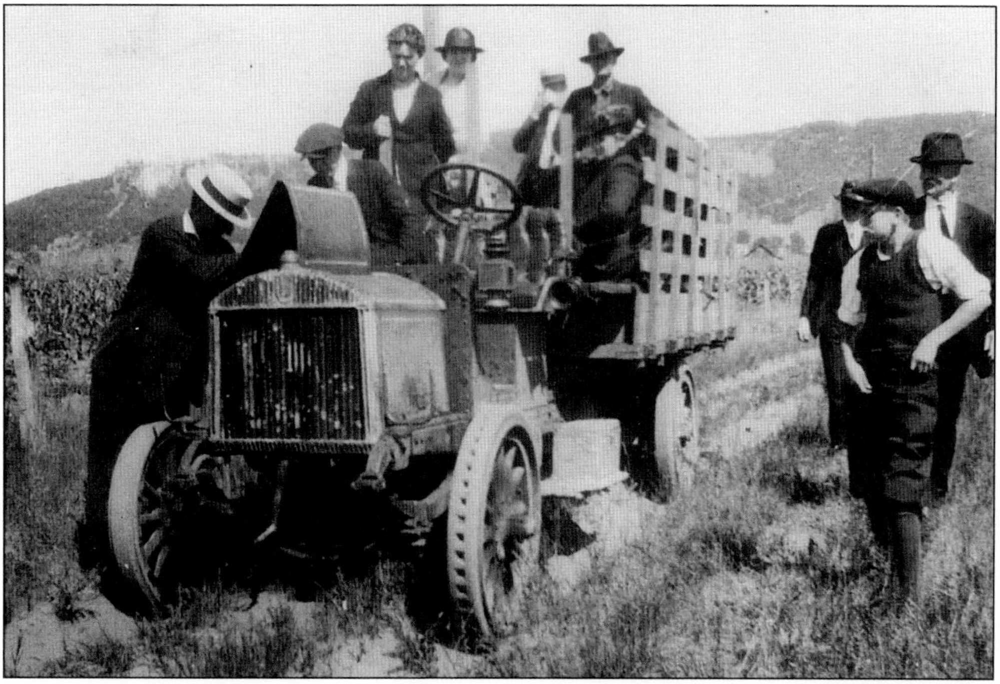

This c. 1920 photo shows the Nels Christianson family, who farmed on Amsterdam Prairie Road, and their new agricultural machine made by the Case Motor Company of Racine.

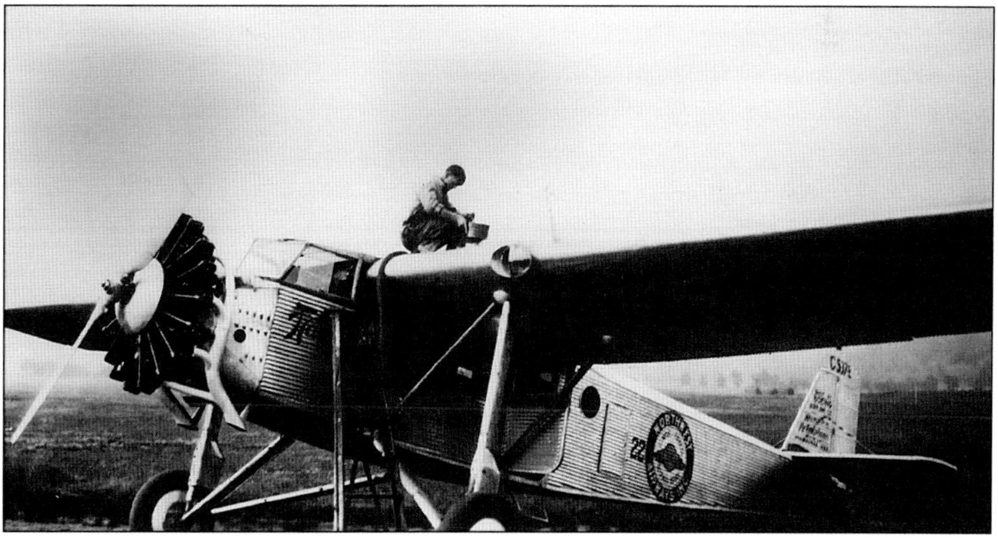

Airmail service was new in 1929, when the camera caught Joe Bedner fueling his single-engine mail plane at the old Salzer Field.

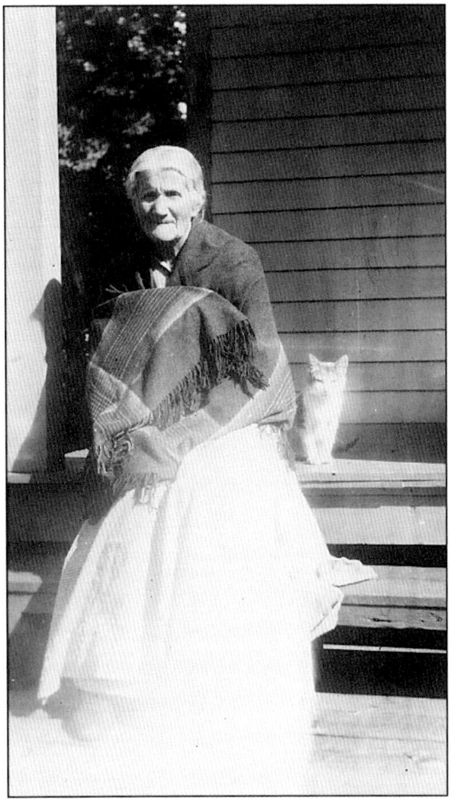

Christina Carisch was photographed *c.* 1903 on the front porch of her home at 1305 West Avenue South. She and her husband Balthazar (shown below *c.* 1900) came to Wisconsin from Switzerland around 1865 and raised nine children.

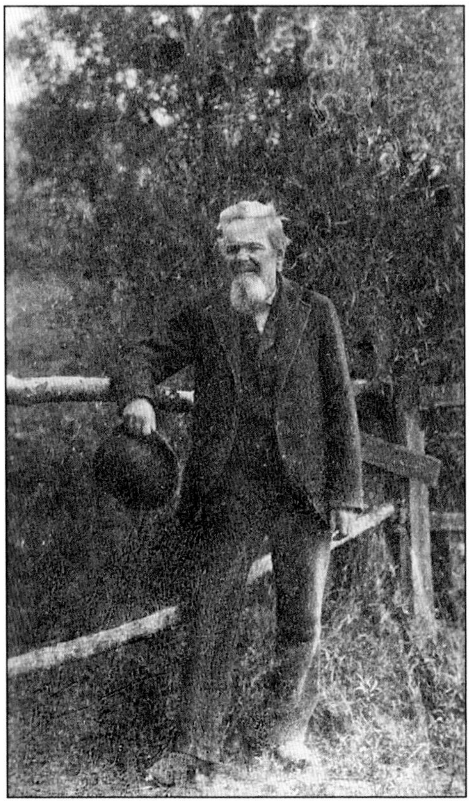

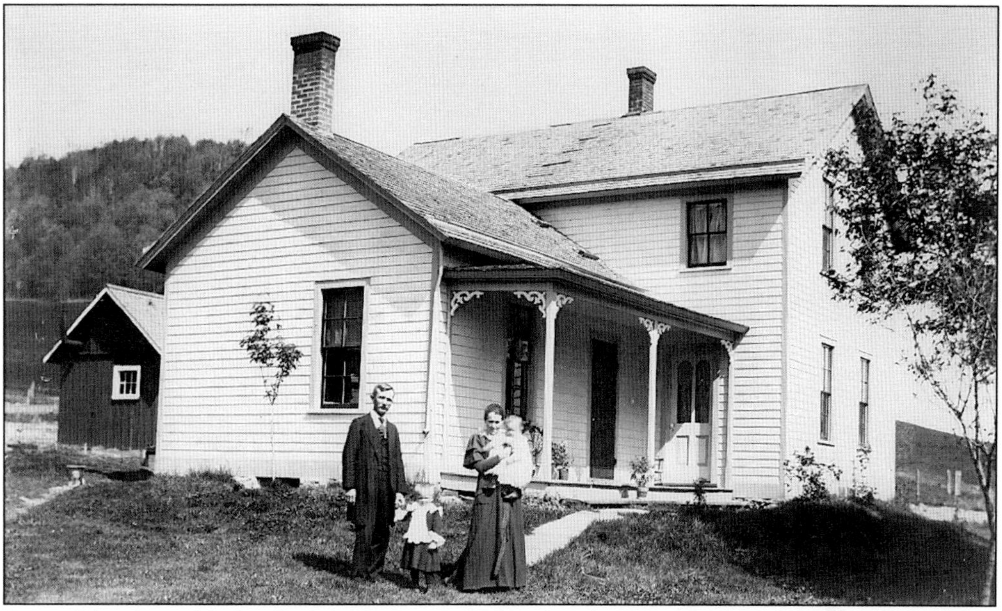

One of the Carisch's daughters, Anna, married E.H. Palechek, a Lutheran pastor. This photo, taken in Esofea, shows the Reverend Palechek with his son Walter, wife Anna, and baby Edna, a few months after Edna's birth in April 1896. Look closely for their dog, Fido.

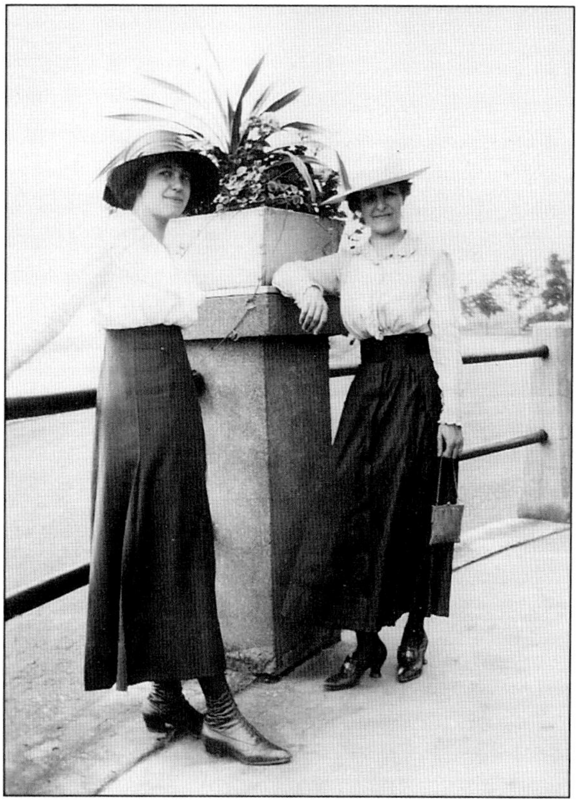

Edna Palechek, the infant in the previous photo, is all grown up in this view. She is pictured with her aunt Laura Carisch (right). Both ladies are dressed in the fashion of the WW I era—simple, ankle-length skirts, white blouses, and big sun-shielding hats.

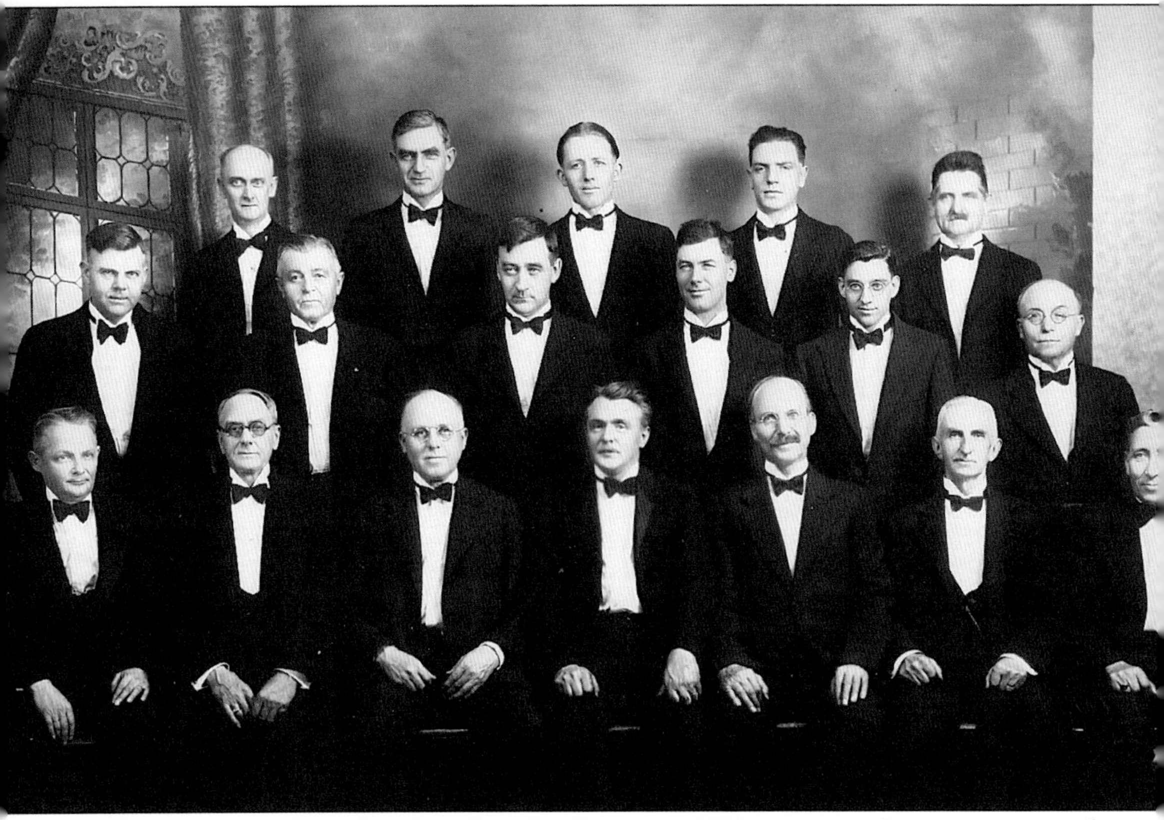

The Normanna Sangerkor formed in La Crosse in 1876 to insure the continuation of Norwegian traditional music, and competitions were still being held well into the 20th century. Shown in this 1930 view are, from left to right, (first row) H.B. Forseth, Theo Dahl, Dr. Yens Rosholt, E.O. Forseth, Nels Haugen, Emil Keibel, and Sivert Hetland; (second row) H.A. Dammen, Olaf Almvig, Dr. M. Sivertson, Will Christianson, Einer Haugsveen, and Hans A. Eide; (third row) Edwin Hoel, J. Thorvald Ranum, Elmer Olson, Thorleif Ranum, and B.L. Skagen.

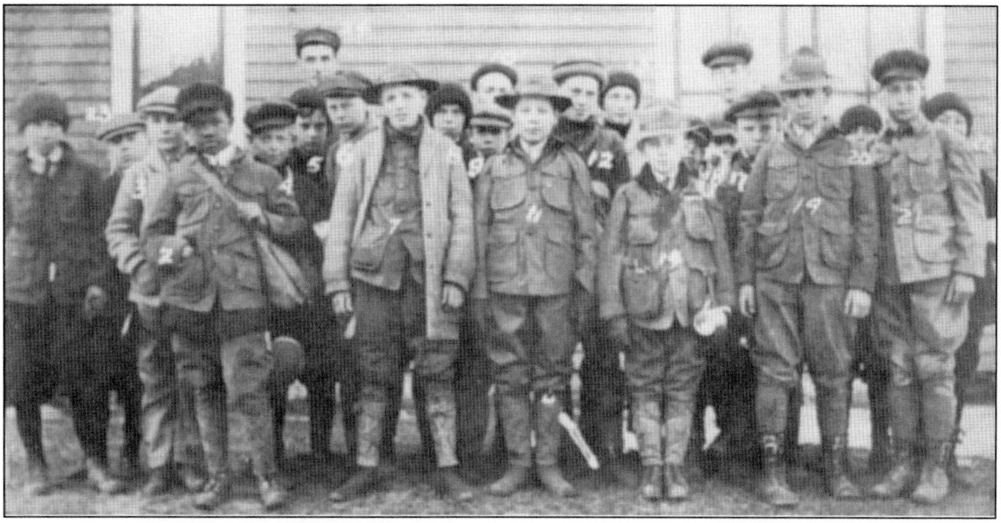

La Crosse's first nationally affiliated Boy Scout troop was organized in 1922, with Harry Spence, the principal of Jefferson school, as the leader. The boys with the most complete uniforms were lined up in the front row as examples.

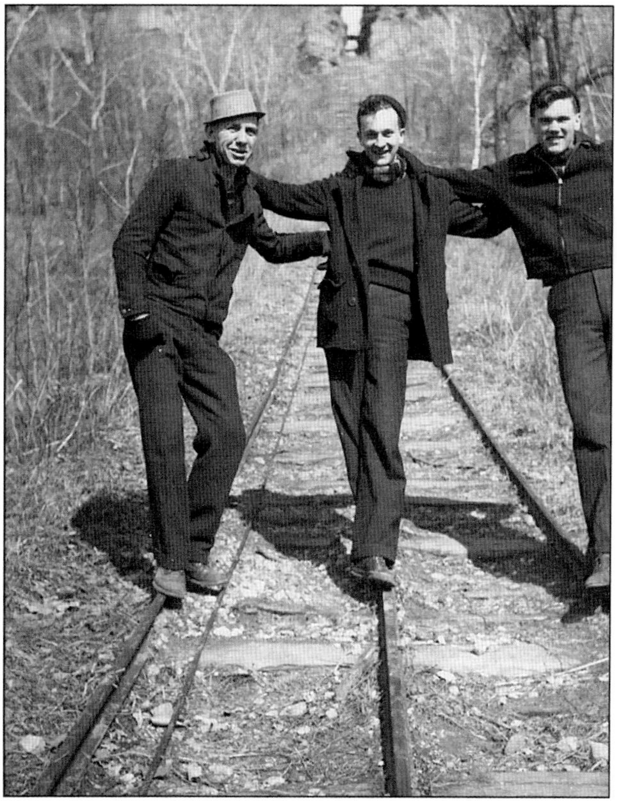

Al Brietzke snapped a photo of these three unidentified men standing on the trolley tracks that lead to the rock quarry on Grand Dad Bluff on March 22, 1937.

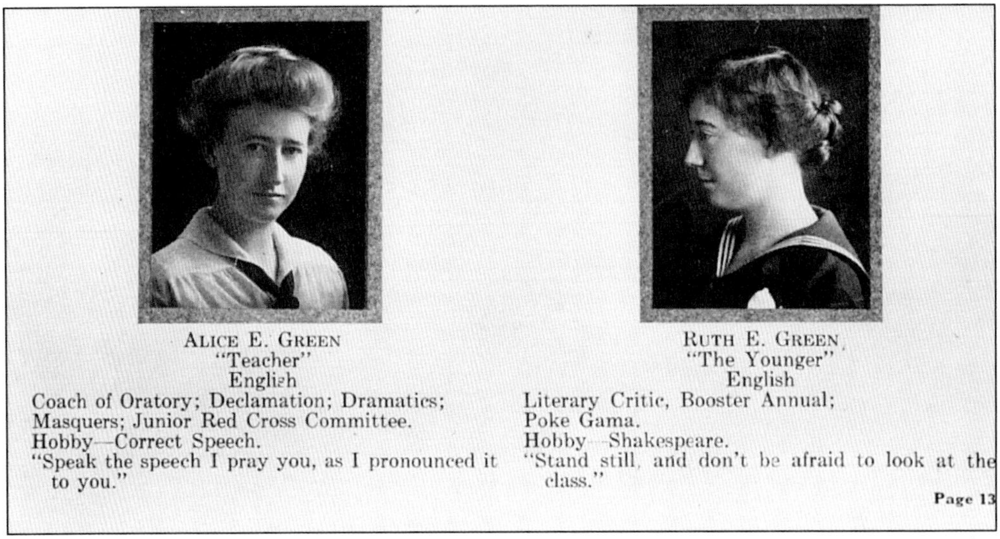

ALICE E. GREEN
"Teacher"
English
Coach of Oratory; Declamation; Dramatics; Masquers; Junior Red Cross Committee.
Hobby—Correct Speech.
"Speak the speech I pray you, as I pronounced it to you."

RUTH E. GREEN
"The Younger"
English
Literary Critic, Booster Annual; Poke Gama.
Hobby—Shakespeare.
"Stand still, and don't be afraid to look at the class."

Page 13

The 1918 La Crosse High School yearbook's faculty page pictured two young sisters who taught English. Alice became the second wife of Frank Hixon, the eldest son of lumberman and financier Gideon and Ellen Pennell Hixon. This 1973 photo (below) shows the same two women, seated in the wash house of the Hixon homestead on Badger Street. Alice Green Hixon donated the Hixon House to the La Crosse County Historical Society as a lovely example of Victorian life.

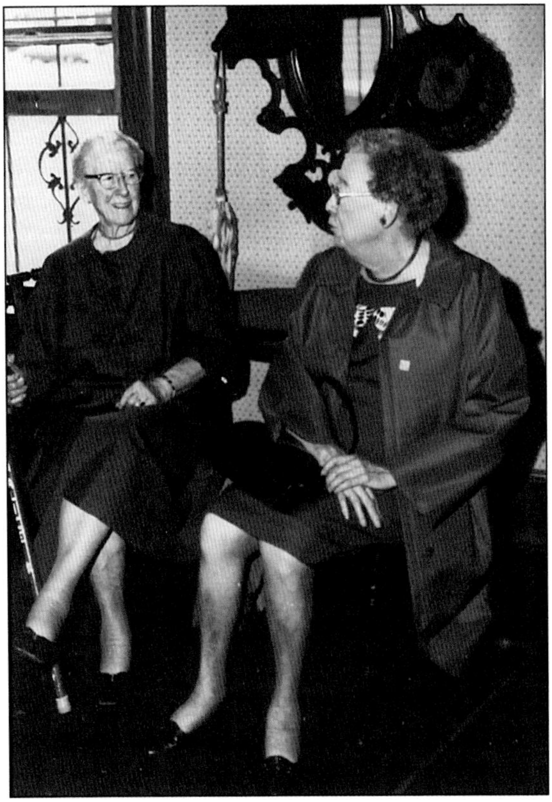

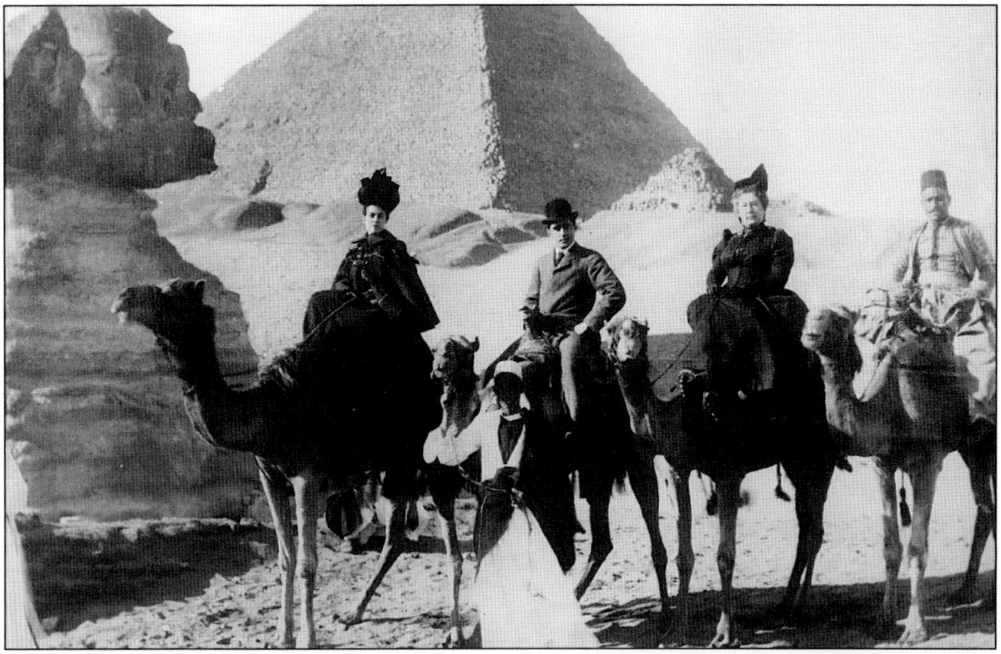

Ellen Pennell Hixon was an adventurous woman; even after the death of her husband, she traveled to many exotic places. This c. 1900 photograph, taken with the Sphinx and pyramids in the background, shows Mrs. Hixon's openness to trying new things such as riding a camel. Shown with her are her niece and companion Mary Crosby, her son Joseph, and two native guides.

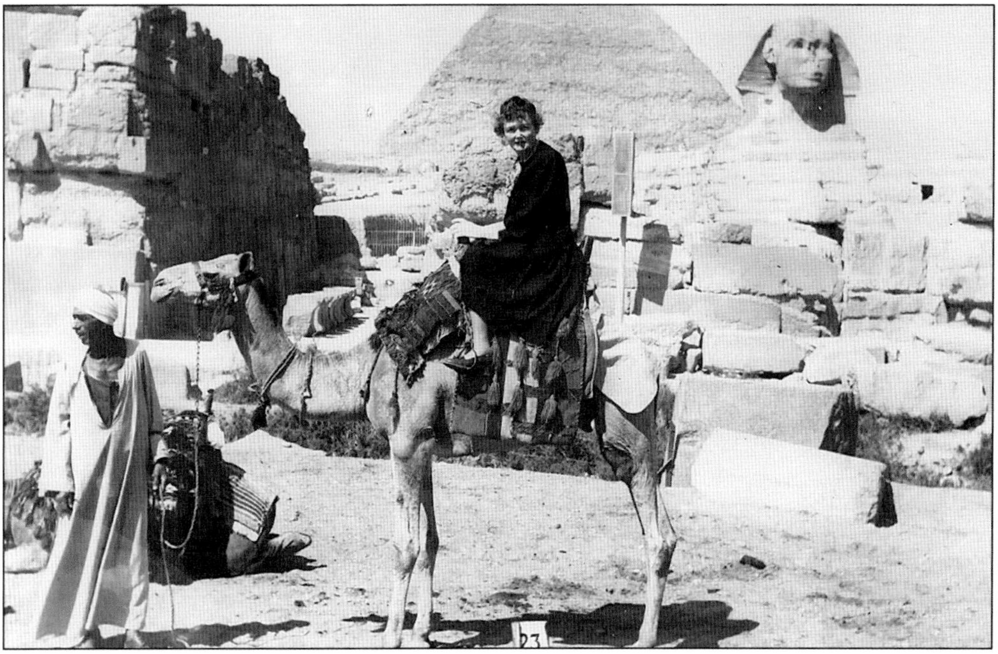

Exhibiting some of the same spunk shown by her mother-in-law years before, Alice Green Hixon poses on a camel at nearly the same spot in 1934. She was also a widow at the time of this trip.

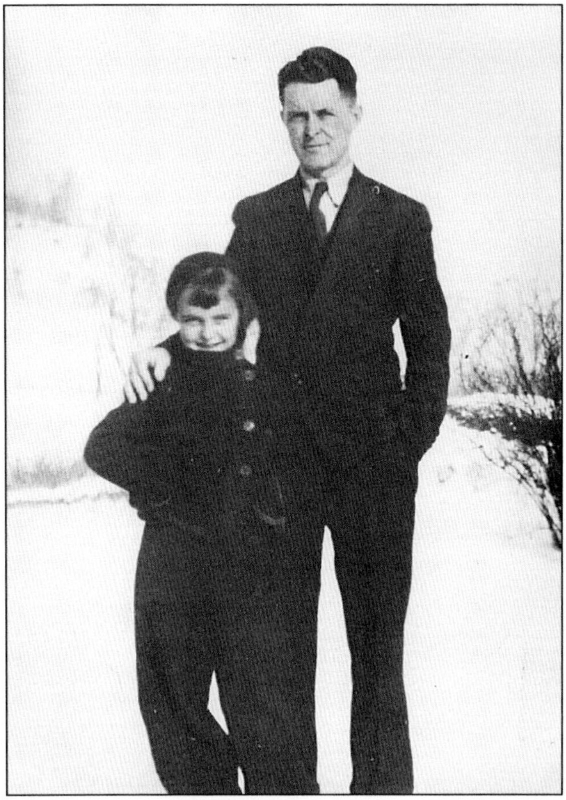

These two photos show Marion (Gavin) Brown as a child and as a young adult. The first shot was taken in La Crescent *c.* 1935, with Marion posed beside her father, local musician Kenny Gavin. The second picture shows her at work in the late 1940s at Byers Flowers (later renamed My Florist). In 1960, Brown bought My Florist from the previous owner, Byron Byers. The shop is still in business, located across the street from Franciscan Skemp Healthcare.

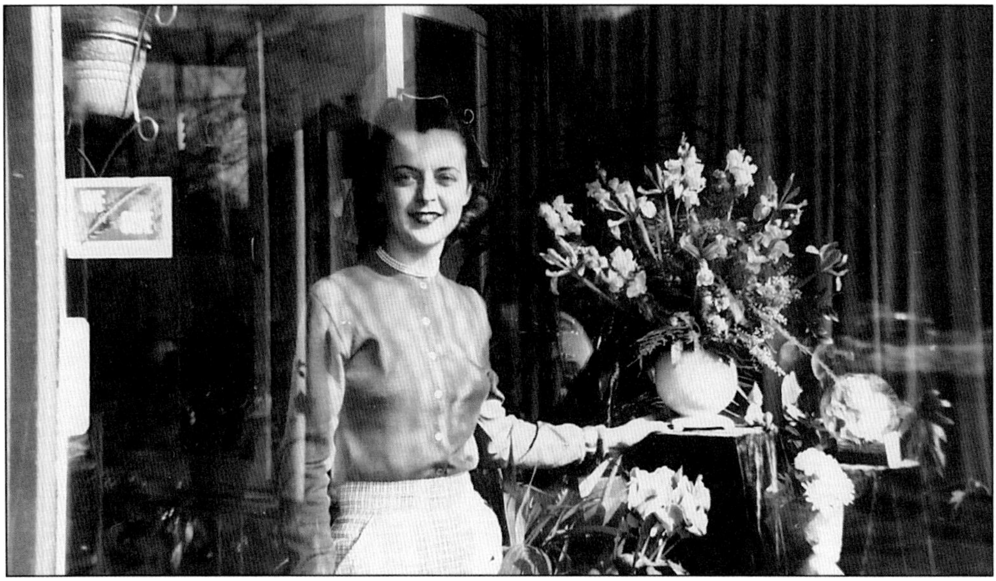

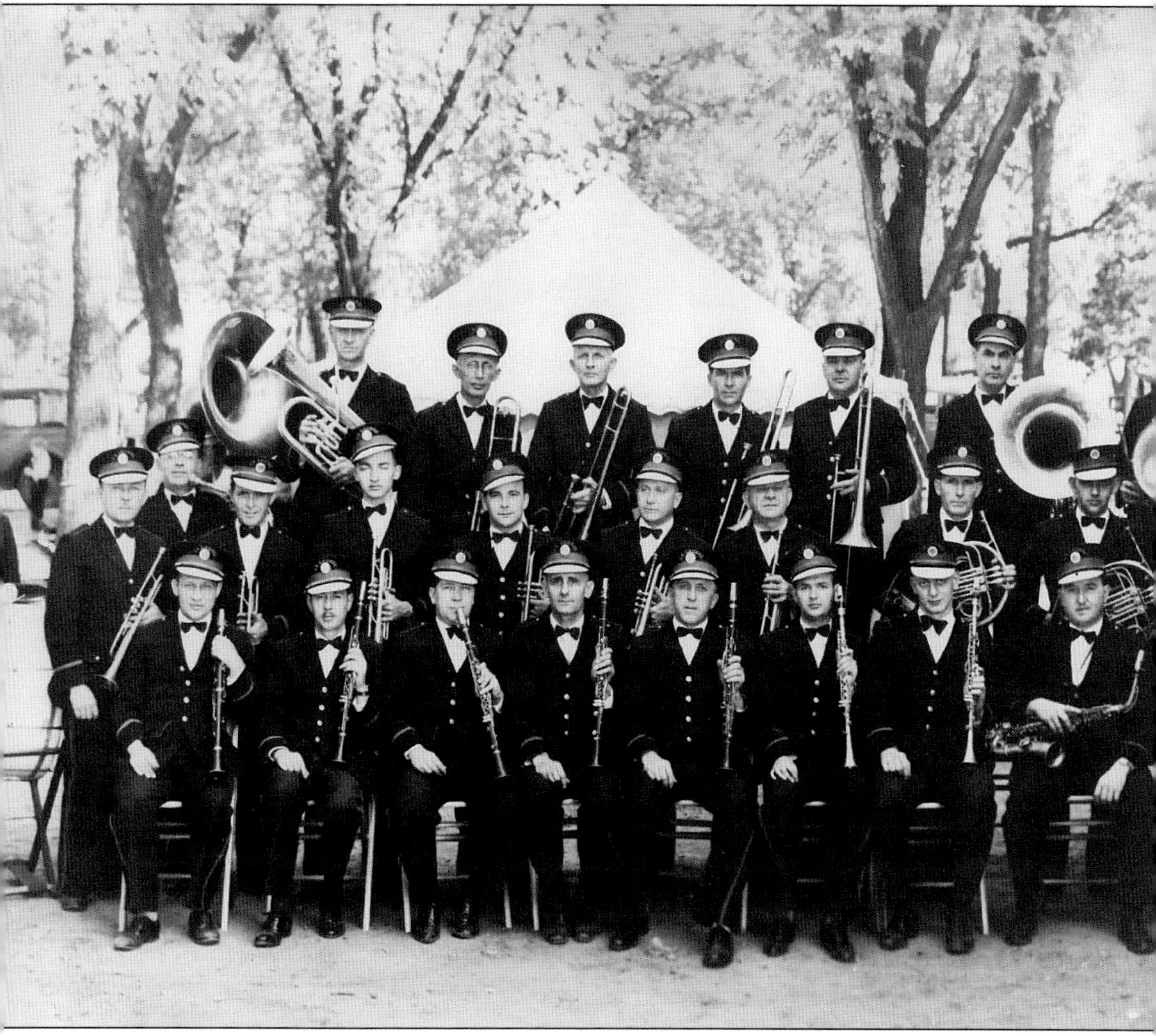

The La Crosse Concert Band is shown here *c.* 1940, posing in Riverside Park. The summer concert series still delights hundreds of music lovers in the open-air park.

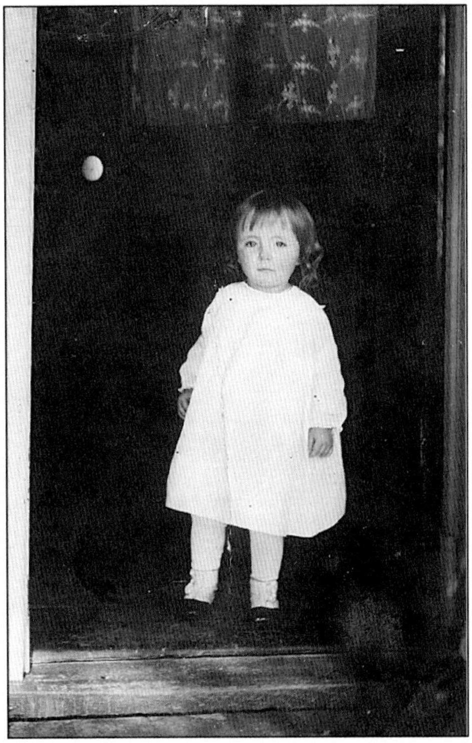

These snapshots of Genevieve (Brown) Ames show her as a young child *c.* 1919, and with her husband, Al Ames, in 1937. Both photos were taken on La Crosse's North Side.

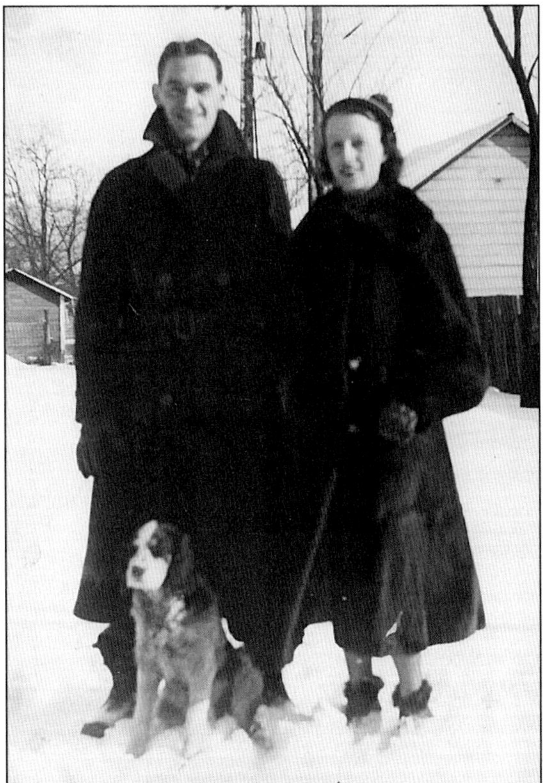

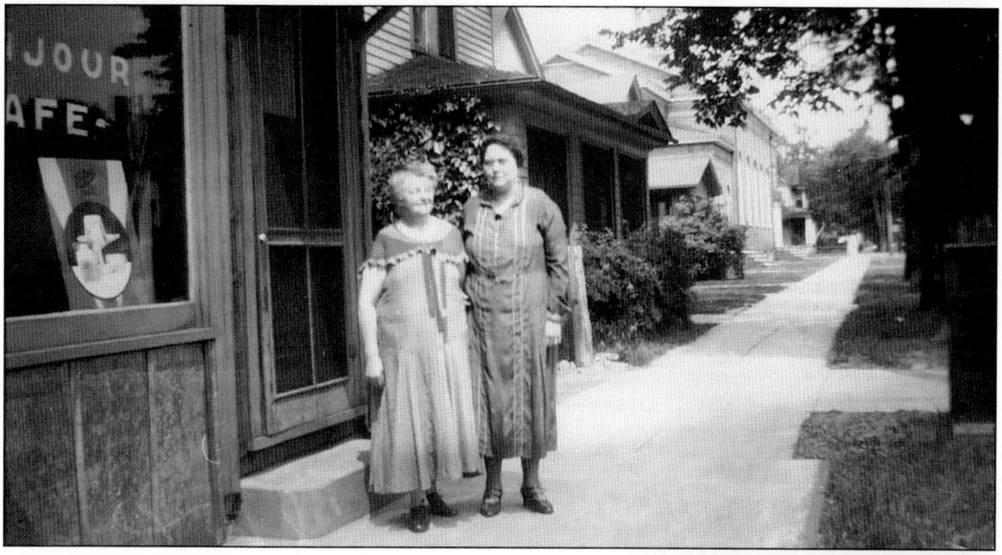

Prior to becoming a flower shop, this site at 1109 Market Street operated as the Bonjour Cafe. The cafe, run by Lenora Jahnke, opened in the late 1920s and remained at that location until the mid-1930s. These two photos are views of the cafe *c.* 1928. The first image reveals some of the Market Street neighborhood as it looked at the time, with the recently built St. John's Church in the background. The people are not identified.

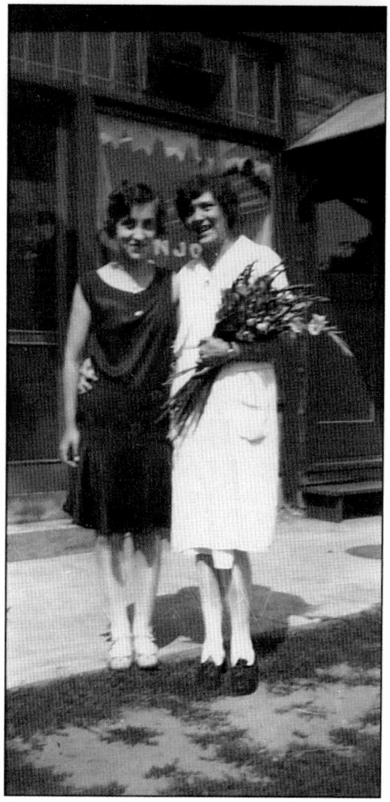

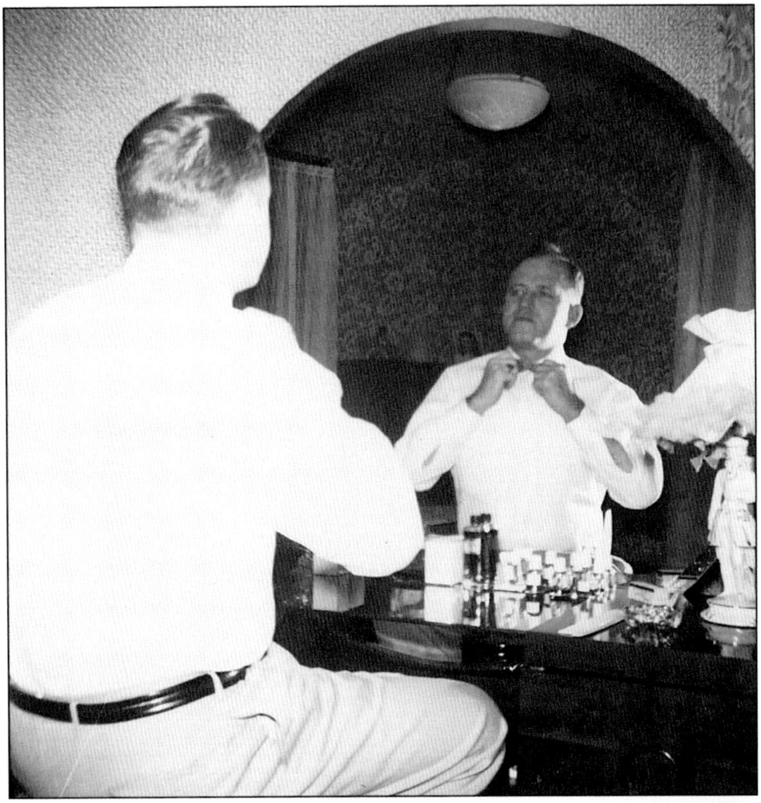

While it certainly was not the case across the board, most Americans who came of age during the 1950s enjoyed nearly boundless employment opportunities and a relative prosperity that contrasted sharply with their childhood memories of the Great Depression. These photos show a young married couple, Dick and Marion Brown, preparing for a night out on the town in 1955.

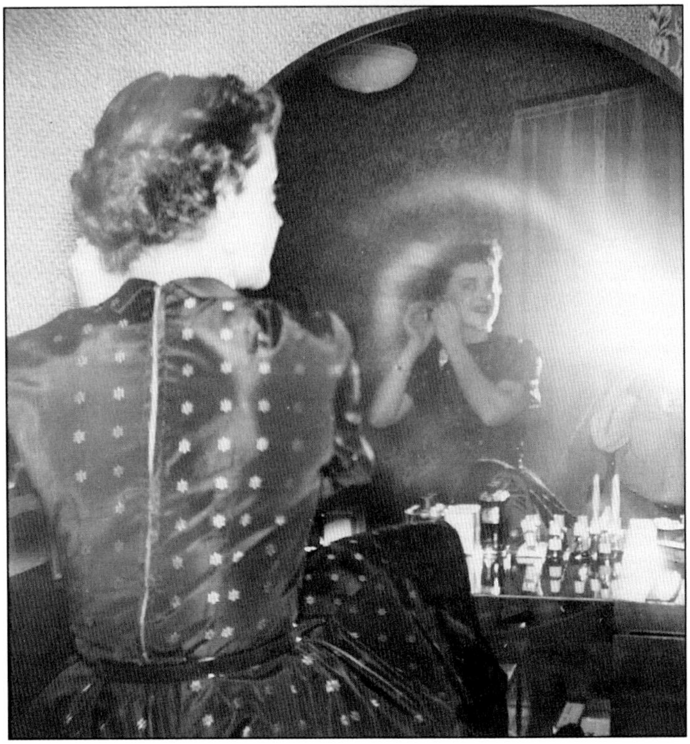

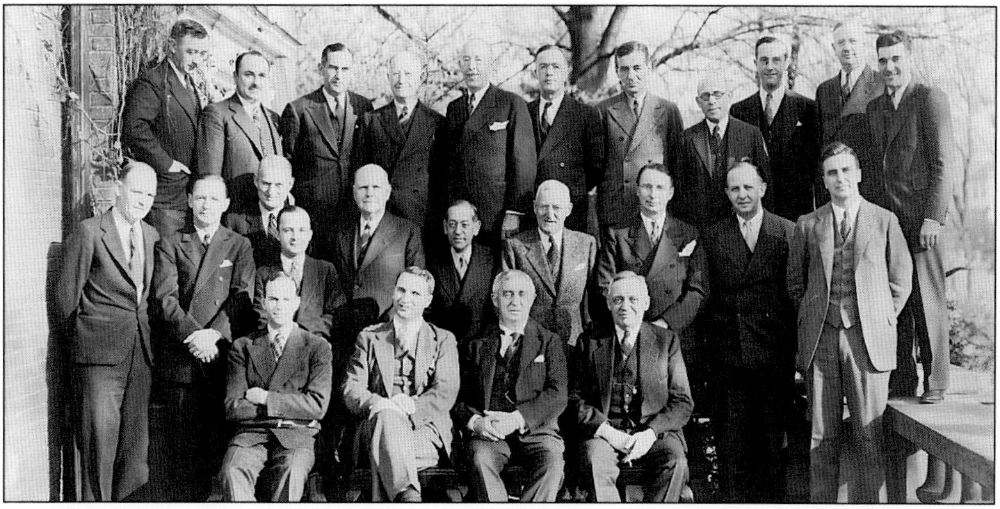

The description on the reverse side of this photograph reads as follows: "November 6, 1937. Lutheran Hospital staff and friends." Pictured from left to right are, (first row) Lloyd L. Fifrick, Sigurd B. Gundersen, Adolf Gundersen, and Ralph Carter; (second row) John C. Harman, Alf H. Gundersen, Erwin C. Schmidt, Robert Slater, Stephen Gsvin, Bernard Dorset, F. Gregory Connell, Gunnar Gundersen, Edward Carlson, and Thorolf E. Gundersen; (third row) Martin Sivertson, Adrien VerBrugghen, Carl Eberbach, Joseph F. Smith, Reginald Jackson Sr., Nels Werner, Jerome Head, Victor Marshall, Reginald Jackson Jr., Paul C. Gatterdam, and Perry T. Walters.

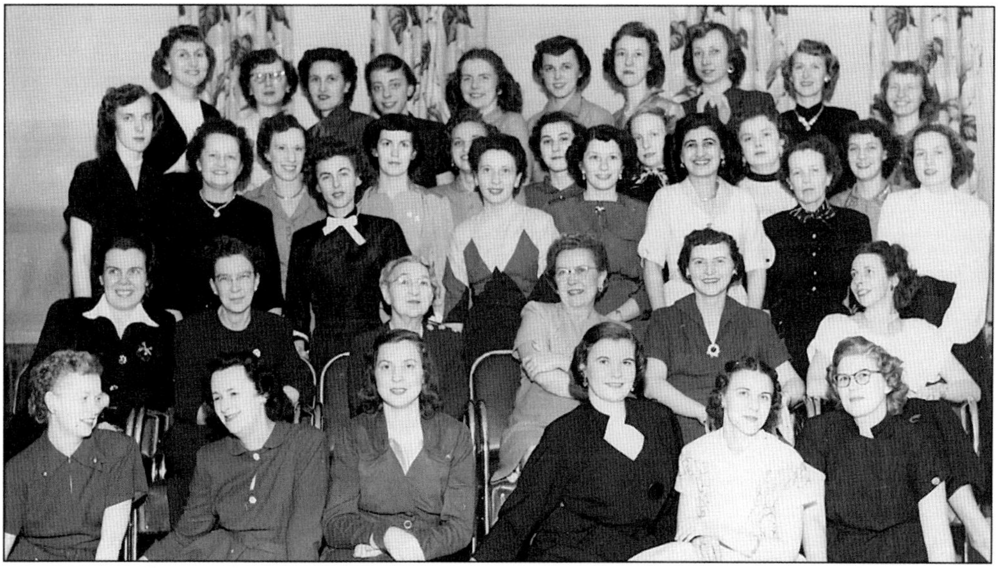

In 1951, Gundersen Clinic threw a Christmas party for its female employees. Pictured from left to right are (first row) Helen Hilden, Mary Crowley, Elinor Waterman, Kay Tuberty, Carol Frisch, and Kay Olson; (second row) Beverly Walsh, Ragna Isaacson Olson, Doris Shesler, Margery Steele, Phyllis Retzlaff, Fran Fregin, ?, Dorothy ?, and Leslie ?; (third row) Marie Maurer, Helen Peterson, Irene Pfaff, Kathryn ?, Dr. Davies, and Beverly Bartlett; (fourth row) Laura Esch, Effie Ellingson, Miss Gabel, Louise Cook, Mrs. Febig, and Mary Higbee; (fifth row) Donna Jones, Diane Jenks, Gwen Straugstelien, Bernice ?, Dorothy Johnson, Olline ?, Rosemary Hickisch, Margaret Spaag, Lorraine Byers, and Doris Hendrickson.

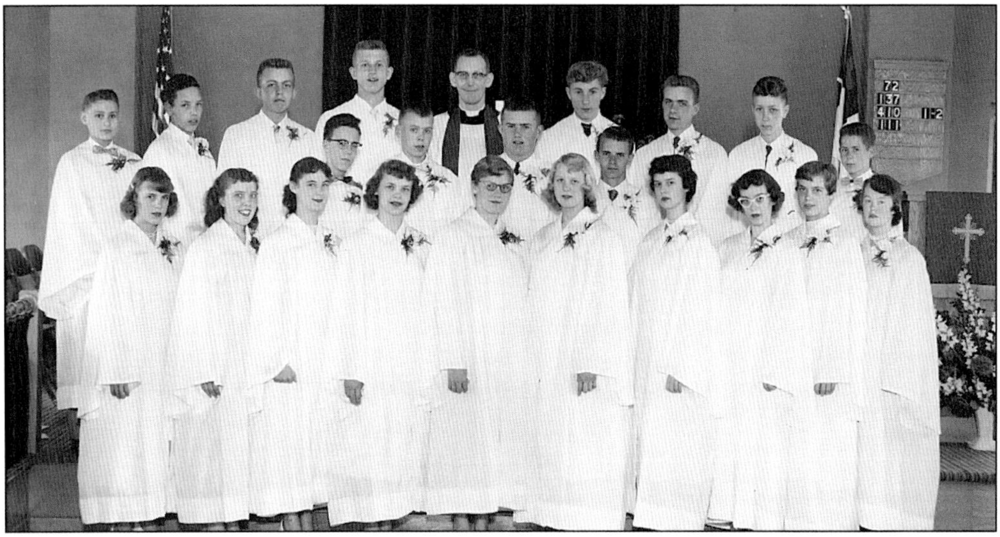

The fashions and hairstyles from the 1950s are evident in this photo of a confirmation class from Our Redeemer Lutheran Church, located at the corner of Weston and Twenty-First Place.

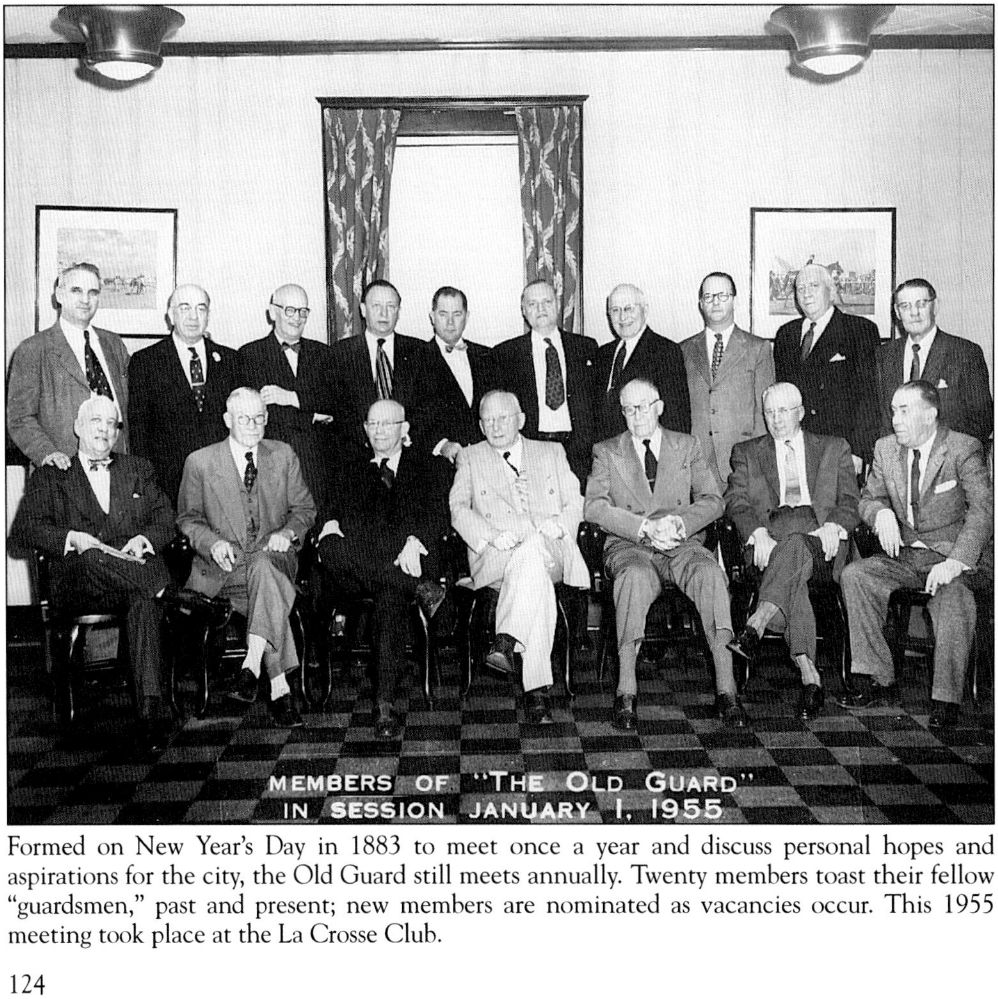

Formed on New Year's Day in 1883 to meet once a year and discuss personal hopes and aspirations for the city, the Old Guard still meets annually. Twenty members toast their fellow "guardsmen," past and present; new members are nominated as vacancies occur. This 1955 meeting took place at the La Crosse Club.

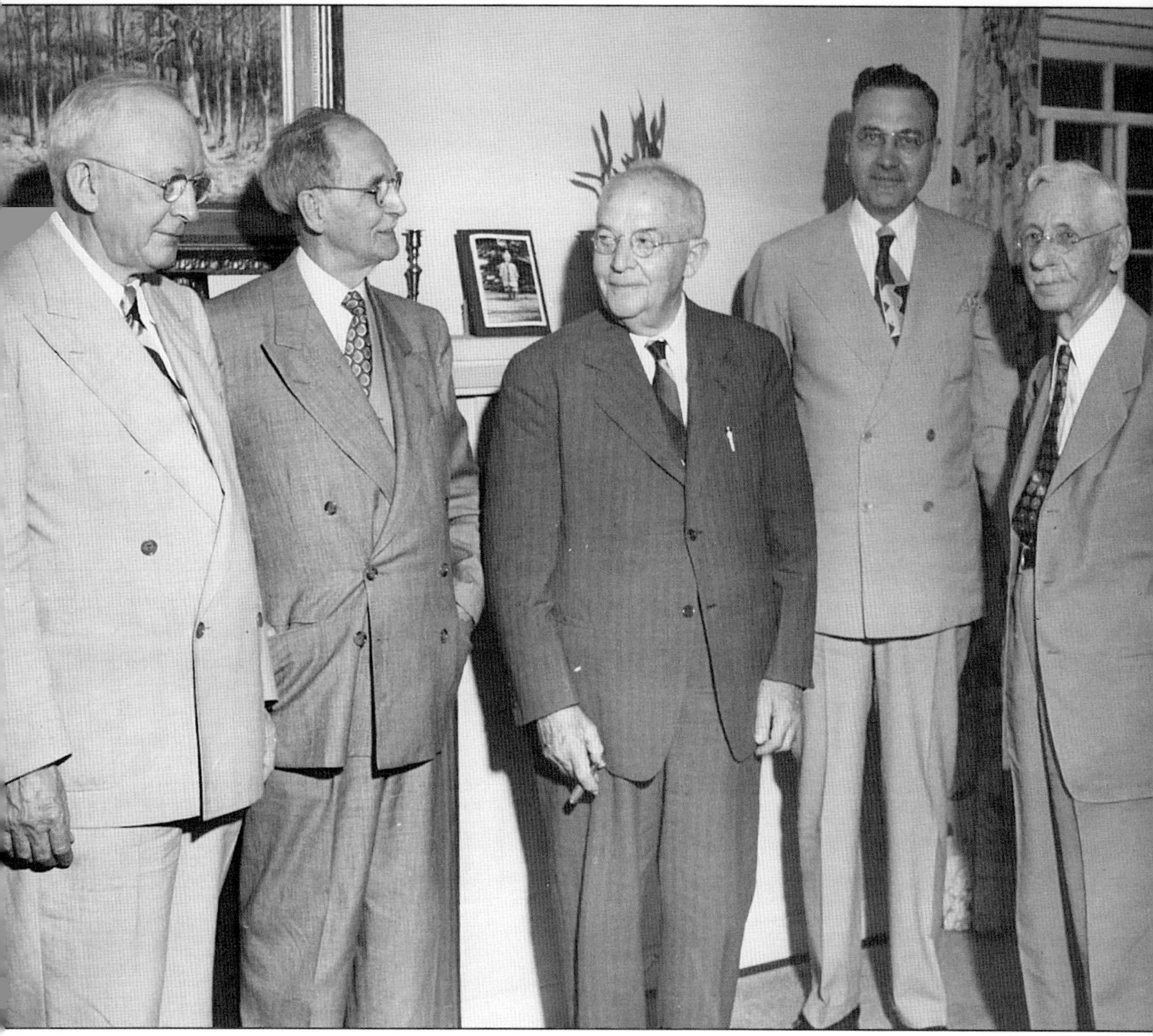

On June 15, 1949, these five La Crosse alumni of the University of Wisconsin class of 1893 met for dinner. They are, from left to right, Will Funke, Mr. Morton, Harry Hirshheimer, Quincy Hale, and Professor A.H. Sanford.

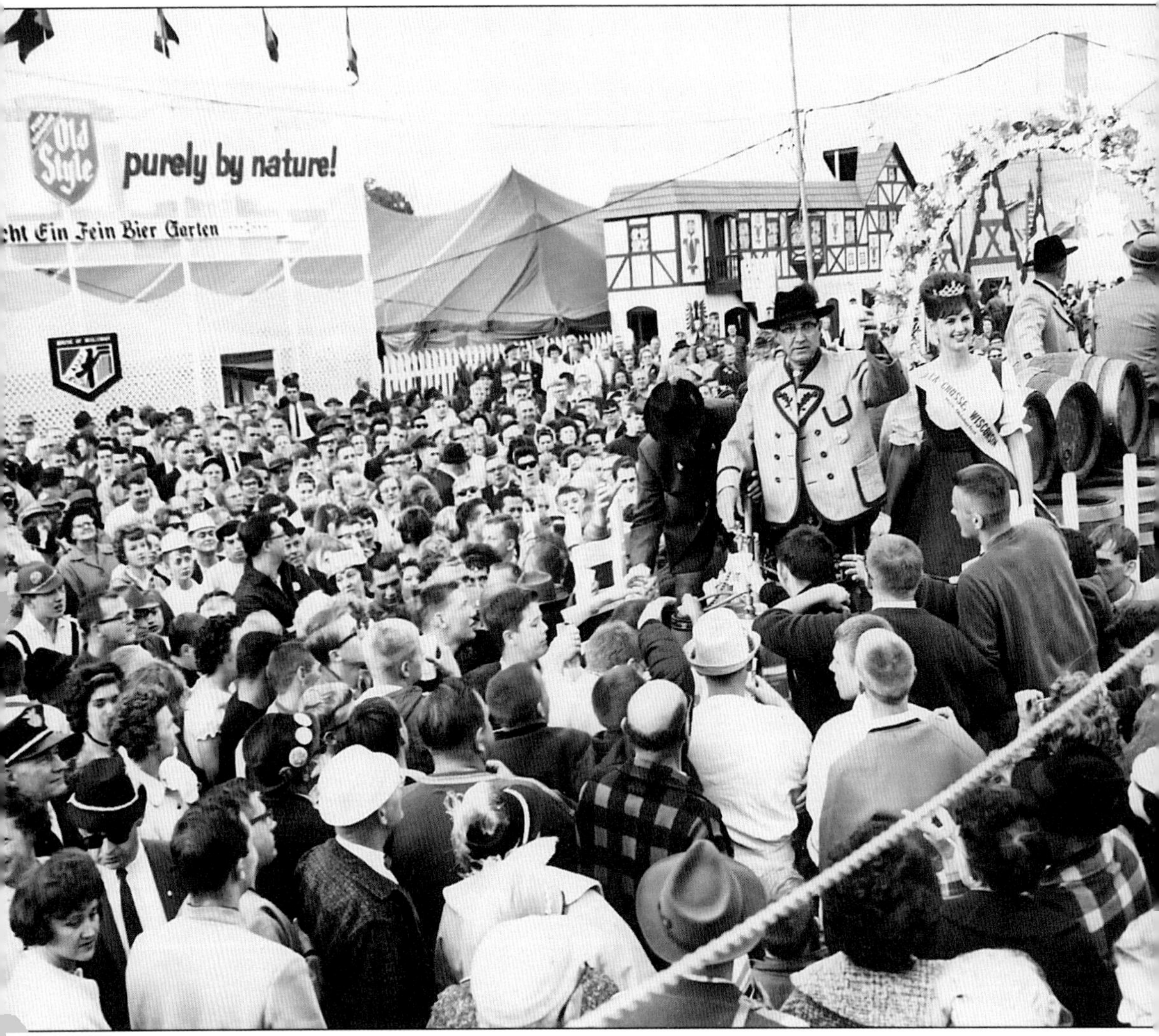

Crowds gathered around the horse-drawn beer wagon for the "Tapping of the Golden Keg" at the 1964 Octoberfest. Decorating the wagon is the outgoing Miss Oktoberfest, Mary Kay Knudson.

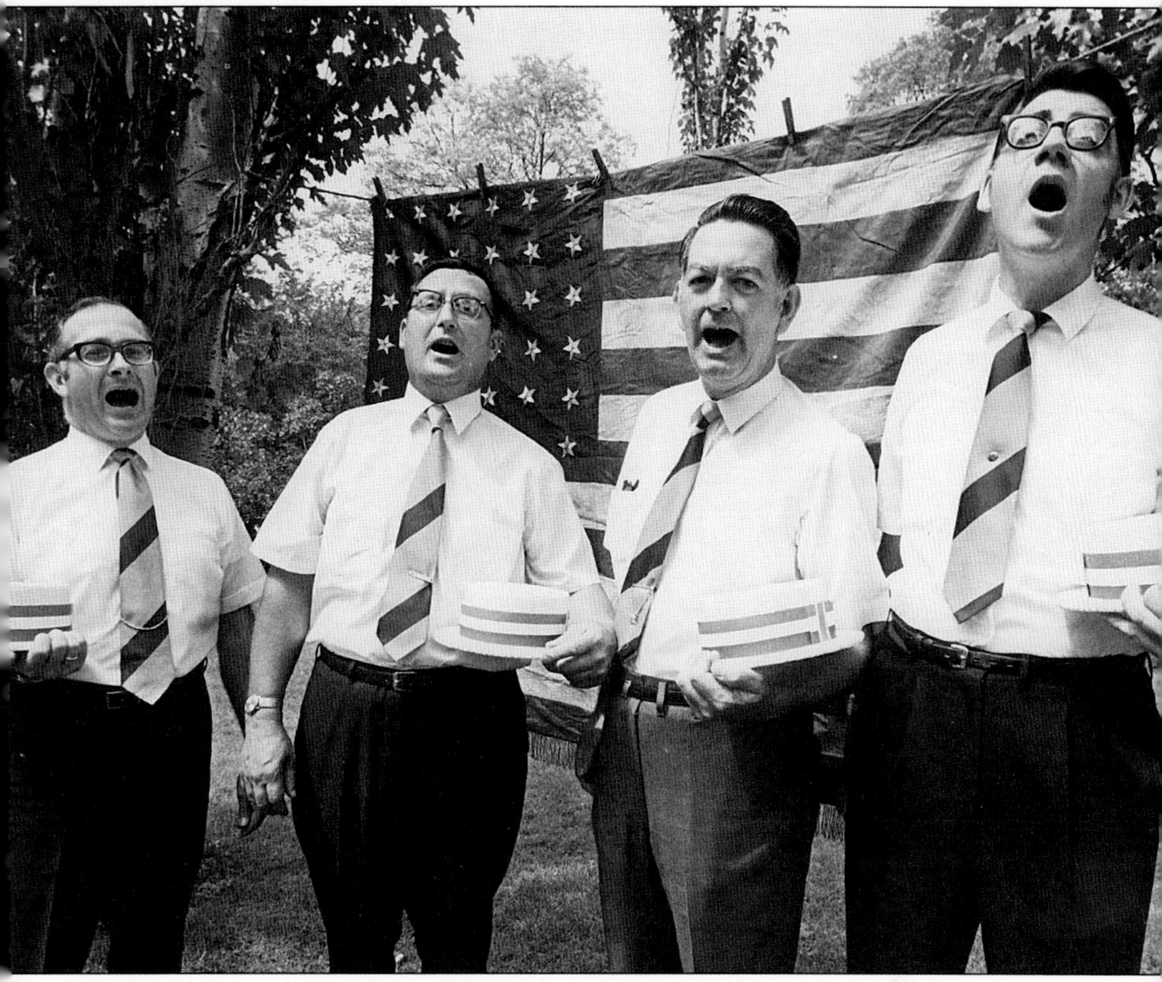

Jim Sherwood, Joseph Dingeldein, Bob Tevis, and Mel Page made up this barbershop quartet. They performed at the Ice Cream Social held on the grounds of the historic Hixon House, on August 16, 1970.

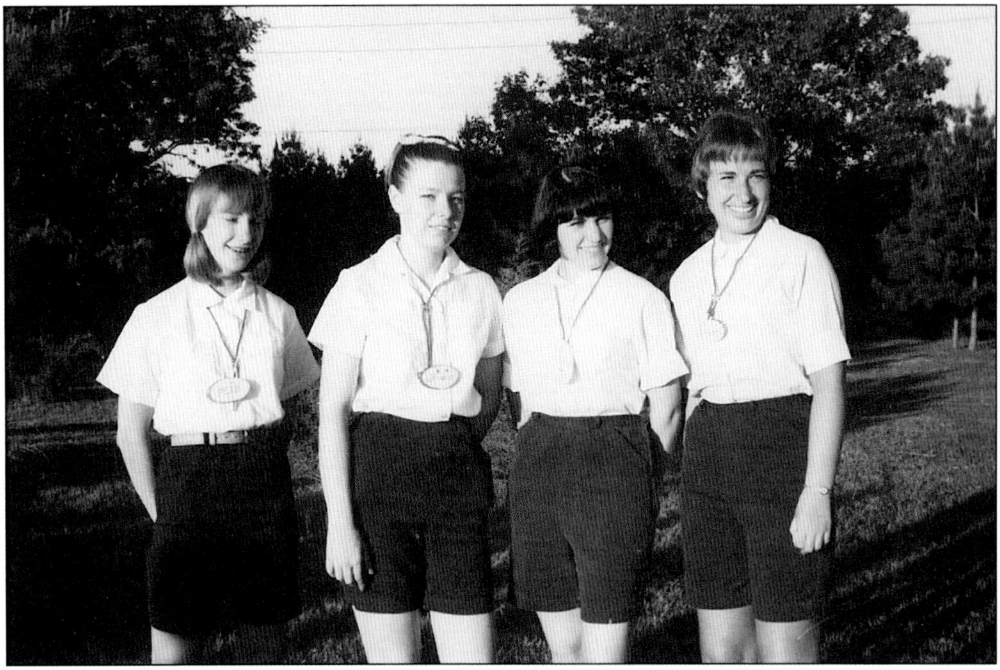

Dressed in their camp uniforms of dark green Bermuda shorts, white blouses, and knee socks, these Girl Scout counselors pose at Mindoro's Camp Ehawee in June 1966. Andrea Sorenson is seen on the right, and the other girls are unidentified.

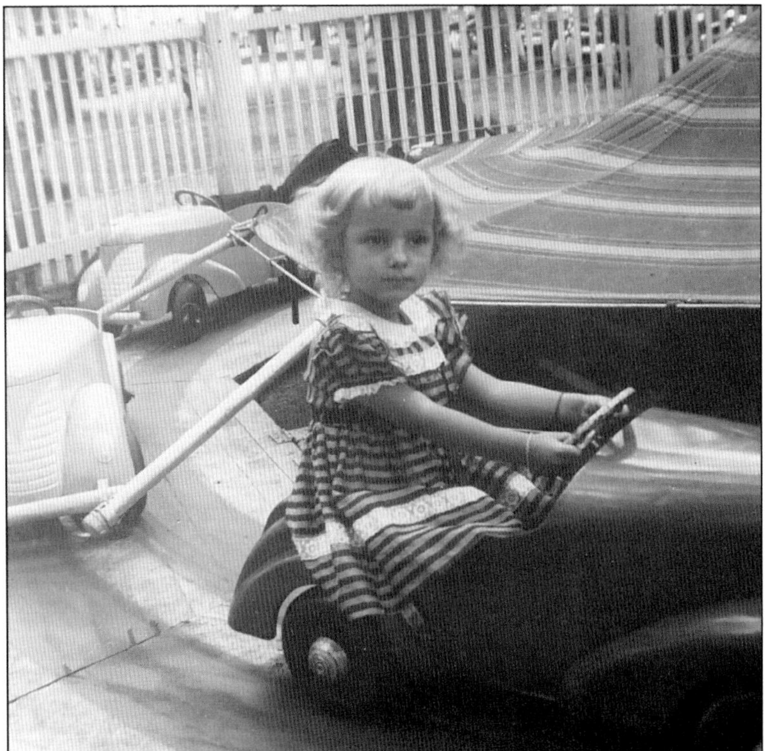

As Jeanne Ames wistfully drove this kiddy car at Myrick Park during the early 1950s, perhaps she contemplated what life (and cars) would be like in the 21st century.